Contents

1 Objects and properties

■ Introduction

This book will prepare you to take GCSE Computer Science offered by the AQA examining board. This qualification involves taking a written exam and completing two programming tasks. Practical programming accounts for 60 per cent of the total course marks.

This book is based around learning programming and creating computer programs. The programming tasks start very simply and get more complicated as the book progresses. Alongside the programming activities you will learn computer theory, which will prepare you for the exam.

The programming language used in this book is called Visual Basic.

■ 1.1 The software you will use

This section will introduce the software you will use during this course.

Visual Basic

An application is a computer program that carries out a task under the control of a computer user. Applications are called apps for short. Apps are examples of computer software. During this course you will create software apps by writing computer code in a programming language called Visual Basic.

You will write the Visual Basic programs with the help of an integrated development environment or IDE. An IDE is a software package with editing features to help you create good programs. The IDE includes a coding window where you type the programs, as you would use a word processor. The IDE has other features as well; for example, you can test your program by running it, and you can design the appearance of the program interface by creating windows with labels and boxes.

The software used in this book is Microsoft Visual Basic. Visual Basic is provided by Microsoft with an IDE called 'Visual Studio'. A free version of Visual Studio is available. It is called 'Visual Studio Express'. This is designed for people who are learning to write programs. Visual Studio Express is a good choice for schools and colleges.

Learning content

3.1.3 Program Flow Control: understand and be able to describe the basic building blocks of coded solutions (i.e. sequencing, selection and iteration).
3.1.8.1 Systems: be able to define a computer system (i.e. hardware and software working together to create a working solution).

Link

Hardware and software – section 1.8

Study tip

Running a program is sometimes called executing the program.

There are several versions of Visual Studio Express. This includes Visual Studio Express 2010 and 2012. You should be able to use this book with either version of the IDE. In places where there are small variations between the two versions, these are briefly discussed to avoid confusion.

Almost all of the activities included in this book can be carried out using other versions of Visual Basic. If you are using an older version, it might be worth considering an upgrade, but if you decide against this, you should not have too many problems. If you have a later version, this should pose no problems, as all the functionality of VB 2010 is maintained.

Microsoft Visual Basic and the development environment are produced and sold by Microsoft. The Visual Basic IDE is an example of a Microsoft Windows application.

In general all Microsoft Windows applications look similar in their appearance. There are many commands and methods that are the same for all Windows applications. You may have used Windows software before, examples include Word and Excel. Practice with Microsoft software will help you to learn skills that will be useful as you work through this book and follow the exercises. Examples of useful skills include using the menus, tabs and icons on the toolbar.

Windows

When you use any windows application, the app opens in a window on the screen. The window can be small or fill the whole screen. In the software window you will see features such as:

- labels and other text to read
- buttons and menus you can click to make choices
- spaces where you can type text and numbers.

Visual Basic lets you create new apps that look like typical Windows software. The app you create will open in a window. The window will have buttons and labels on it. If you design it well it will look like a professional software application.

In Visual Basic a software window is called a **form**. The items that appear on the form, such as labels and buttons, are called **objects**. The characteristics of an object, such as its colour, position, size, etc., are called the **properties** of the object.

> ### Key terms
>
> **Form**   A software window that can hold objects.
>
> **Object**   An item in the software window. There are other kinds of 'object', but for now we will just use the term to mean the objects that appear on a form.
>
> **Property**   A characteristic of an object that can be altered by a computer program.

■ 1.2 Begin Visual Basic

In this section you will write a simple Visual Basic program that will open a software window. In the window, a message will be displayed. Creating this simple application will introduce you to the IDE and you will use it to make software that carries out tasks. First, read through the information below and look at the images which show what will be on the screen as you work. Then follow the instructions in the box headed Activity to carry out the task.

Your teacher will explain how to start up the Visual Basic IDE. The opening screen looks like this.

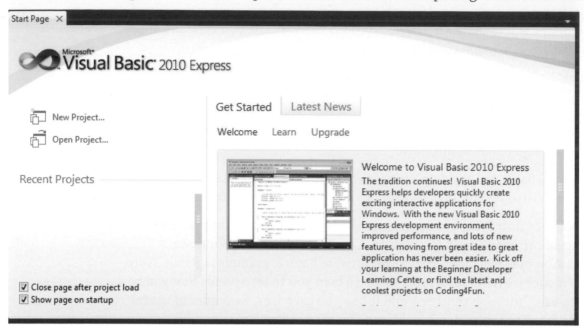

If you click on the words New Project..., the New Project window opens. This is where you choose a name for your project.

Make sure Visual Basic is selected on the left of the screen and Windows Forms Application in the centre of the screen.

Now you must think of a name for your programming project. Here are some rules about naming projects.

- The name must start with a letter.
- The name can include numbers and spaces.
- The name can't include punctuation marks such as ? and /.

Here are some suggestions about choosing a good name.

- The name should remind you of what the program does.
- It is good practice to start the name with a capital letter. Capital letters are allowed
- Include your name or initials in the project name, if the storage area is shared with other people.

In this example, a good name would be My First Program.

When you click on the 'OK' button you may see a window that asks you to select a storage location for your project. You should use your personal storage area, for example on the network. If you are not sure your teacher will let you know what storage location to use. Select the storage location and click on the 'Save' button to complete the action.

At the end of this section is an activity. You will be asked to start Visual Basic and begin a new project. When you do this you will see the Visual Basic IDE. It looks something like this.

Solution Explorer

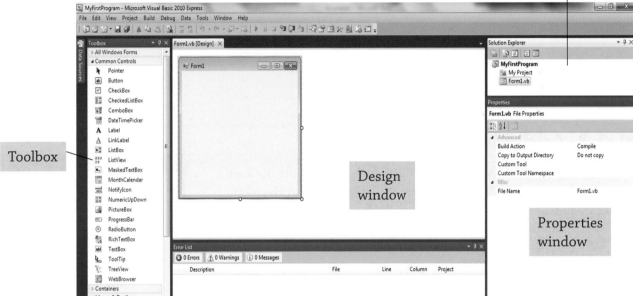

Toolbox

Design window

Properties window

The IDE workspace is divided into several parts:

- At the top of the screen is a menu bar. There are menus called File, Edit, View and so on. If you click on any of these words, a drop-down menu will open.
- Below the menu bar is a toolbar. On the toolbar are icons (little pictures) that offer different software options.
- Most of the screen is a large working area called the main windows space. It is divided into several smaller windows. The names of these smaller windows are given in the screenshot.

You will use these windows as you create programs:

- Toolbox (in this example it is on the left of the screen)
- Properties window (in this example it is on the lower right of the screen)
- Solution Explorer (it is above the Properties window)
- Design window (this is the main area in the centre of the screen).

Study tip

If you cannot see the windows such as Toolbox and Properties then open the View menu at the top of the screen. A menu of choices will open. Select the name of any window that you cannot see on the screen. When you select the name of a window it will appear on the screen.

In the Design window there is a single form called *Form1*. It looks like an empty software window.

Activity Start Visual basic

Carry out these tasks.

- Start Visual Basic.

- Click on New Project... .

- Make sure that the option Windows Forms Application is selected in the centre of the screen.

- Enter a name for your new project at the bottom of the screen. The suggested name is My First Program.

- Click on OK.

- Look at the IDE, and find the four windows described in this section.

- If any of the windows are not there, use the View menu to select a window and make it appear.

■ 1.3 Add a label to a form

To make a Visual Basic application you attach labels, buttons and other items to forms. These items are called 'objects'. In the next activity you will add a label to the form. Labels are objects that are just used to display text messages for the computer user to read.

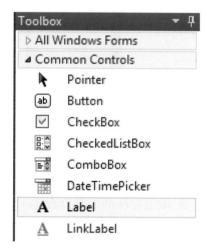

Toolbox controls

To put objects onto a form you use software tools called 'controls'. The controls are held in the Toolbox, which is on the left-hand side of the screen.

There are many different controls in the Toolbox. Look in the Toolbox window and check some of the controls that it holds. This will give you some ideas about the types of objects you can add to a form.

In the activity that follows you will add a label to the form. You can add a label to a form either by dragging the Label control from the Toolbox onto the form or you can double-click the Label control. Both of these methods will add a label to the form.

If you add a label to a form, the computer will give it a name to identify it. The computer will call the first label that you add *Label1* the next *Label2* and so on. In section 1.4 you will learn how to change the name of an object, but for now just use the name the computer has given.

Properties

The characteristics of an object, such as its appearance and functions, are called its properties. As well as adding an object to a form you can change the properties of the object. One property you can easily change is the position of an object. To change its position you just click and drag the object around on the form to whatever position you want.

To change other properties you must use the Properties window, which is on the right-hand side of the IDE.

The Properties window can be seen in the next screenshot. The window displays the properties or features of *Label1*. The list of properties may be arranged by categories or in alphabetical order. It is usually easier to find the property you want if you use alphabetical order. Clicking on the A→Z button at the top of the Properties window puts the list in alphabetical order.

Click on the A→Z button to put in alphabetical order

Properties

Label1 System.Windows.Forms.Label

⊿ Appearance

BackColor	Control
BorderStyle	None
Cursor	Default
FlatStyle	Standard
Font	Microsoft Sans Serif, 8.25p
ForeColor	ControlText
Image	(none)
ImageAlign	MiddleCenter
ImageIndex	(none)
ImageKey	(none)
ImageList	(none)
RightToLeft	No
Text	**Label1**

Some of the properties that you can change include:

- **Text**: Whatever you type as the *Text* property will be shown on the object. In this case, as the object is a label, this will be the contents of the label.
- **ForeColor**: This is the colour of the text. Click on the small arrow to the right of the property to open a window of colour options. Choose any colour for the text of the label.

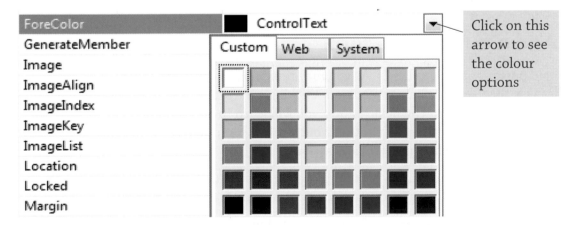

Click on this arrow to see the colour options

- **Font**: Font means the size and style of text. You can change the font used in the label by clicking on the button with three dots on it, to the right of the *Font* property. A window opens where you can choose the style and size of text.

Activity Add a label to a form

Carry out these tasks.

- Make sure Visual Basic is open with My First Program open on the screen.
- Look at the Toolbox on the left-hand side of the screen.
- Find the Label control in the Toolbox.
- Drag the Label control onto the form to create a label called *Label1*.
- Click on *Label1* to select it.
- Drag the mouse to move the label about on the form, and move it to a central position on the form.
- Look at the Properties window on the right-hand side of the screen.
- Find the *Text* property.
- Delete the text 'Label1' and replace it with the message 'This is my first software application.'
- Press the ENTER key.
- Select the *ForeColor* property.
- Click on the small arrow on the right of this box.
- A selection of colours will open. Choose a colour for the text.
- Select the *Font* property.
- Click on the small button showing three dots on the right of this box.
- Choose any font, style and size.
- Click on OK.

■ 1.4 Add a button to a form

Forms can hold buttons as well as labels. As you may remember from using other software packages the user can click on a button. Clicking a button is used to select options or to close a window. In the next chapter you will learn to add computer code to a button so that when the user clicks the button, the computer performs an action. For now this button won't perform any actions.

There is a control in the Toolbox called Button. Dragging this control onto the form creates a new button, called *Button1*. You can change the properties of the button.

- Position: You have seen how you can drag an object about on a form to change its position.
- Size and shape: When a button is selected it appears with little squares on the corners and the sides. These are called resize handles. By dragging the resize handles you can change the size and shape of the button.

■ *Text*, *ForeColor*, *Font*, etc.: These properties can be changed by using the Properties window, as you learned when you created a label.

Naming objects

You have learned how to add objects to a form. You have added labels and buttons. When you add an object the Visual Basic IDE gives the object a name. The name is generated automatically, for example *Button1*, *Label1* and so on.

You can choose your own names for the objects. It is better to give descriptive names to the objects in your program. That makes it easier for you to remember the name of the different objects. It will help you to write your code without errors. It will also make it easier for other people to read and understand your program.

To make your code easy to understand, choose names that begin with a three-letter reminder of what type of object it is.

■ The name of a button will begin with *btn*.
■ The name of a label will begin with *lbl*.

The name of an object is one of the object properties. Like the other properties, you can change it in the Properties window. It is shown in brackets at the top of the window (see the next screenshot). Simply delete the existing name (*Button1*) and enter a descriptive name. Because the button has 'OK' on it, a good name would be *btnOK*.

You can also change the name of *Label1* to *lblMessage*.

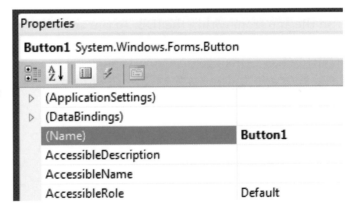

Activity Add a button to a form

■ Find the Button control in the Toolbox.

■ Drag this control to *Form1* to create a button on the form called *Button1*.

■ Change the position of *Button1* on the form.

■ Change the size of *Button1*.

■ Change the text of *Button1* to 'OK'.

■ Select a suitable colour and font.

■ Change the name of *Button1* to *btnOK*.

■ Change the name of *Label1* to *lblMessage*.

■ 1.5 Run the app

You have created a simple app. It has two objects: a label and a button. You have not added any extra computer code to the app, so it will not carry out any actions. It is just a display. The display the user sees when an app is running is sometimes called the user interface. So you have created a simple user interface, but you have not added any functionality to that interface yet.

Now you can try out the app, and see how it works. Running an app means telling the computer to display the interface, and carry out any functions. There are two ways to run an app.

When the app is being developed you can test it by running it within the IDE. This is sometimes called debugging the app, as it gives you a chance to find any errors or bugs in the computer code.

When an app is completely finished you can compile it to make a stand-alone app, which you can distribute to other users. You will learn more about compiling an app later in the book, in chapter 27.

Link

Compiling an app – chapter 27

For now you will run the app from within the IDE. To run an app, click on the Start Debugging button on the toolbar at the top of the screen. The button has a small green arrow/triangle on it. Clicking on it will run your app and you will see *Form1* with the label and button that you created.

To stop the app from running click on the Stop Debugging button, which is the button on the toolbar with a small blue square. If you click on this tool it will stop the debugging process.

You are very unlikely to get a message saying there is a bug or error in this program. Later, as you add programming code, you may find that there are errors in your work. Debugging your app gives you a chance to check it and remove errors.

Activity Run the app

- Make sure Visual Basic is open, with your project on the screen.
- Click on the Start Debugging button.
- Look at the user interface you have created.
- Click on the Stop Debugging button to close the app.

1.6 Save your work

Finally, you must save your work. At the moment the simple app, which you have created, is held in the computer's active memory. If you close down the IDE then the app will be lost.

To ensure an app you create is saved to use another time you must save it to a storage area attached to your computer. You may save your work to a memory stick, to the hard disk of the computer, or to network storage. Your teacher will explain the storage arrangements at your school or college.

The 'Save All' button looks like a stack of storage disks. This will save your current work, and all files associated with it. For now your app is simple and has only one file.

Clicking the Save All button opens the Save Project window, which looks like this.

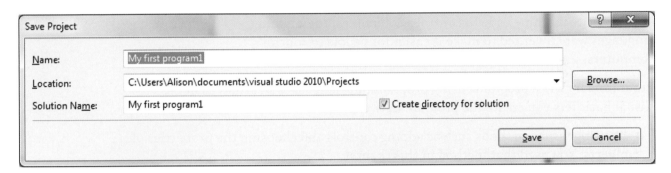

In this window you can name the project and choose a suitable storage location. Click on the Save button to complete the action.

Activity Save the app

- Click on the Save All button.

- Look in the Save Project window and make sure the name of your project and the save location are correct. Change these details if you need to.

- Click Save.

- You may exit Visual Basic as your work is now saved.

Study tip

You may have seen the 'Save Project' form when you first entered the name of the project. If you have already seen this form and selected a storage location, you won't see it a second time.

Study tip

Get into the habit of saving your code regularly while you are working. Do not wait until the end of a project. A hardware problem, a power cut, or an error in your project, could cause your system to stop working temporarily. Any code that is not saved might be lost.

■ 1.7 Programming basics

In this section you will reflect on the practical programming task that you just completed. This section will discuss some programming concepts that will help you to understand the work that you completed.

Programming languages

You wrote a program using the Visual Basic programming language. A program is a set of instructions that makes a computer carry out an action. The action the computer carried out in this case was quite simple – it showed a window with a label and a button.

Computers are controlled by an electronic number code called 'machine code'. It is based on binary numbers. But you do not need to write machine code to control a computer. Programming languages were invented to make it easier for people to control computers.

Link

Binary numbers – chapter 4

Programmers write programs using programming languages such as Visual Basic. Visual Basic lets you create the program in two ways:

- By using visual methods such as adding controls and choosing the properties of objects. You used that method in this chapter.
- By entering new computer code from scratch. You will begin to use that method in chapter 2.

When you have created a program, the instructions you have created must be converted into machine code, so that the computer understands them. When you 'run' the machine code, the computer will carry out the instructions.

The program code is converted into machine code by a piece of software called a compiler. The compiler creates a new machine code file. The machine code file is a working software application. You can run the application any time you like.

A compiler which turns your Visual Basic program into a machine code app is part of the Visual Basic package. When you run the program by clicking on the debug button, the compiler creates a machine code file and runs it right away so you can see its effect.

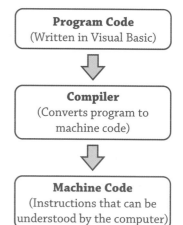

Program Code
(Written in Visual Basic)

Compiler
(Converts program to machine code)

Machine Code
(Instructions that can be understood by the computer)

Later in this book you will learn how to compile the app to make a permanent working software file, which you can save to a CD or share with friends.

Link

Compiling an application – chapter 27

Debugging

It is common for computer programs to have errors in them when they are first written. Errors in computer programs are sometimes called bugs. Finding and correcting the errors in programs is called **debugging**.

In this chapter you created a very simple application in Visual Basic. You used the debugging tool to run the program code, and to check that it worked properly. The debugging tool interpreted the program (turned it into machine code) and then it ran the program (carried out the instructions).

If your program ran as you wanted it to, then it did not have any errors in it.

> **Key term**
>
> **Debug** To check through a program for errors and correct them.

> **Link**
>
> Types of error – chapter 22

■ 1.8 Hardware and software

This book will help you learn about the features of computer systems. This section introduces the hardware and software that make up a computer system. You will learn more in future chapters.

Hardware

Hardware is a general word for the devices that make up a computer system, such as the keyboard and the computer screen.

There are four types of hardware device:

- Input: puts information into the computer system.
- Processing: the central processor of the computer, which carries out the work.
- Storage: stores information in electronic form.
- Output: shows or produces results.

All computers include all four types of hardware.

> **Key term**
>
> **Hardware** The pieces of equipment that make up a computer system.

> **Link**
>
> Computer systems – chapter 10

Software

The instructions that tell the computer what actions to perform are held as machine code inside the computer system. **Software** is a general term for any collection of machine code instructions.

In this chapter you created a simple piece of software, which displayed a message on the screen. A piece of software that carries out a defined task is called a software application or app. As you work through this book you will create a series of apps.

> **Key term**
>
> **Software** The instructions that make a computer function in the required way.

Computer systems

A functioning computer system comprises hardware and software. You may be familiar with computers such as desktop PCs and laptops. Nowadays there are also many smaller portable and handheld computer devices available. Examples include tablet computers such as the iPad, and e-book readers such as the Kindle.

Most modern mobile phones include a computer processor. The word for a phone with a built-in processor is a 'Smartphone', but many people just call them 'phones' nowadays. Smartphones can run apps – these are small computer programs often written by freelance programmers.

Many of the familiar objects around us have a computer processor built into them. For example, washing machines and central heating systems are often computer-controlled. In addition larger public systems, such as the electricity supply or the lights which control traffic flow, are computer-controlled.

Industrial systems are frequently controlled by computers. Examples include the robots in car factories and control of power stations and mining operations. Computers are also used in scientific research and exploration, from monitoring the climate and detecting earthquakes, to recording signals from outer space.

In short, computer systems are embedded in almost every aspect of modern life. It is important to understand them, their strengths and their limitations. People who can work with computers are at an advantage in finding a useful role in adult life.

Find out more about computer systems in chapter 10.

■ Chapter end

Overview

In this chapter you created a simple Visual Basic app. It consisted of a form that held two objects – a label and a button. The objects had properties such as position, text and colour.

- You added objects to a form.
- You changed some of the properties.
- You checked the app using the debugging tool, which interprets the code and runs it.

You learned that computer systems are made up of both hardware and software. Hardware is a general name for the objects that make up a computer system. Software is a general name for the instructions that tell the computer how to act.

■ Questions

Answer these questions to demonstrate your learning:

1 Give the name of any software application you have used that has a windows interface.
2 Describe two objects that can be added to a form.
3 Describe two properties of an object.
4 Describe two different ways you can add an object to a form.
5 How would you change the size of a button on a form?
6 If you change the font of a label, how would the appearance of the label change?
7 Explain the meaning of a bug in computer code.
8 What is the difference between compiling and running computer code?
9 Name two items of hardware.
10 Why is it important to save an app before closing Visual Basic?

Further activity

Practice activities can be carried out if you finish the work in this chapter with time to spare. You can also carry out these activities in your own time to help with learning and to improve your skills.

Extension activities will let you increase your skills, through independent learning. These activities are not essential in order to tackle the assessed activities but they will increase your skills.

Practice activity: Here is a user interface with several buttons and labels. Start a new project called Example Interface. Use the skills you have developed in this chapter to create this interface. Give the objects suitable names.

The second label continues over several lines. To allow this, select the label, find the property called *AutoSize* and change it from 'True' to 'False'.

Save your work.

Extension activity: Move the mouse to the toolbar at the top of the IDE. Find an area to the right of the toolbar, where there are no tool icons. Right click in this area. You will see a list of toolbars. The Standard toolbar is selected.

Click to select the Layout toolbar. The tools on the Layout toolbar allow you to align and distribute the objects on a form. If you have time, familiarise yourself with these buttons and how they allow you to work with the design of the form.

2 Event-driven programming

■ Introduction

In the last chapter you created a simple app with a user interface. In this chapter you will add a small amount of computer code to make the interface respond to user actions. This is an example of event-driven programming, as the program will respond to events.

You will also find out about coding errors, and how the user interface helps you to identify and correct errors.

■ 2.1 Ways of programming

In the last chapter you learned that computer programs are written in a computer language and then converted to machine code, which the computer understands.

Traditionally computer programs were written as a sequence of instructions. The instructions were typed in by the programmer and then converted into machine code. The instructions would be carried out by the computer in the order they were given. The program would perform the actions in this order every time it was run.

Modern computer languages are more flexible than this. They offer visual tools and features that make it easier to create the programs. The programs that you create are designed to respond to a range of different events, such as the choices of the computer user.

Visual Basic – like other similar computer languages – can be described as:

– an object-oriented programming language
– an **event-driven programming** language.

In this section you will learn what those expressions mean. You will then create a short piece of Visual Basic computer code, which is linked to an object and controls an event.

Object-oriented programming

Visual Basic is a programming language that lets you create objects. In chapter 1 you used the Visual Basic system to create a form with a label and a button. The form, the label and the button are all examples of objects.

In programming an object is an item that:

- has properties
- is linked to particular actions and events.

A key feature of object-oriented programming is that there are common types (or classes) of object. All objects of the same class have many features in common. For example, in Visual Basic a button is a class of object. All buttons have certain basic properties that are fixed, and other properties that you can change. Properties that you can change include the text, location and appearance of the object.

In chapter 1 you created a program called My First Program. You used the Visual Basic system to alter the properties of the objects. For example, you changed the text of the label and the button.

> **Study tip**
>
> This chapter gives a simple overview of objects and events, suitable for a beginner. Programming is a complex subject, and if you continue your studies in computer science you will learn a lot more about these issues.

Event-driven programming

A traditional computer program is a series of instructions. When you run the program the instructions are carried out in order. An event-driven program is different from that. An event-driven program can include many different instructions, but they are not carried out until an event happens.

So, an event-driven program responds to events. The types of events that might make the program respond include:

- A stimulus from the environment, such as a rise in temperature or a noise
- A stimulus from the computer, such as a disk error
- A signal from a timer
- A signal from the computer user, such as using the mouse to click on a button.

In this book you will mainly create event-driven programs which respond to signals from the computer user.

■ 2.2 Open the saved app

In chapter 1 you created a simple app called My First Program. It had an interface but no functionality. In this chapter you will add code to that program.

First you must open the file you saved last time. When you start up Visual Basic you will see the Start Page, which will list all recent projects that you have worked on. The project you worked on last time, My First Program, should be on that list. By clicking on the name of the project you will select and open it.

If you share storage space with other users you may not see your program in the list of Recent Projects. If so, click on Open Project... and use the navigation system to locate the storage area where you saved your work last time, and select your file.

Activity Open the saved app

- Start Visual Basic.

- Find the name of your file in the Recent Projects list.

- Click on the file name to open it.

■ 2.3 Add code to an object

My First Program is open on your screen. The form has two objects on it – a label (*lblMessage*) and a button (*btnOK*). In this section you will write a simple piece of computer code linked to the button. The code will make the program end when you click *btnOK*.

If you double-click on any object on a Visual Basic form a second tab will open. This Code Editor tab shows the code that is linked to that object. In this tab you can type any new code that you want to add. The image shows what you will see on the screen.

There are two tabs.

- One tab is called Form1.vb [Design]. If you click on this tab you will see the layout and design of *Form1*.
- The other tab is called Form1.vb. If you click on this tab you will see the code that is linked to *Form1*.

If you have not already done so, double click on *btnOK* to display the code shown in the screenshot.

Take a look at the code in this tab. Visual Basic has automatically generated some code for *Form1*. The code is displayed in the tab using text of various colours. Some of this code is linked to *Form1* and some of the code is linked to *btnOK*.

You can make changes to the code if you need to but Visual Basic is quite good at creating the right code for what you need. Generally you will add new code, but you will not usually need to change the code that is already there.

The *Form1* code

At the top of the code you will see the line

```
Public Class Form1
```

The words *Public* and *Class* are key words in Visual Basic. Key words have a fixed meaning in Visual Basic code. They are shown in blue text. The word *Public* tells you that the code in *Form1* is not hidden or restricted. The word *Class* tells you that the code defines the object class for *Form1*.

The next word is *Form1*, which is the name of the object. As this is the name of an object rather than a key word it is shown in a different colour.

At the bottom of the code you will see the following words.

```
End Class
```

This line marks the end of the code for *Form1*.

The code for *btnOK*

Inside the *Form1* code is another piece of code. This code is linked to *btnOK*. The *btnOK* code is held inside the *Form1* code, just like *btnOK* is held inside *Form1*.

The first line of the *btnOK* code looks like this:

```
Private Sub btnOK_Click (...
```

The words *Private* and *Sub* are key words. They are in blue text. The word *Private* means that *btnOK* is only accessible through *Form1*. It is not a public object. The word *Sub* means that the code is a sub-procedure. You will learn more about sub-procedures in chapter 18.

Link

Procedures – chapter 18

The word *btnOK* is the name of an object. *btnOK_click* is the name of an event. The event occurs when a user clicks on *btnOK*. So this code will be activated when a user clicks on *btnOK*.

Following the words *btnOK_Click* is some more code inside brackets. This code is automatically generated. You do not need to change it. In general this code will not be used in your programming tasks and as you are a new programmer you can ignore it.

The last line of the *btnOK* code looks like this:

```
End Sub
```

This line marks the end of the code for *btnOK*. Now you will add more code to *btnOK* so that when the user clicks on this button, it has the effect of closing the user interface and ending the app.

The single-word command *End* has the effect of ending the app, and closing the open form. When you carry out the activity at the end of this section you will add this command to the code for *btnOK*.

Editing code

You can edit the code in the coding window just as you would edit a word-processed document. You move the cursor, create new lines, insert and delete text, and use copy and paste. If you are not clear about how to use these features, take time for more practice with word processing.

Indentation

If you look at the code listing on the screen of your computer, you will see that the lines of code are not all positioned in the same way. Some codes are set in from the left margin. In other words they are 'indented'.

Indentation is used to improve the readability of programs. You have learned that the code for *btnOK* belongs within *Form1*. This is shown by the indentation. The code for *Form1* is not indented. The code for *btnOK* is indented. That shows that *btnOK* is part of *Form1*, and is held inside it.

You don't have to add indentation to your code, as it is added automatically by the computer as you type. Pay attention to what indentation is added. This will make the structure of the code easier to understand.

Adding comments

You have learned to improve the readability of your code by using sensible names for objects. Another way to improve readability is to include comments. Comments are explanations written by the programmer. Comments explain what a line or small section of code is for. Comments are ignored by the software. They are only for human readers.

Comments are useful in many different ways:

- They help you to clarify your intentions as you write code.
- They help you to remember the purpose of the code you wrote, if you come back to it later.
- They help other programmers to understand your code when they read it or work with it.

To show that a line is a comment, for the software to ignore, you begin it with a single quotation mark. That is all – you don't even need to close the quotation at the end of the line

For example

```
'This is a comment
```

If the comment goes over several lines, put a quotation mark at the start of each line.

To show that it recognises the line is a comment, Visual Basic puts it in green characters.

Use of colour

The Visual Basic IDE uses coloured text to show different parts of the code:

- Blue characters are used for visual basic key words such as *End* or *Sub*.
- Green characters are used for comments: these will not be read by the computer.
- Red characters are used for text strings.
- Black characters are used for other values such as the names of objects and events.

Visual Basic will use colour automatically. You don't have to do anything to make it happen. Look out for the use of colour as you develop program code. In this book samples of computer code are printed in the colours that you should see on your computer screen.

Activity Add code to *btnOK*

In this activity you will add code to *btnOK*. This code is linked to the event *btnOK_Click*. In other words the code will be activated when the user clicks on *btnOK*. The code will close the interface and end the app.

- If you have not done so already, double-click on *btnOK* to open the Code Editor tab.
- Compare the contents of the Code Editor tab and the Design tab.
- In the Code Editor tab, find the code for *btnOK_Click*.
- Move the cursor to the blank line between *Private Sub btnOK_Click* and *End sub*. If you don't see a blank line in this position, press ENTER to create a blank line.
- Type *End*.
- Above the code you just entered, add the comment 'Ends the app.

The completed code now looks like this:

```
Public Class Form1

    Private Sub btnOK_Click(ByVal …
        'Ends the app
        End

    End Sub

End Class
```

Your screen will show more code than shown here. The extra code follows the words:

```
    Private Sub btnOK_Click(ByVal …
```

This additional code is not shown here, and in this book we will leave this code out, when listing programs. You do not need to change this code. It is added automatically by the software when you write a program. The three dots following ByVal will remind you that extra words appear. Do not edit or delete this code, as that may stop your program from working properly.

- Click on the Save All button to save your work.
- Run the app using the Debugging tool.
- Click on the OK button. You will see the app respond to this event and close.

■ 2.4 Errors in computer code

Every computer language has rules. These rules are called the syntax of the language. When you write program code it must follow the syntax of the language you have chosen. If your program does not follow the rules of the language this is called a **syntax error**.

This is not the only type of error that is possible when you are programming. There are three main types of programming error:

1 Syntax errors break the rules of the programming language. Visual Basic displays an error message if you type a line of code with a syntax error in it.
2 Run-time errors occur when the program code does not have a syntax error, but it instructs the computer to carry out an impossible action. The program will stop or crash when you try to run it.
3 Logic errors mean there are no syntax or run-time errors, but the software does not do what you want it to do.

You will learn more about finding and correcting errors as you continue with this book.

It is unlikely that you have made an error in this code, as it is very simple. However it is good to understand how to find and correct errors in a program.

In the last section you added the single new code word *End* to the program. In this section you will see what would happen if you mistyped this word, for example typing *Endd* instead of *End*.

Endd is not a Visual Basic key word. The computer is not able to understand this word, or follow the instructions. If you type a word wrongly, so that it is not a correct code word, Visual Basic spots the error. The Visual Basic **IDE (Integrated Development Environment)** displays many clues to show you that there is an error.

The main working area will look like the screenshot on page 23.

There are four clues on this screen that tell you that your code includes an error:

1 The word *Endd* is not shown in blue text, because it is not a Visual Basic key word.
2 The word *Endd* has a wiggly blue line under it. That lets you know that the computer does not understand the word.
3 The computer has added brackets () after the word *Endd*; that is because it thinks it might be the name of a procedure. You will learn more abut procedures in chapter 18.
4 At the bottom of the screen is an error message that says 'Endd is not declared.' This means you have used the word *Endd*, but you have not explained what it means.

Key term

Syntax error A mistake in a computer program that breaks the rules of the computer language. A syntax error prevents the program from being converted to machine code.

Key term

IDE (Integrated Development Environment) Software that provides features to help a programmer create computer code.

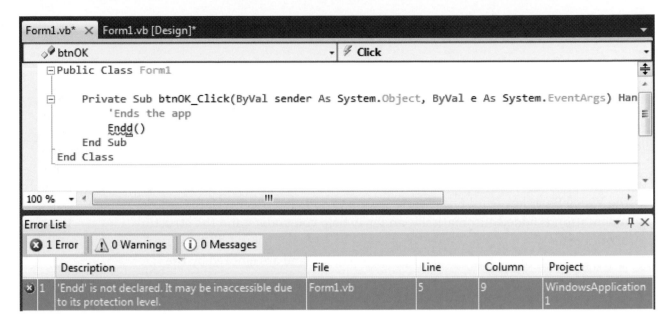

So, the IDE has given you many clues that your code has got an error in it. Supposing you ignored these clues and tried to run the app anyway? The Debugging tool would not be not able to interpret the code or run the app because the app has a syntax error. You would see an error message that says 'There were build errors. Would you like to continue?'

In summary, the IDE has many ways to let you know if there is an error in your program. You can edit the code to correct the error. When you have corrected the error, the error warnings disappear and the app will run.

Errors are not always this easy to find. Throughout this book you will learn more about finding and correcting errors.

Study tip

If you do not see the error list, as shown here, open the View Menu and select Error List.

Activity Find and correct errors

- Move the cursor to the code for *btnOK_Click*.

- Change the word *End* to *Endd*.

- Notice the error messages that appear on the screen.

- Click the Start Debugging button to try to run the app.

- You will see an error message that says 'There were build errors. Would you like to continue?' Click on 'No'.

- Correct the error and run the app again.

■ Chapter end

Overview

In this chapter you learned that Visual Basic is an object-oriented and event-driven programming language. Code is linked to objects, and activated by events such as the user clicking a button. You added code to the object called *btnOK*. When the user clicks on the button, the code is carried out.

You learned that:

- the Visual Basic key word *End* causes the app to end, and the interface to close
- indentation is added automatically, and may help you understand the structure of your code
- comment lines begin with a single quotation mark, and are ignored by the computer
- the IDE identifies errors, and gives you the opportunity to correct them
- there are three main types of computer code error: syntax errors, run-time errors and logical errors.

■ Questions

Answer these questions to demonstrate your learning:

1 Explain why Visual Basic can be called an object-oriented language.
2 Explain why Visual Basic can be called an event-driven language.
3 What is the difference between what you see in the Design tab and the Code Editor tab of a developing application?
4 In the code line *Public Class Form1* what does the word *Form1* represent?
5 What does the code line *End Sub* do?
6 A sub-procedure begins with the words *Private Sub btnSelect_Click*. What event will cause the code in this sub-procedure to be carried out?
7 Describe two ways that you can spot a syntax error in your code.
8 Give three advantages of adding comments to your code.

Further activity

Practice activities can be carried out if you finish the work in this chapter with time to spare. You can also carry out these activities in your own time to help with learning and to improve your skills.

Practice activity: In the practice activity in chapter 1 you created a new project called Example Interface. Add a second button to the form, with the text *Exit* on it. Add code so that this button ends the app and closes the interface.

3 Changing object properties

Introduction

In chapter 1 you learned that Visual Basic apps make use of objects: objects include forms, labels and buttons. All objects have properties, which include the size and position of an object, and the text it displays. In this chapter you will learn to add code to a program that alters a property of an object in response to an event. Specifically, you will make a message appear when the user clicks a button.

3.1 Changing the *Visible* property

The Design tab shows the current form and all the objects on the form.

If you select any object on the form, then the properties of that object are shown in the Properties window. In this example (see screenshot) the *lblMessage* object is selected. The properties of *lblMessage* are shown in the Properties window.

The properties are shown in alphabetical order. The final property in the list is *Visible*, which is highlighted in the screenshot. If the *Visible* property is set to True, then the label will be visible to the user when the app is run. If the *Visible* property is set to False, then the label will be hidden from the user.

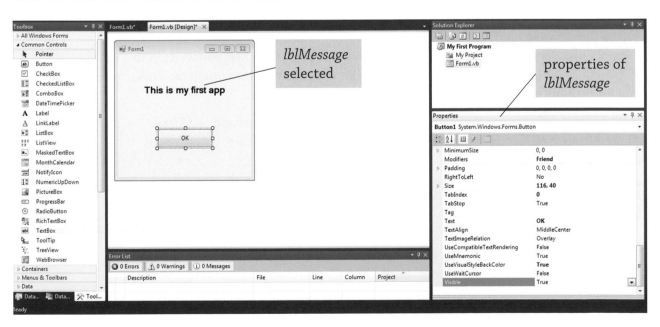

There are two easy ways to change a property of an object.

- Double-click on the property value (such as True) and it will change to the next option. Keep double-clicking to cycle through the various options.
- Click on the arrowhead next to the property value. A short menu of options will appear and you can click on the one you want to select.

Some properties have many options, some have only two. The *Visible* property has only two options: True and False.

Activity Change the *Visible* property

- Start Visual Basic.

- Find the name of your file in the Recent Projects list.

- Click on the file name to open it.

- Select *lblMessage*.

- Change the *Visible* property of *lblMessage* to False.

- Run the app. You will see that *lblMessage* is not visible to the user.

■ 3.2 Add a button to make *lblMessage* visible

In this activity you will learn how to add a new button to the form, which makes *lblMessage* visible again.

Create a button object

You can add as many buttons and labels as you wish to a form. The name of an object should tell you what the object does. That will help you when you write your code. A good name for the button that makes the message visible is *btnShow*. This name is used in this example, but you can use any name you like.

If you double-click on any object, the code tab opens, and you can add code that is linked to that object. If you haven't added any code for that object yet, then an empty sub-procedure will appear.

The next screenshot shows an example of this. You can see the code for *btnOK_Click*, which you entered in the last section. Below the code for *btnOK_Click* is some new code that begins *Private Sub btnShow_Click*.

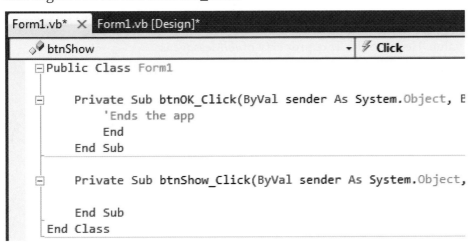

You should already know the meaning of this code. It tells you that this is a sub-procedure that will be carried out when the event *btnShow_Click* happens. In other words, whatever code you add to this section will be carried out when the user clicks *btnShow*.

Referring to objects and properties

If you want to refer to an object in your code, you just type the name of that object. In this case you want to create code to alter the properties of *lblMessage*, so you would type *lblMessage*.

You can refer to any property of that object by typing a full stop, and then the name of the property. For example

- The *Visible* property of *lblMessage* is called *lblMessage.Visible*
- The *Text* property of *lblMessage* is called *lblMessage.Text*
- The *Font* property of *lblMessage* is called *lblMessage.Font*

And so on.

Assign a value to an object property

When writing visual basic code you often need to **assign a value** to an object property or other item. Assigning a value means that a new value is given to the item. The code overwrites the old value of the item and imposes a new value. In this example you will alter the value of the property *lblMessage.Visible* from False to True.

The command that assigns a value is the equals sign. The general structure for this command is as follows.

- Enter the name of an object property.
- Type the equals sign.
- Enter the value you want to assign to that property.

> ### Key term
>
> **Assign a value**   To give a value to a named item, such as the property of an object, or a variable.

When you assign a value such as a number value or True or False, you simply enter that value. So, the code to assign the value True to the *Visible* property of *lblMessage* is:

```
lblMessage.Visible = True
```

The code to assign the value 'Hello' to the *Text* property of *lblMessage* is:

```
lblMessage.Text = "Hello"
```

Notice that double quotes " " are used around a string of text. The quotes and text appear in red.

IntelliSense

The Visual Basic IDE includes a very useful feature called IntelliSense. As you enter Visual Basic code, IntelliSense will help you by showing you a drop-down list of choices about what to type next.

Here are some of the ways that IntelliSense might help you as you are working on this task.

- If you type the name of an object and then a full stop, IntelliSense knows that the next word must be a property of the object. Therefore it lists all the properties of the object. The image shows an example of this. You can select the property you want from the list.
- If you type an equals sign, IntelliSense knows the next word must be a value you can assign to the property. Therefore it shows you a list of all the possible values to choose from. In the case of the *Visible* property, there are only two possible values: True and False.

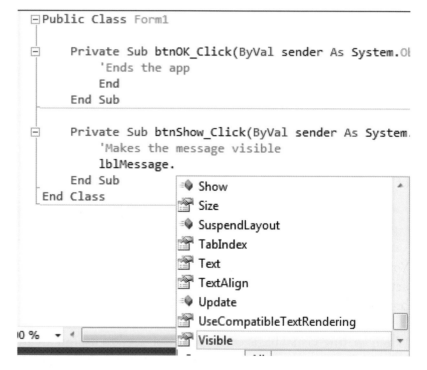

You can ignore the help if you want to, but in general it is very useful and will make it easier for you to write correct code. As you type code, you may like to make use of the choices that the computer displays.

Activity Add a button that makes *lblMessage* visible

- Make sure My First Program is open.

- Change the text of *btnOK* to read 'End' instead of 'OK'.

- Add a second button, with the text 'Show message'.

- Set the name to *btnShow*.

- Double-click on *btnShow* to open the Code Editor tab.

- Move the cursor to the blank line below *Private Sub btnShow_Click*.

- Type the name *lblMessage*.

- Type a full stop.

- Select *Visible* from the list of properties.

- Type an equals symbol, =.

- Select True from the list of options.

- Enter a comment line above the code, explaining what the code does.

- Save your program and then use 'debug' to run the code.

You should find that the program runs. When you click on the Show message button, the label becomes visible. The End button will close the application.

If you get any error messages or other problems you may have made a mistake in typing the code. Check your work very carefully to find the error.

- When you are happy with your work, save the program.

■ 3.3 Practice your skills

You have learned how to assign a value to the property of an object. In the next activity you will practice these skills. You will add a third button to the form. This button will hide the label, by setting the *Visible* property to False.

The completed interface and the full code for this project is shown at the end of this chapter.

Activity Add a button that makes *lblMessage* invisible

- Use the skills you have learned to add a third button to the form, and choose a suitable layout. The screenshot shows a suggested arrangement.

- Alter the text of *btnHide* to read 'Hide message'.

- Enter code so that when the user clicks on *btnHide*, *lblMessage* is not visible.

- Add a comment explaining the purpose of the code.

- Save the file and run the app to see if it works.

If there are any errors or problems with your code, make corrections. Remember to save again if you make any changes.

■ 3.4 Computer systems

Computer systems can be described in terms of their input and output, and in terms of **data processing**. In this section you will look at both ways of describing a computer system.

Key term

Data processing
Transforming data into information by organising it and making it more useful.

Input and output

In this chapter you have developed a simple app that performs a single function – it displays or hides a message. The app responds to the actions of the user. If the user clicks on a button then the message is displayed. If the user clicks on another button the message is hidden.

Although it is very simple, the app demonstrates a key function of computer systems. They accept input and produce output. In this case the input is a click of the mouse. The output is a message displayed on the screen.

This diagram shows the basic structure of any computer system.

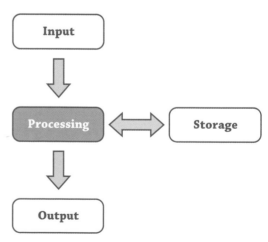

- **Input:** Every computer system receives input in order to control its operation. In some cases this may be input from a user, through a keyboard or mouse. In other cases the computer receives input from the environment, such as detecting movement or temperature.

- **Output:** Every computer system produces some kind of result. Examples include a screen display, a warning sound, or a change to the actions of a machine or robot.
- **Processing:** The processing is whatever internal action the computer carries out to transform the input into the output. You will find out more about the internal structure of the computer processor in chapter 17.
- **Storage:** Computer storage is used to save any data and software needed by the computer system.

You will see that the basic four-part structure of a computer system matches the four basic types of hardware that are available. The hardware of any computer system must include input devices, output devices, storage devices and a processor.

The type of processing that can be carried out by a computer depends on the software that is in place. The simple app that you wrote is an example of software. The app accepts input and, depending on what input is received, produces output that is displayed on the computer screen.

So, software is a set of instructions, created by a programmer, that allows the computer system to accept input and produce output. Every piece of software is different. Different software makes the computer carry out different actions.

As you learn Visual Basic you will create many different pieces of software. In each case, pay particular attention to what input the software accepts, what output the software produces, and what processing is carried out to transform the input into output.

Producing your own software will help you to have a stronger understanding of the meaning of all of these key terms.

Links

Storage – chapter 4
Input devices – section 10.2
Output devices – section 10.3
The processor – chapter 17

Data and information

Data is a general term for facts and figures. Data is a plural word, so it is correct to refer to 'some data' or 'items of data'. Items of data are input to a computer system. Before they are input, items of data have not been processed or organised.

In contrast, information means data that has been processed or organised by the computer. Information is the output from a computer system. Information has been processed to make it more useful to the human user.

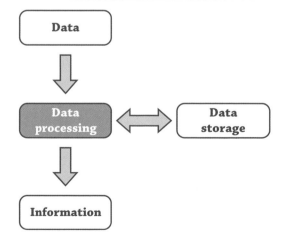

Data processing is the process of transforming data into information. It happens inside the computer. Data processing is the main purpose of a computer. Computers take data input, which is not fully organised or processed, and process it to make it more useful to human users. The diagram shows a typical computer system processing data to create information.

Computers are used in many different ways. The type of output varies a lot. But in all cases the output of a computer is useful in some way. That is why people make and buy computers – because they are useful.

Computers are digital electronic devices. That means all the data and software inside the computer system is held in electronic **digital** form. When items of data are input to the computer system they are converted to electronic digital form. When information is output from the computer system it is converted from electronic digital form to some other form. You will learn more about this in the rest of this book.

> ## Key term
>
> **Digital**   Digital data is stored inside the computer in the form of on/off electronic signals.

> ## Link
>
> Data storage – chapter 4
> The computer processor – chapter 17

■ 3.5 Examples of computer systems

All computer systems fit this model: data input is processed to produce information output.

Business information systems

Computers are used very widely in business. Computers are used to control finance and accounts, to keep stock records, to calculate employee pay, and for many other business functions.

Typically in a business computer system, input is typed into the computer by a user with a keyboard. The user will type in the day-to-day facts and figures that are important to the business. For example, a user of a business accounts system will enter data about money received or spent by the business.

Business computer systems produce reports and other forms of information that are useful to the business. For example, an accounts system will process data about the amount of money coming into the business, and the amount of money spent. The accounts system will report on how much money the business has left in its account. This is very useful information.

Industrial control systems

Industrial control systems are used to control robots and other machines in factories, power stations, mines and other places where raw materials are extracted or processed to make the items we need.

Typically, in an industrial system, input comes into the computer from sensors that detect features of the environment such as temperature, pressure or the position of moving parts. The computers will use this data to control the actions of machines. Machines may carry out actions such as heating, cutting, assembling or transporting. At the end of the process there is a useful output product.

Other systems

Computers are also used in medicine, science, education, law enforcement, transport and many other areas of day-to-day life.

In all cases, computer systems transform input into output. The output of the system is something that is useful to the human user.

Benefits of computer systems

Before computers were invented, all of this work was carried out by human beings. For example, accounts were calculated on paper, and industrial processes were controlled entirely by human workers.

The advantages of using computers include the following.

- Computers process data into information very quickly.
- Computers can operate day and night without rest.
- Computers do not get bored by repetitive tasks.
- If they are set up properly computers are accurate and precise.

Computers cannot be used for all types of work.

- Computers cannot carry out caring or supporting activities, such as nursing or parenting.
- Computers cannot respond creatively to new events.
- If a computer system is not set up correctly, it can make serious mistakes.

You can see that it is important to make sure that computer systems are set up properly, or they can be inaccurate or even dangerous.

> **Link**
>
> The need for robust and reliable systems – chapter 10

■ Chapter end

The interface

Here is the user interface for My First Program. The names of all objects are shown.

Full code listing

Here is the full listing of the code that goes with My First Program. Note that the lines which begin Private Sub have a lot of extra code which has been omitted from this listing. This additional code is added automatically by the computer. You do not need to edit this code.

```
Public Class Form1

    Private Sub btnOK_Click(ByVal sender As -
        'Ends the app
        End
    End Sub

    Private Sub btnShow_Click(ByVal sender As -
        'Makes the message visible
        lblMessage.Visible = True
    End Sub

    Private Sub btnHide_Click(ByVal sender As -
        'Hides the message
        lblMessage.Visible = False
    End Sub
End Class
```

Overview

- In this chapter you learned that Visual Basic code can be used to assign a value to an item. You assigned a value to one property of an object. You assigned the value True to the *Visible* property of the *lblMessage* object. The code is

```
lblMessage.Visible = True
```

- You learned the basic structure of all computer systems. All computers systems include input, processing, storage and output. There are hardware devices to carry out each of these functions. The type of processing that is carried out depends on the software that is in place.
- Another way to describe a computer system is by describing how it turns data into information. In business, industry and other contexts, computers are extremely useful. Computers have some advantages and some disadvantages compared to human workers.

■ Questions

Answer these questions to demonstrate your learning:

1 Describe how you can change the properties of an object using the IDE, without coding.
2 A program had an object called *lblTitle*. The programmer wanted to refer to the *Font* property of the object. How do you refer to the *Font* property of *lblTitle*?
3 What are the two possible values of the *Visible* property of any object?
4 What symbol is used to assign a value to an item?
5 How can the IntelliSense feature help you when you are writing code?
6 Draw a diagram setting out the relationship between input, output and other major features of a computer system.
7 What is the difference between data and information?
8 How would we describe the work of a computer system in terms of data and information?
9 Compare a typical business use of computers to a typical industrial use of computers. What are the differences in input and output of these two types of computer system?
10 Describe one advantage and one disadvantage of a computerised system compared to a human worker.

4 Data storage

■ Introduction

In this chapter you will learn about how data and software are stored on a computer system. There are several different types of data storage and you need to understand how the computer stores data in order to write programs.

■ 4.1 Primary storage

The processor of a computer is the item of hardware that carries out data processing. The work of the processor is carried out electronically. Inside the processor all data and software are processed in the form of electronic numbers. These numbers are made of electronic signals that can be in two states: on or off. All data is processed in the form of these on/off signals.

On/off electrical signals can be represented as binary numbers. Binary numbers are made of 1s and 0s. Find out more about binary numbers in section 4.4.

Primary storage is the area of computer storage that is connected directly to the computer processor. It is very quick and easy for the processor to take data and software from primary storage. The data travels down short connections called data buses.

Primary storage inside a computer system is also called computer memory. There are two types of primary storage: ROM and RAM.

ROM

ROM stands for Read Only Memory. 'Read-only' means that the data in ROM can be read by the computer, but not changed. The digital contents of ROM are permanently fixed, often in the factory where the computer was made, by physically building the on/off digital signals into the computer's transistor circuits.

ROM has one very big advantage over other parts of primary storage. It is permanent and does not lose its contents when the computer is switched off. That means it can be used to store the start-up software that makes the computer boot up when it is switched on.

On a typical PC the start-up software stored in the ROM is called the BIOS. That stands for Basic Input/Output System. The BIOS has the job of starting up the

Learning content

3.1.8.4 Memory: know the differences between non-volatile and volatile memory; understand the purpose of both types of memory and when each should be used.

3.1.8.5 Secondary storage: understand what secondary storage is and be able to explain why it is required; describe the most common types of secondary storage; understand how optical media, magnetic media and solid state work.

3.1.10 Data representation: understand that computers use the binary alphabet to represent all data and instructions; understand the terms bit, nibble, byte, kilobyte, megabyte and gigabyte; understand that a binary code could represent different types of data such as text, image, sound, integer, date, real number; understand how sound and bitmap images can be represented in binary; understand how characters are represented in binary and be familiar with ASCII and its limitations.

system hardware, and loading the operating system from wherever it is stored (typically the hard disk of the computer). The BIOS also makes sure that the keyboard, screen, and other input and output devices communicate properly with the computer processor. That means that the computer is ready to go and you can start typing and using the mouse.

The big disadvantage of ROM is that its contents cannot be changed. The contents of ROM are fixed in the factory, and never change after that. This means that ROM cannot be used to store new software or data when the computer is in use.

RAM

RAM stands for Random Access Memory. The computer processor can access any part of RAM while the computer is switched on. In general the more RAM a computer has, the more powerful the computer. RAM is read–write memory. This means the computer processor can read the data in RAM, and also put new data into RAM.

RAM is used to store the software currently in use by the computer. It is also used to store the data that is in use at that time. So, for example, if you were using a word processor to write a report, the word-processing software would be in RAM. The text of the report would be in RAM. But work you did on a previous day would not be in RAM.

RAM is entirely electronic. If the computer is switched off, or the electrical power is cut off, the contents of RAM will be lost. Memory that will lose its contents when the power is turned off is called **volatile** memory.

The main advantage of RAM storage is that it is quick and easy for the processor to read the data and instructions that are stored there, and to store new data. The main disadvantage is that the contents of RAM are volatile – they are lost if the computer is turned off. For this reason, when you are using the computer you should always save your work to secondary storage before you close down the computer. If you were working on a report and the power went off, your unsaved work would be lost. If you exited from the software without saving the report to storage, then your work would be lost.

The table compares the advantages and disadvantages of ROM and RAM.

	ROM	RAM
Advantages	**Non-volatile**. The data in ROM is not lost when the computer is switched off. Because it is primary memory, ROM can be accessed very rapidly by the processor.	**Read–write**. New data can be stored in RAM at any time. Because it primary memory, RAM can be accessed very rapidly by the processor.
Disadvantages	**Read-only**. New data cannot be stored in ROM.	**Volatile**. The data in RAM is lost when the computer is switched off.

Virtual memory

Nowadays many people have several different software applications open at the same time: for example, a web browser, a word processor, and a computer game might be running at the same time. There is often not enough room in RAM to store all the software that is in use.

'Virtual memory' is a way for the computer to manage a lot of software with limited RAM. The processor combines RAM with secondary storage to create a larger memory store, and the software that is in use is stored partly in RAM, and partly in secondary storage.

In the next section you will learn about secondary storage.

■ 4.2 Secondary storage

Computer systems include **non-volatile** storage. This is storage that does not depend on electricity. It is also called secondary storage. Data and software in secondary storage will not be lost when the power is turned off.

Secondary storage has advantages and disadvantages compared to primary storage.

- Advantages: secondary storage is read–write storage and it is non-volatile, so it has advantages over both ROM and RAM.
- Disadvantages: it takes longer for the processor to access the contents of secondary storage. In general, data and software are copied into RAM before processing.
- As you have seen, virtual memory combines RAM and secondary storage. In this case, typically, the commands which are used less often are kept in secondary storage, because it is slower for the computer to access them.

There are three main ways that digital signals can be stored, without the need for electricity:

- magnetic storage
- optical storage
- solid-state storage.

Magnetic storage

In magnetic storage the electronic signals from the computer are converted into magnetism. The on/off electronic signals are converted into positive and negative magnetic charges. Magnets do not need electricity. A magnetic charge is retained when electricity is switched off. It is easy to change a magnetic charge, which means data stored magnetically can be easily changed and deleted. This means that magnetic storage is an example of non-volatile, read–write storage.

There are three main types of magnetic storage.

- **Magnetic tape** holds the magnetic charge on continuous plastic tape, which is wound up into dense spools. Magnetic tape is cheap, high-volume storage, but slow access. It is mainly used for large backups.

- **Floppy disks** hold the magnetic charge on a soft plastic disk inside a hard case. Floppy disks used to be very popular for storage, but they have low capacity and are rarely used now.
- **Hard disk drives** (HDDs) hold the magnetic charge on a stack of metal disks. They have high capacity and are widely used nowadays. In general, hard disks are fixed inside the casing of a computer. This is called an 'internal' hard disk. Because an internal hard disk is typically fixed inside the computer, it can only store data from that computer, unless other computers are connected by a direct data link. **An external HDD** is held in a separate case and is plugged into the computer. That means it can be easily moved from one computer to another.

Optical storage

In optical storage the electronic signals from the computer are converted into microscopic indentations, known as pits, burned into the surface of a CD, DVD or Blue-ray disk. A laser beam shone onto the surface of the disk detects the presence of these pits. This is how the disk is read by the computer. DVDs and Blue-ray disks use smaller and more precise pits, so they can store more data than CDs.

Optical storage does not depend on electricity. Once the pits have been burned on to the disk the data is permanently in place. Optical storage is cheap to make and distribute and generally quite robust (hard to damage). Disks can be easily taken out of one computer and inserted into another. That means optical storage disks are a good way to share data and software. CDs, DVDs and Blue-ray disks are often used to distribute music or films, as well as copies of software to install on a computer.

A disadvantage of optical storage is that once the pits have been burned into the disk they cannot be erased. This means the data on an optical disk cannot be changed once it is has been burned. Once the disk is full, no more data can be stored on the disk.

> ### Did you know?
>
> Rewritable CDs are available. This technology is called CD-RW. A rewritable CD is coated in a dye which becomes transparent when it is heated to a particular temperature. When you want to reuse the CD the coating is reheated and returns to its original state.

Solid-state storage

Solid-state storage is the most modern of the three main types of storage. It stores electronic signals by trapping electrons in microscopic transistors. Because electrons are so small, solid-state storage can hold a great deal of data in a very small device. The most common use of solid-state storage is as flash memory in a USB flash drive. Flash memory is compact, robust and reliable. The arrangement of trapped electrons can be altered at any time so it is easy to change or delete the data held in flash memory. A USB flash drive can be plugged into any modern computer, so this type of storage is very suitable for carrying files around and moving them between computers. A lot of pupils use a flash drive to store their school work.

The advantages of solid-state memory are that it is compact, robust and portable.

The main disadvantage of flash memory is that it is more expensive than other forms of storage, though prices are coming down as the technology is developed. One concern is that the memory may decay as electrons escape from the transistor circuits. As solid-state storage is quite a new invention, nobody is quite sure whether this will be a long-term problem.

Solid-state storage can be used to make hard disk drives. A solid-state drive is known as an SSD. An SSD may be found in more expensive laptops and hand-held devices. At the moment an SSD is about ten times more expensive than an ordinary HDD of the same storage capacity. This may change.

A third type of hard drive combines both magnetic and solid-state storage. This is called a hybrid drive. Manufacturers of hybrid drives say they use less power and are more reliable than HDDs, but less expensive than SSDs.

■ 4.3 Data representation

You have learned that all data is held inside primary storage in the form of electronic signals that can be in two states: on or off. When the data is copied to secondary storage these signals are converted into some other system – magnetic charge, small optical holes, or microscopic transistors that hold electrons. All of these systems can be in two states.

Measuring storage capacity

A single on or off signal inside a computer is called a bit. This stands for binary digit.

A single digit cannot store anything significant, so in computer systems bits are typically used in groups of eight. A group of eight bits is called a byte. A byte is enough memory to store a single text character or letter. The capacity of computer memory is typically measured in bytes. Half a byte (four bits) is sometimes called a nibble.

You need a lot of bytes to store most types of modern data. So, we talk about bytes using large numbers. Some of the major units used to measure the size of computer storage are shown in the next table.

Quantity	Size	Comment
1 kilobyte (kB)	1024 bytes	Even a short typed document will use several kilobytes of memory.
1 megabyte (MB)	1024 kilobytes	One digital photo may use several megabytes of memory, depending on how large and detailed it is.
1 gigabyte (GB)	1024 megabytes	One gigabyte of storage could hold a large collection of images and documents. Sixteen hours of MP3 songs (based on a file size of 1 MB per minute) uses about a gigabyte of storage. When you compare computer storage, the capacity of each type of storage is often expressed by saying how many gigabytes it will hold. A regular DVD holds about four or five gigabytes of data although DVDs are now available that will hold more data than this.
1 terabyte (TB)	1024 gigabytes	This can store a great deal of data. A terabyte of storage could hold about 16,500 hours (690 days!) of MP3 songs (based on a file size of 1 MB per minute), or a large number of books and movies.

Storing data

You have learned that all types of data inside the computer system must be stored as binary numbers. Data that is stored in number form is called digital data. Standard systems are used to convert data into digital form. In this section you will learn about these systems.

Text data is stored digitally using a system called **ASCII**. ASCII stands for 'American Standard Code for Information Interchange'. It is pronounced 'As-key'. There is an ASCII number code for each character in the western alphabet as well as other common text characters such as punctuation marks. For example the code for 'A' is 65, 'a' is 97, 'b' is 98 and so on. Nowadays a larger coding system called 'Unicode' is used internationally. Unicode is a greatly extended coding system. It includes codes for other character systems, such as Arabic and Chinese writing. The Unicode for letters in the western alphabet remains the same as ASCII code.

Machine code

Computer instructions are stored using a number code called machine code. Every action that the computer processor can perform (such as storing data or adding numbers together) has its own unique number code. When you write a program it must be converted into machine code before the computer can carry out the instructions.

Storing images

Images, including pictures and photos, must be converted into digital form before they can be stored or processed by a computer. Cameras and mobile devices take digital photos. Computer images that you make using graphics software are digital. Digital images are made of **pixels**. A single pixel is the smallest part of a picture that can be altered. You may think of a pixel as a tiny dot, and a picture is made up of thousands or millions of these dots. In a printed image, a pixel is one dot or point of ink. In a screen image it is one point of light.

There are several different ways that the computer can store images. These are called different image formats. One common format is bitmap. A bitmap file stores the position and colour of each pixel in the image. That means each bitmap image takes a lot of storage space. Higher resolution images use more pixels to make the same size image, so they are clearer and more detailed but use more storage space.

A disadvantage of bitmap graphics is that if you make the image larger, all the dots in the image get larger. Instead of being one pixel, each dot expands to cover several pixels. The image does not get more detailed. The image can look blurred or grainy.

> ### Did you know?
> It has been estimated that Wikipedia holds 4 or 5 terabytes of data.
>
> The first 20 years of observations by the Hubble Space Telescope comes to more than 45 terabytes of data.

> ### Key term
> **ASCII (American Standard Code for Information Interchange)** a code used to convert characters into numerical form for computer storage and transmission.

> ### Key term
> **Pixel** Pixel is short for 'picture element'. It is the smallest changeable part of a picture.

An alternative way of storing an image uses 'vector' graphics. Vector graphics store mathematical formulas which define the curves and other shapes that make up the image. This uses less storage space than a bitmap image. Another advantage of vector graphics is that they are scalable. That means they can be made larger or smaller with no loss of image quality, because the mathematical formulas can be recalculated by the computer to create images of all different sizes. A disadvantage of vector images is that it can be challenging to make a vector image. Every image is made from shapes and curves.

Vector images are typically used for graphic designs and drawings. Bitmap images are used for screenshots and photos.

The characteristics of an image such as brightness and colour are stored using a number code. In a bitmap image the brightness and colour of each dot will be stored. In a vector image the brightness and colours of each shape within the image are stored.

Some image formats use a long number code to store the different colour values. These images can use a wide range of colours, so they can look more realistic and subtle. But they take more storage space.

Storing sounds

Sound can also be stored using digital codes. You may know that sound is made of sound waves, which travel through the air. A recording device detects these sound waves and turns them into digital form. The digital information records the shape of the changing sound wave.

There are many different audio coding systems, called formats. There is a trade-off between the amount of space used by a format and the sound quality of the result. Some audio formats use more storage space, but produce higher quality results. Some audio formats use less space, but the quality of sound is worse.

- The system used on most personal audio devices is called MP3. This is a compressed format. That means some of the detail of the sound is removed, to make the file smaller. The MP3 format uses less storage space than many other audio formats – but it has only moderate sound quality. Audio compression which results in a loss of sound quality is called 'lossy compression'.
- An alternative audio format is WAV. WAV files are not compressed. They retain more detail of the original sound than the MP3 format, but they take up more storage space. Because WAV files are so large, they are not used on most portable devices, or on websites. BBC radio uses WAV audio formats.
- A third type of audio file is compressed, but the compression does not result in a loss of sound quality. This is known as 'lossless compression'. There are a number of rival formats with competing claims about quality.

Storing moving images

Moving images, for example in films and on TV, are made by storing a series of still images. The equipment shows each image for a fraction of a second, and this tricks the eye into seeing movement. In the past each still image was stored in sequence on a reel of film. Physical film stock of this kind is rarely used nowadays. Instead the images are represented in digital form. The digital files can be transmitted or stored using computer systems.

Examples including digital TV, video clips on YouTube, and DVDs of films that you can buy. Many modern phones can take short video clips. Video clips of events, perhaps taken by passers-by, are often seen in the news. Moving images on the Internet help us to see what it is like to live in other countries, or to experience disasters and wars.

A video clip is made of still images. The quality of a video clip depends on the quality of the images. It also depends on the quality of the sound track. You have already learned about image and sound quality. Higher resolution images are composed of more pixels, with a greater range of colours. High quality video makes use of this type of image.

Because video is made of millions of images, video clips can take up a lot of storage space. Methods are available to compress video files, so they take up less space, but this often causes loss of image quality.

Quality v. storage space

You have learned that there are a range of different formats which can be used to store pictures, sounds and moving images. Some formats store more detail and variety. These formats produce high quality results. However, they use more storage space. This is called high resolution. Other formats store less detail, and produce lower quality results, but use much less space. This is called low resolution.

Different formats are more suitable for different purposes. Images and sounds used on small portable devices are often stored in low-resolution formats to save space. Large screens and expensive sound systems generally use high resolution storage methods, to produce impressive high quality sounds and images.

■ 4.4 Binary numbers

You have learned that all data in primary and secondary storage is represented by two-state signals. When we describe this data we show the signals as 1s and 0s. Of course, if you looked inside computer memory you wouldn't see 1s and 0s, this is just a way of describing the digital content.

A number system that uses only 1 and 0 is called **binary**. So when we want to show the way that data and software are stored inside the computer we use binary numbers. In this section you will learn about binary numbers.

> **Key term**
>
> **Binary**   Numbers in base 2. They are formed from the digits 1 and 0 only.

Binary and decimal

The normal number system that we use is called decimal. Decimal means base 10. Decimal numbers are made up of ten different digits: the digits 0 to 9. The value of a digit depends on its position in the number. The digit on the right counts the number of units, the next digit counts the number of tens, the next digit counts the number of hundreds, and so on. Each column heading is ten times larger than the previous column.

Hundreds	Tens	Units
4	5	2

To work out the value of a number you multiply the digit in each column by the column value, and add the results together. This example shows four hundreds, five tens, and two units.

$$4 \times 100 = 400$$
$$5 \times 10 = 50$$
$$2 \times 1 = 2$$

So the decimal number 452 has the value 400 + 50 + 2.

Binary numbers use only two digits: 1 and 0. As with decimal numbers, the value of each digit depends on its position in the number. The digit on the right shows the number of units. The next digit shows the number of twos, the next digit shows the number of fours and so on. Working from right to left, each column heading is two times larger than the previous column.

128	64	32	16	8	4	2	units
0	0	0	1	0	1	0	1

To work out the value of a number you multiply the digit in each column by the column value, and add the results together. In this example there is a 1 in the 16 column, 1 in the 4 column and 1 in the units column.

$$1 \times 16 = 16$$
$$1 \times 4 = 4$$
$$1 \times 1 = 1$$
$$16 + 4 + 1 = 21$$

So, 00010101 is binary for the decimal number 21.

Remember that inside the computer bits are organised in groups of eight. A group of eight bits is called a byte. When writing binary numbers you typically show all eight bits, including any 0s on the left hand of the number.

The largest binary number that can be represented by a single byte of data is 11111111. This represents 128 + 64 + 32 + 16 + 8 + 4 + 2 + 1, which equals 255. Numbers that are larger than 255 are stored using several bytes linked together. Negative numbers and fractions are stored using more complex binary systems.

Convert binary to decimal

To convert a four-bit binary number to decimal, use a grid that shows the first four binary values.

8	4	2	units

Now follow these steps.

1 Insert the four-bit binary number into the grid. If the number has fewer than four bits, then fill up the columns on the left with zeros.
2 Then add together the values of all columns containing a 1.

Example: convert 0101 from binary to decimal.

■ Insert the number into the grid.

8	4	2	units
0	1	0	1

■ Add together the value of columns containing a 1.

$$4 + 1 = 5$$

So, this conversion shows that 0101 in binary is the same as 5 in decimal.

To convert binary numbers longer than four bits, use a grid with more columns.

Convert decimal to binary

To convert a decimal number to binary is a similar process. Begin with the grid as before. In this example I have used one more column than before.

16	8	4	2	units

Now follow these steps:

1 Start at the furthest left column, in this case the column with the value 16.
2 If you can subtract this value from the number, without giving a negative result, then write a 1 in the column. If you can't subtract the value, then write a 0.
3 Continue through all the columns from left to right, subtracting the values.

Example: convert 12 from decimal to binary.

■ The first column value, 16, is too large to subtract from 12, so enter a 0.

16	8	4	2	units
0				

■ The next column value, 8, can be subtracted from 12, so enter a 1. The remainder after this subtraction is 4.

16	8	4	2	units
0	1			

■ The next column value is 4. This can be subtracted exactly. Enter a 1.

16	8	4	2	units
0	1	1		

■ The number is now reduced to 0, so complete the grid with zeros.

16	8	4	2	units
0	1	1	0	0

So, 12 in decimal is the same as 01100 in binary.

■ 4.5 Hexadecimal numbers

Hexadecimal is base 16. It uses 16 different digits, shown by the numbers 0, 1 to 9, and the letters A to F.

Half a byte is four bits. It is sometimes called a nibble. Four bits can store exactly 16 different digits. That means it is very easy to convert between binary and hexadecimal, and both number systems fit in well with the way computer storage is organised.

> **Key term**
>
> **Hexadecimal**   Numbers in base 16.

The next table shows the binary, hexadecimal and decimal versions of the first 16 numbers.

Binary	Hexadecimal	Decimal
0000	0	0
0001	1	1
0010	2	2
0011	3	3
0100	4	4
0101	5	5
0110	6	6
0111	7	7
1000	8	8
1001	9	9
1010	A	10
1011	B	11
1100	C	12
1101	D	13
1110	E	14
1111	F	15

People who work directly with computer systems would find it difficult to work with binary numbers. It is difficult to tell the difference between two long binary numbers. If you were typing in binary numbers all the time, it would be easy to make a mistake.

Instead, computer programmers and engineers typically use hexadecimal numbers. Each hexadecimal digit represents a four-bit binary number. It is much easier to convert between binary and hexadecimal than between binary and decimal.

Converting from binary to hexadecimal

There is an exact match between every four-bit binary number and every hexadecimal digit. The binary–hexadecimal table shows this.

To convert a binary number to hexadecimal follow these steps.

1 Split the binary number into groups of four bits.
2 Under each group of four bits write the equivalent hexadecimal number.

So, for example, convert 10100101 into hexadecimal.

- Split into groups of 4.
  1010   0101

- Write the hexadecimal underneath.
  1010   0101
  A   5

So, 10100101 in binary is A5 in hexadecimal.

> **Study tip**
>
> To convert a single binary digit into hexadecimal, use the table on the previous page to look up the value.

Converting from hexadecimal to binary

To convert hexadecimal to binary write the four-bit binary value under each hexadecimal digit.

So, for example, convert F8 into binary.

F   8
1111   1000

So, F8 in hexadecimal is the same as 11111000 in binary.

Convert hexadecimal to decimal

The digits 0 to 9 have the same meaning in both decimal and hexadecimal. The letters A, B, C, D, E and F in hexadecimal represent the numbers 10 to 15 in decimal.

Hexadecimal	Decimal
A	10
B	11
C	12
D	13
E	14
F	15

> **Study tip**
>
> Hexadecimal numbers do not always include letters. The numbers 0–9 are written the same in hexadecimal and decimal. Be careful that you know which number system is in use.

If you remember this grid you will be able to convert any one-digit hexadecimal number into decimal.

If you need to convert a two-digit hexadecimal number then remember the following.

- The digit on the right stands for units.
- The digit on the left stands for 16s.

Enter the digits into the grid. Multiply the digit by the column value, and add the results together.

Example: convert the hexadecimal number 3B to decimal.

16s	units
3	B

- The first column shows the digit 3 in the 16s column. So this digit stands for 3 multiplied by 16.
  $3 \times 16 = 48$

- The next column shows the digit B in the units column. B represents 11 in hexadecimal. So this digit stands for 11 multiplied by 1.
  $11 \times 1 = 11$

- Add the two values together.
  $48 + 11 = 59$

So, the hexadecimal number 3B is the same as the decimal number 59.

Convert decimal to hexadecimal

To convert decimal to hexadecimal is quite straightforward. The numbers from 0 to 9 are the same in both systems. The decimal numbers 10 to 15 convert to the hexadecimal digits A to F.

If you need to convert a decimal number larger than 15 into hexadecimal, then divide by 16, and record the remainder.

Example: convert the decimal number 92 to hexadecimal.

- Divide the number by 16.
  $92 \div 16 = 5$ (remainder 12)

- Write the number of 16s in the grid.

16s	units
5	

- The remainder is 12. This is the number that should go in the units column. 12 in decimal is written as C in hexadecimal, so write this in the units column.

16s	units
5	C

So 92 in decimal is written as 5C in hexadecimal.

■ Chapter end

Overview

In this chapter you learned about how computers store data.

You learned about primary and secondary storage. Primary storage is made up of ROM and RAM. ROM is non-volatile read-only memory. RAM is volatile read–write memory.

Secondary storage has advantages over ROM and RAM as it is permanent memory that can store data and software even when the computer is switched off. There are three main types of secondary storage: magnetic, optical and solid-state.

You also learned that data is stored in the form of on/off signals that make digital numbers. These may be represented using the binary number system. A single binary digit is called a bit. Bits are usually processed in groups of eight, called bytes.

You learned about conversion between binary (base 2), decimal (base 10) and hexadecimal (base 16).

■ Questions

Answer these questions to demonstrate your learning.

1 What does RAM stand for?
2 What does read-only mean when referring to computer storage?
3 What is volatile storage?
4 What are the three main types of secondary storage?
5 What is ASCII code, and what is it used for?
6 How does a bitmap file store a digital photograph?
7 Explain the difference between a bit and a byte.
8 Roughly how many bytes are there in a megabyte?
9 Why are binary numbers particularly useful as a way of describing the contents of computer storage?
10 What is the advantage of hexadecimal over decimal as a way of representing binary numbers in an easy-to-read form?

Further activity

Practice activities can be carried out if you finish the work in this chapter with time to spare. You can also carry out these activities in your own time to help with learning and to improve your skills.

Here is a table showing the ASCII code for the letters A, B and C. The code is shown in decimal, binary and hexadecimal.

Letter	ASCII code		
	Decimal	Binary	Hexadecimal
A	65	0100 0001	41
B	66	0100 0010	42
C	67	0100 0011	43

Extend this table to show all the letters of the alphabet.

5 Constants

■ Introduction

In this chapter you will learn to create a named area of storage called a constant, and save a value in that storage area. The value of a constant is defined in the program code. When you save the program code, the value of the constant is saved.

Learning content

3.1.1 Constants, variables and data types: understand when to use constants in problem-solving scenarios.

■ 5.1 Saving program code

You have learned that within the computer there is RAM and secondary storage.

- RAM: Electronic primary storage, closely connected to the processor. It is volatile and the contents are lost when the computer is switched off.
- Secondary storage: The contents are retained when the computer is turned off.

Link

Primary storage – section 4.1
Secondary storage – section 4.2

When you are working on writing a program the code you enter is stored in RAM. When you save the program (by clicking Save) the program is copied to secondary storage. If you switched the computer off without saving your program it would be lost. RAM is volatile, meaning that it disappears when the electricity is turned off.

Also, if you close Visual Basic without saving, your work will be lost. That is because the computer only keeps current active work in RAM.

So, you must always remember to save your program before you stop work for the day. You should save your program at regular intervals while you are working, in case there is a computer fault or the electricity fails.

■ 5.2 Constant: a named storage area

Data that you input is kept in RAM as you work at the computer. Unless it is saved to secondary storage your input will not be retained when the computer is turned off. In different programs that you build you will learn different ways to save data to secondary storage.

In this section you will learn to save data as a **constant**.

- A constant is a named storage area. Giving a name to the constant is called declaring the constant.
- You can put any value you like into the named storage area. That is called assigning a value to the constant.

Key term

Constant A named area of storage that holds a value that does not change.

Once you have declared a constant, and assigned a value to it, then wherever the code contains the name of the constant, the computer will use the value assigned to the constant.

■ 5.3 Declare a constant

In this chapter you will create a constant to store your own name. Then wherever the constant appears in the code, the computer will substitute your name.

To create a constant you must:

- choose a name for the constant
- choose a **data type**
- declare the constant
- assign a value to the constant.

> **Key term**
>
> **Data type**   Data stored using a particular storage method. Different storage methods allow different types of data to be stored.

Choosing a name for the constant

When you declare the constant you can give it any name. The constant name must begin with a letter of the alphabet. The name must only contain upper and lower case letters, numbers and the underline character. You can't include a space in the name of a constant.

These are valid constant names.

UserName

User_Name

Name1

Name_1

Choose a sensible name for any constant that you declare. The name should make it clear what value is assigned to the constant. In this example you will declare a constant called UserName.

Choosing a data type for the constant

You learned in the last chapter that the computer uses different systems to store different types of data as electronic numbers. The computer stores number values as binary numbers. There are several different binary number types used to store larger numbers and fractions. In later chapters you will learn about some of the data types that are available.

The computer uses ASCII code to store text characters (letters of the alphabet). A string is any series of characters that the computer can store using ASCII code. This means if you create a constant using the string data type, then any string of characters can be stored in that constant. In this chapter you will declare a constant of the string data type.

> **Link**
>
> ASCII – section 4.3

A string is always shown inside double quotation marks. All the following are valid strings.

"Alison"

"Harry Potter"

"GCSE Computer Science"

The maximum length of a string is over a billion characters. You could store the text of a whole book as a string if you wanted.

Declaring the constant

You will declare the constant at the top of the code for *Form1*. When a constant is declared at the top of *Form1* it can be used in any of the code on *Form1*, including any of the sub-procedures.

To declare a constant you enter the following text as one line of code:

- the keyword *Const*
- the name of the constant
- the keyword *As*
- the data type of the constant.

So the code

```
Const UserName As String
```

means 'Declare a constant called UserName of string data type.'

Assigning a value to the constant

To complete the line you must assign a value to the constant. You learned in chapter 3 that the equals sign is used to assign a value to any item.

So the code:

```
Const UserName As String = "John"
```

means 'Declare a constant called UserName of type string, and assign the value "John" to that constant.'

Similarly, the code:

```
Const UserName As String = "Sian"
```

means 'Declare a constant called UserName of type string, and assign the value "Sian" to that constant.'

Activity Declare a constant

- Start Visual Basic and load My First Program

- Open the Code Editor tab.

- At the top of *Form1*, just below the first line, enter the following code:

```
Const UserName As String
```

- Complete the line by entering an equals sign and your own name in quotation marks. In this example I have used the name 'Alison' because that is my name, but you should use your own name.

```
Const UserName As String = "Alison"
```

- Add a comment line to explain the function of this code

Here is what the completed code looks like. Your code should show your name instead of mine.

```
Public Class Form1

    'Assign the user's name to a constant called 'UserName'

    Const UserName As String = "Alison"
```

■ 5.4 Output the constant as label text

You have now declared a constant and assigned a value to it. The constant is called *UserName*, and your own name is stored there.

You can now use that constant in your code.

Output a value as a text property

You have learned that the *Text* property of an object, such as a button or a label, is the text that is displayed by that object. If you assign a value to the text property of an object then that value will be displayed by the object. Therefore, one way to display the constant you have just declared is to assign the value of the constant to the *Text* property of a label.

The way to refer to the property of an object is to give the object name, then a full stop, then the property. So, the *Text* property of *lblMessage* is called:

```
lblMessage.Text
```

The way to assign a value to a property is with an equals sign. So, the following command assigns the value stored in the *UserName* constant, to the text property of the *lblMessage* object.

```
lblMessage.Text = UserName
```

This method of assigning a value to a *Text* property of an object is a very common way to display output in Visual Basic.

Combining two strings

You can also combine the *UserName* constant with other strings of text, to give a more complex message. For example, instead of just displaying your name, the label could show your name plus a message such as 'Greetings Alison' or 'Greetings John'.

To combine more than one string you simply add the strings together using the & symbol.

```
"Greetings " & UserName
```

Combining two strings together like this is called 'concatenation'. Notice three points about the quoted string.

- The string is shown in red characters.
- The string is enclosed in double quotation marks. This is the general rule when you include strings of text in your code.
- The string includes a space inside the quotation marks. That is so that there is a space between the word 'Greetings' and your name.

Adding two or more strings together like this is also called **concatenating** the strings. The full code to concatenate the two strings, and to assign that combined string to the text property of *lblMessage* is as follows.

```
lblMessage.Text = "Greetings " & UserName
```

> **Key term**
>
> **Concatenating** To add two or more strings together to create a longer string. The & symbol is used.

Add code to a sub-procedure

You now have to decide where to add this code. Currently the sub-procedure for *btnShow_Click* contains one line of code: the code that makes *lblMessage* visible.

```
lblMessage.Visible = True
```

You will add the line above that code, so that when you click *btnShow* two things happen.

- The label displays the output string.
- The label becomes visible.

Activity Output a constant as label text

- Move your cursor to the code for *btnShow_Click*, above the following line.

```
lblMessage.Visible = True
```

- Type the following code.

```
lblMessage.Text = "Greetings " & UserName
```

- Run the program and see what happens when you click on the Show message button.

- Save your code.

■ 5.5 Output a constant using a message box

You have seen how to output a string by assigning it to the *Text* property of a label. There is another way to output a string. This is to use a message box. A message box will display a message to the user, plus an OK button. The message box will stay open until the user clicks the OK button. That is to make sure the user has time to read the message.

The code *MsgBox( )* creates a box on the screen with a message in it. Whatever appears in between the brackets will appear in the message box.

For example, if you enter this code:

```
MsgBox("Goodbye " & UserName)
```

the message that appears in the message box will be the string "Goodbye" plus whatever value is stored in the constant *UserName*.

You will enter this code in the code for *btnOK_Click* above the code *End*, which ends the program. That means that when the user clicks *btnOK* they will see the goodbye message in a message box, and then the program will end.

Activity Output a constant in a message box

■ Move your cursor to the code for *btnOK_Click*.

■ Above the word *End* add a new line of code.

```
MsgBox("Goodbye " & UserName)
```

■ Run the program and see what happens when you click on the Exit button.

■ Click on the OK button to close the message box.

■ Save your code.

■ 5.6 Advantages of using a constant

You have seen how you can assign a value to a constant. Whenever you enter the name of the constant in your code, the computer will use the value that has been stored in that constant.

But why not just enter the value itself, instead of using a constant? Using a constant has several advantages:

■ Easier to make changes. Using a constant makes it easier to make changes to your program later. If you need to change the Username, you only need to change the single command that assigns a string to the *UserName* constant. The value of *UserName* will be changed throughout the program. That could save you a lot of work.

- Makes your code more readable. You should choose a descriptive name for the constant. This makes your code easier to read.
- Fewer opportunities for error. Because the value of the constant is only entered once, in the constant declaration, there is less opportunity to make a mistake. If you had to enter the string in many different places throughout your program, there are many chances of mistyping.
- Shorter. A string can be up to a billion characters long (though that is not recommended!). You can store a long string as a constant with a short name. Then, you only need to type the short constant name into your code. The computer will substitute the long string everywhere you use the constant name.

Here is an example of how the use of a constant improved a computer program. A programmer created an app that calculated how much VAT (value added tax) should be charged on purchases. He stored the value 15 per cent in a constant called *VATRate*. He used this constant throughout his program, instead of entering 15 per cent in hundreds of different lines. This had several advantages:

- Easier to make changes. When he wrote the program the VAT rate was 15 per cent. Later the rate of VAT changed to 17.5 per cent. The programmer only had to change one line of his code: the line where the constant was declared.
- More readable. Anybody reading the program could clearly see that he was using *VATRate* as a key value in his program, instead of wondering why the value 15 per cent was used throughout.
- Avoiding errors. He only had to enter 15 per cent once, in the statement that assigned a value to the constant, so it was easy to avoid an error, and to check that the correct value had been used.

■ Chapter end

Full code listing

A student called Tequisha created a program following the instructions in this book. She included comments in her code.

Here is a complete listing of her program code.

```
Public Class Form1

  'My first program by Tequisha

  Const UserName As String = "Tequisha"

  Private Sub btnOK_Click(ByVal sender As -

    'Clicking btnOK displays a message and closes the app

    MsgBox("Goodbye " & UserName)

    End

  End Sub
```

```
Private Sub btnShow_Click(ByVal sender As -

    'Clicking btnShow displays a greeting message in the main form

   lblMessage.Text = "Greetings" & UserName

   lblMessage.Visible = True

  End Sub


Private Sub btnHide_Click(ByVal sender As -

    'clicking btnHide hides the message in the main form

   lblMessage.Visible = False

  End Sub

End Class
```

PLEASE NOTE: There is a long string of text in brackets following the name of each subprocedure. This text begins

```
(ByVal sender As System.Object, ByVal e As
```

This text is too long to quote in full every time, and you will not need to change it for your ordinary programming work. So in future when listing code, this extra text will be left out. Just concentrate on the lines which are important for current purposes.

Overview

In this chapter you learned how to declare a constant and assign a value to it. The general structure for declaring a constant.

```
Const «name» As «dataType» = "«value»"
```

Instead of the words in angled brackets « » you would enter the constant name, data type and value.

To output a constant you can assign the value stored in the constant to the text property of a label. The general structure for this command is given below.

```
Object.Property = Constant
```

You can join strings together using the & symbol, which is called concatenation. The result is a long string.

Another way to output a string is to use a message box. The command for a message box is given below.

```
MsgBox(«value»)
```

Instead of «value» enter a constant name, a string or a concatenated string.

■ Questions

Answer these questions to demonstrate your learning.

1 Give two rules you would follow when deciding on the name for a constant.
2 Write out the code you would use to declare a constant called *MyAddress*, which stores your address.
3 Write out the code you would use to assign the constant *MyAddress* to the text property of *Label3*.
4 Write out the code that will output the constant *MyAddress* in a message box.
5 Explain two advantages of using a constant in a program.
6 What does concatenate mean, and how do you concatenate two strings?
7 If a line of a program starts with a single quotation mark, what does the computer do?
8 Give one way that the use of colour helps you to understand Visual Basic code.

Further activity

Practice activities can be carried out if you finish the work in this chapter with time to spare. You can also carry out these activities in your own time to help with learning and to improve your skills.

Extension activity: Visual Basic has a constant called *vbNewLine*. If you concatenate strings with this constant, then they will appear on different lines when they are displayed.

For example, this code assigns a multi-line string to the constant *MyAddress*.

```
Const MyAddress As String = "22 Browning Avenue" & vbNewLine &
"OXTON" & vbNewLine & "XT7 8GY"
```

Use this method to input your own address into the constant *MyAddress*, and display it as a label on a form.

If you complete this extension activity, save your program file using a new file name.

6 Variables

Introduction

In the last chapter you learned how to use a constant to store a value that could be used in your program. In this chapter you will learn how to use variables. If you want a user to input a value while the program is running, you will store it in a variable.

Learning content

3.1.1 Constants, variables and data types: describe the difference between a constant and a variable; understand when to use constants and variables in problem solving scenarios.

6.1 The difference between constants and variables

What is a constant?

In the last chapter you learned that a constant is a named area of storage with a value assigned to it. You declare a constant by:

- giving it a name
- giving it a data type
- assigning it a value.

Whenever the name of the constant is used in your code, the computer will use the value that has been assigned to the constant. This value will be the same every time the constant is used. It will stay the same every time you run the program. That is why it is called a 'constant'.

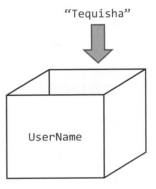

The image shows a diagram of what happens when you declare a constant. A named storage 'box' is created in computer memory and a value (in this case the string "Tequisha") is placed in the box.

What is a variable?

A **variable** is a named area of storage. But unlike a constant, it has no fixed value assigned to it by the program. It is an empty storage area. While the program is running the variable can be used to store different values. The value stored in a variable can be different every time the program runs. It can also be changed while the program is running.

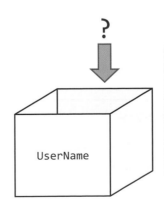

Key term

Variable A named area of storage that holds a value that may change during or between programs.

The value in the variable can be input by the user, or it can be calculated by the computer. In this book you will learn about both ways of assigning a value to a variable.

■ 6.2 Create the user interface

In this chapter you will create a new program. It will allow the user to input his or her name. The name will be stored in a variable. Because the name will be stored as a variable, it can be different each time you run the program.

A good way to start a programming project is to think about the values that need to be input and output, and design a user interface. The next screenshot shows the interface design. The form has three objects – two buttons and a label. The names of these objects are shown. When the user clicks on *btnEnter* they will be able to input a value. The value will be displayed by the label *lblMessage*. *btnEnd* will end the app.

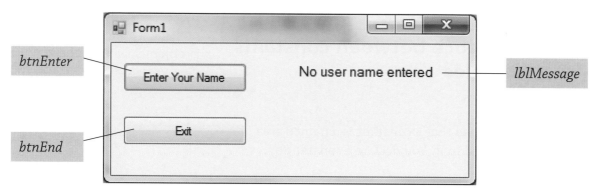

The first activity is to create this form.

Activity Create a user interface

■ Start Visual Basic, make sure Windows Forms Application is selected and click on New Project.

■ Enter the project name User Name Display.

■ Add one label and two buttons to create a form that looks like the example user interface given here. Give suitable names to the objects.

■ Add code so that clicking *btnEnd* causes the program to close.

■ Run the program using the Debugging tool to make sure it works.

■ Save your work.

■ 6.3 Declare a variable

Now you will declare a variable called *UserName*. To declare a variable you use the word *Dim*, which stands for dimension. You give the variable a name and a data type.

For example:

```
Dim UserName As String
```

This line declares a variable called *UserName*. The variable is of type *String*. That means the variable can be used to store any string of text. Notice that the declaration does not assign a value to the variable. The variable is empty storage space until a value is input.

Once the variable has been declared as an empty storage area, you can use the variable in the program. In the next two section you will write code to

- allow the user to input a value to the variable
- output the value stored in the variable.

> **Study tip**
>
> An initial value can be assigned to a variable when it is declared, but it is not fixed. It can be changed later.

Activity Declare a variable

- Make sure the program User Name Display is open on your screen.

- Open the Code Editor tab that shows the program code.

- Move the cursor to the top of the program, just below the line *Public Class Form1*.

- Enter the line:

```
Dim UserName As String
```

- Save your work.

■ 6.4 Assign a value to the variable

In the last section you declared a variable called *UserName*. Declaring this variable set up a named storage area. In this section you will assign a value to the variable. Assigning a value to a variable will put a value into the named storage area. The value will be text which is input by the user.

Variable =

The equals sign is used to assign a value to a variable.
To assign a value to *UserName*, enter the name of the variable and the equals sign.

```
UserName =
```

Whatever value comes after the equals sign will be assigned to the variable. For example, if you entered this command:

```
UserName = "Alison"
```

then the string "Alison" would be assigned to the variable. But this is not what you want. You want the user to be able to input any text. Whatever text the user inputs will be assigned to the *UserName* variable.

InputBox

To enable the user to enter some text you will use the command *InputBox*. This is a very useful command. It causes the computer to display an input box on the screen. Whatever the user types in that box will be assigned to the variable.

To assign the user input to the variable you give this command:

```
UserName = InputBox()
```

But this command is not completed yet.

InputBox message

You will see that there are some brackets following the word InputBox. Inside these brackets you enter a message to the user. The message is called a 'prompt'. It is a message to the user telling them what to type.

The completed command looks like this.

```
UserName = InputBox("Enter your name")
```

Result of this command

The result of this command is shown in the next screenshot. An input box appears.

- The message 'Enter your name' is shown in the input box.
- There is space for the user to enter some text.
- There are two buttons which say 'OK' and 'Cancel'.

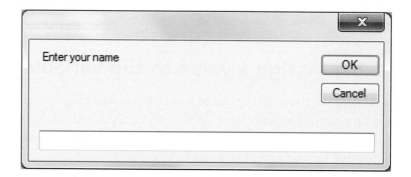

If the user enters his or her name and clicks on the OK button, then the text entered will be assigned to the variable *UserName*.

Activity Input a value to a variable

- Open the tab that shows the Form design.

- Double-click on *btnEnter*.

- In the procedure *btnEnter_Click* enter the following code.

```
UserName = InputBox("Enter Your Name")
```

- Run the program using the Debugging tool to make sure there are no errors.

- Save your work.

■ 6.5 Display the variable

In chapter 5 you learned two ways to output a string value.

1 You can assign the string value to the *Text* property of a label.
2 You can use a message box.

In the next activity you will use both these methods to display the value stored in the variable *UserName*. You should have the skills to complete this. If you can't remember how to do these things, check back to chapter 5.

Use of quotation marks

This is a reminder about how you use quotation marks.

■ If you want to output a string then you have to enclose the string in double quotation marks.
■ If you want to output the contents of a variable you do not put quotation marks around the variable name.

Variable names, key words and object names are not put in quotation marks. Quotation marks are only used when you want a literal string to appear just as you have quoted it.

Activity Output a value

■ Go to the section of code linked to *btnEnter*. Type a second line of code below the last.

```
lblMessage.Text = "Your name is " & UserName
```

■ Enter code linked to *btnEnd* so that the words 'Goodbye' and UserName will be displayed in a message box when the user exits the program.

■ Add comments to your code to explain what each section of the code does.

■ Use the Debugging tool to make sure the code runs properly.

■ Save your work.

There is a full listing of the completed code at the end of this chapter. You can check your finished work against this.

If you run this program several times you will see that you can enter any string of characters as the *UserName* variable. Whatever value you enter will be displayed as the text of *lblMessage*.

■ 6.6 Scope of variables

Before you can use a variable in any command, you have to declare the variable. In the program you just wrote, the command to declare the variable was:

```
Dim UserName As String
```

This line appeared at the top of the form code, before the code for *btnEnter_Click* and *btnEnd_Click*. A variable that is declared at the top of a form can be used by all the objects within that form. *UserName* was used by *btnEnter* (this button allowed the user to input a value to the variable). The variable was also used by *btnEnd* (this button displayed the variable in a message box).

You could also declare a variable within the code of a particular object, such as a button. But in that case the variable can only be used by that object. It cannot be used in other parts of the program code. The part of the program where a variable can be used is called the **scope** of the variable.

If you declare the variable at the top of a form, then its scope is all the objects within that form. This is shown in Figure 1.

However, if you declare a variable within the code for a single object, then the variable can only be used in the code for that object. This is shown in Figure 2.

In the activity you will test this idea. You will move the variable declaration from the top of the form, into the code for *btnEnter*. You can use cut and paste commands to move the code, or you can delete and retype. By moving the variable declaration, you change the scope of the variable. The scope of the variable is limited to *btnEnter*, which causes errors in your program.

Scope errors

If you try to use a variable outside of its scope you will cause errors in your program. As you carry out the activity look out for these errors.

1 The term *UserName* in the *btnEnd* code is underlined with a blue wavy line. This is because the computer does not know what that word means. The variable was declared in the code for *btnEnter*. This means that it is not recognised in the code for *btnEnd*.

2 There is an error message at the bottom of the screen that reads:

Error1: UserName is not declared. It may be inaccessible due to its protection level.

If you try to run the code you will see more error messages. These error messages are because there is a mistake with the scope of the variable.

Overview of 'scope'

Here is what you have learned about variable scope.

1 A variable must be declared before it is used.
2 The scope of the variable depends on where it is declared.

Key term

Scope The scope of a variable or constant is the section of computer code where it is recognised.

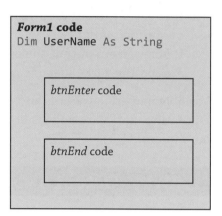

Figure 1. In this example, the scope of *UserName* includes all code and objects within *Form1*.

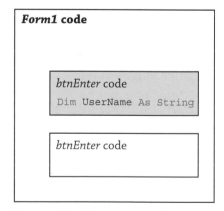

Figure 2. In this example, the scope of *UserName* is limited to *btnEnter*. The variable can only be used in the code for *btnEnter* and nowhere else.

3 If the variable is declared at the top of a form, then it can be used by any object in the form. Its scope is the whole form.

4 If the variable is declared within the code for an object, then it can only be used by the code for that object. Its scope is limited to the object.

Some programs have more than one form. In that case you have to decide whether the scope of a variable is within one form, or across the whole program. You will learn more about using multiple forms later in the book.

Link

A project with more than one form – chapter 16.

Activity Testing variable scope

Now you will test this idea.

■ Make sure the program User Name Display is open on the screen and you are looking at the Code Editor tab.

■ Select the text of the variable declaration from the top of the form, and move it to the code for *btnEnter* (you can use cut and paste to do this).

■ Notice the error messages that appear when you make this change.

■ Correct the error by returning the variable declaration to its proper place.

■ 6.7 Naming constants and variables

You have learned that constants and variables should be given clear descriptive names that tell the reader what value is stored in that constant or variable.

The rules for naming constants and variables are:

■ the name must start with a letter
■ the name can't include a space, full stop, exclamation mark (!), or the characters @, &, $, #
■ the name can't exceed 255 characters in length – but never use anything like this length of name
■ the name of a constant or variable should never be the same as a keyword or other word used in your code.

As well as these strict rules, there are some general guidelines:

■ Make sure the variable name is not too long or complicated.
■ Make sure the variable name explains what is stored in the variable.
■ Use upper and lowercase letters to make the variable easier to read.

Some programmers include the data type in the name of the variable. Find out more about variable names and data types in chapter 7.

Link

Variable names and data types – chapter 7

■ 6.8 Pseudocode

Pseudocode is a simplified way of writing computer programs. It is quicker to write than computer code.

But pseudocode is not a working programming language. It cannot be turned into machine code that will run on a computer. It is only used to plan or set out the structure of a computer program.

Pseudocode might be used in many different circumstances. For example:

- to try out a programming idea on paper
- to share ideas with other programmers
- to keep a record of the structure of your program.

In other words, pseudocode is used as a way of setting out the logic and workings of a program, without actually writing working code.

What can pseudocode do?

Using pseudocode you can describe most of the features of a computer program. These are:

- the values that are input and output from a program
- the variables that are used and what values they hold
- structures such as loops, which you have not learned yet.

In this section you will learn how to write some pseudocode.

What is missing from pseudocode?

Because pseudocode is not a working programming language, it does not have all of the features you will be familiar with. Pseudocode does not include features such as:

- definition of an interface with buttons, text boxes, etc.
- the code which starts and finishes a program
- variable declarations
- details of how values are input and output (such as Message Box and labels).

In other words, there is a lot missing from pseudocode.

Advantages

Pseudocode has some advantages compared to writing in a programming language:

- You write it quickly because it is very short.
- You can set out the logical structure of a program in a straightforward way, leaving out unnecessary details.
- Programmers who know different programming languages can use pseudocode to share their ideas.

Disadvantages

But pseudocode has a number of disadvantages:

- Pseudocode does not compile into a working application.
- If you have created pseudocode, you still have to do more work to turn it into a functioning program.
- A program which works in pseudocode may not translate perfectly into code in your chosen language.
- Pseudocode is not 'event-driven' or 'object-oriented'; there are no objects or properties or events such as button-click. So a pseudocode program will not have all the functionality of Visual Basic.

6.9 Write some pseudocode

It is quick to write pseudocode. In many chapters of this book you will look at the pseudocode equivalent of the Visual Basic code you write.

Values and variables

Just like in Visual Basic, pseudocode lets you assign values to variables. But there are differences:

- In pseudocode a little arrow like this ← is used to assign a value to a variable. This is different from Visual Basic which uses the equals sign.
- In pseudocode you do not need to declare a variable or give it a data type. Just use the variable when you need it.

A statement to assign a value to a variable is set out like this:

```
variable ← value
```

Just like in Visual Basic, string values are shown in quotation marks. So the command to assign the value 'London' to the variable *Hometown* would be:

```
Hometown ← "London"
```

Input and output

The key words INPUT and OUTPUT are used. These are the first pseudocode key words you have learned. In pseudocode, key words are written in UPPER CASE.

Unlike Visual Basic there is no need to describe the input or output methods (such as Message Box or Label.Text). The command to write output is simply:

```
OUTPUT message
```

So to output the message 'Enter your home town' you would write:

```
Output "Enter your home town"
```

The command to accept user input and assign it to a variable is:

```
variable ← USERINPUT
```

So the code to input a value and assign it to the variable *Hometown* is:

```
Hometown ← USERINPUT
```

Putting the two commands, together gives this short pseudocode program.

```
OUTPUT "Enter your name"
UserName ← USERINPUT
```

Make sure you understand what this program does.

Comments

To include a comment in pseudocode begin the line with the symbol #. Just like comments in Visual Basic, these lines will have no effect on the flow of the program.

Example of pseudocode

In this chapter you created a short program. You designed an interface and wrote code. A full code listing is set out at the end of this chapter.

Here is the same program in pseudocode. One line is a comment:

```
OUTPUT "Enter your name"
#assign input to variable UserName
UserName ← USERINPUT
OUTPUT "Goodbye "
OUTPUT Username
```

You can see that the program is much shorter in pseudocode than in Visual Basic.

Activity Simple pseudocode

Create a pseudocode program which:

- displays the message 'Enter the name of your home town'

- stores user input as a variable called Hometown

- outputs a message saying 'Have fun in ...' and the name of the Hometown.

■ Chapter end

Full code listing

Your completed code may look something like this. Notice the use of different coloured text to show key words (blue), names of objects and variables (black), strings (red) and comments (green).

```
Public Class Form1
    'Declare the variable UserName
    Dim UserName As String

    Private Sub btnEnter_Click(ByVal sender As –
        'User input to the variable UserName
        UserName = InputBox("Enter your name")
        lblMessage.Text=
        "Your name is " & UserName
    End Sub

    Private Sub btnEnd_Click(ByVal sender As –
        'Display userName and exit
        MsgBox("Goodbye " & UserName)
        End
    End Sub

End Class
```

If your code does not look like this, go back and check your work.

Overview

In this chapter you learned how to:

- declare a variable
- input a value and assign it to a variable
- output a variable.

You declare a variable with the following type of command. In this case the variable is called *UserName* and the data type is *String*.

```
Dim UserName As String
```

You can input a value to a variable using an *InputBox*. The *InputBox* command looks like this (in this case the variable is called *UserName* and the prompt to the user is 'Enter your name'):

```
UserName = InputBox("Enter your name")
```

You can output a variable using the *MsgBox* function, as follows:

```
MsgBox(UserName)
```

You can also assign the variable to the text property of a label:

```
lblMessage.Text = UserName
```

You also learned that the location of a variable declaration sets the scope for the variable. If the variable is declared at the top of a form, then it can be used by all the objects on the form. If the variable is declared within the code for a particular object then it can only be used by the code for that object.

You learned that pseudocode is a simplified coding language used to set out the general structure of a program. A program written in pseudocode is much shorter and simpler than one written in Visual Basic. However, it cannot be turned into machine code that can run on a computer.

■ Questions

Answer these questions to demonstrate your learning.

1 Explain the difference between a constant and a variable.
2 Give the code to declare a variable called *MyPet* of type string.
3 Give the code to use an input box to enter a value into the variable *MyPet*.
4 Explain two ways to output the value in the variable *MyPet* so the user can read it on the screen.
5 A programmer declared a variable. She needed to use the variable in two different sub-procedures on the same form. Where should she declare the variable?
6 Give two rules you should follow when picking a name for a variable.
7 Explain how quotation marks are used when assigning a value to a string variable.
8 The string "Mansfield" is assigned to the variable *MyTown*. Explain what the user will see on the screen when this code is run by the computer.

```
MsgBox(MyTown)
```

9 What is the pseudocode equivalent of the Visual Basic code shown in question 8?
10 Give the pseudocode command that will assign the value "Basketball" to the variable FavouriteSport.

Further activity

Practice activities can be carried out if you finish the work in this chapter with time to spare. You can also carry out these activities in your own time to help with learning and to improve your skills.

Practice activity: Create a user interface with a single button and a label. When the user clicks the button an input box appears asking them to input the place they live in. After they enter this value the label on the form will display a message saying 'Have fun in …' and the name of the place they live. You will need to use a variable to store the place name. Give the button and the label suitable names.

7 Data types

Introduction

In the last chapter you worked with simple string variables using the input box function. In this chapter you will learn about using multiple variables of many different data types. You will learn new ways to assign values to variables using text boxes to collect user input. You will begin to look at how programs are structured and developed.

Learning content

3.1.1 Constants, variables and data types: understand when to use variables in problem-solving scenarios; understand the different data types available; be able to explain the purpose of data types within code.

7.1 Data types

So far you have used variables of one data type: a string. A string variable can be used to store any text. The computer stores the string using ASCII code (part of the Unicode system).

But there are many other ways for the computer to store data. There are many different data types. It is important to select the right data type that matches the type of data you want to store in a constant or variable. When you declare the constant or variable you must declare the correct data type.

The next table shows some of the most useful data types in Visual Basic.

To store this data	Use this data type
Any group of text characters	String
A single text character	Char
True or False	Boolean
A whole number with no decimals	Integer
A number that can include decimals	Decimal
Any date	Date

There are other data types available. The ones shown in this table should be enough for all the work you need to do for GCSE Computer Science.

You will use all of these data types as you follow the exercises in this book.

Link

ASCII and Unicode – chapter 4

Did you know?

Many professional programmers include the data type as part of the name of a variable. So, a string variable to store a surname would be called *strSurname*. An integer variable to store an age would be called *intAge*.

You can use this as a naming convention in your work. It is not used in this book.

■ 7.2 User questionnaire

In this section you will create a simple input questionnaire. It will accept three different items of data from the user and store these values in three variables.

- First name
- Surname
- Age

It will then output the variables in a message box.

Planning the program in pseudocode

In pseudocode you do not need to declare variables or select data types. The pseudocode version of this program is very simple.

```
#Input the values

FirstName ← USERINPUT

Surname ← USERINPUT

Age ← USERINPUT

#Output the values

OUTPUT FirstName

OUTPUT Surname

OUTPUT Age
```

Turning the plan into a working program

Now you can produce a complete working Visual Basic program which matches this.

In developing a program you will follow these steps:

- Create a user interface.
- Declare variables.
- Assign values to variables.
- Output the results.

We will take these steps one at a time.

Create a user interface

In chapter 6 you wrote a program that used one variable of the string data type. You assigned a value to that variable using the *InputBox* function. The *InputBox* function is useful if you need to assign a value to a single string variable. But *InputBox* cannot be used for more than one variable at the same time and it cannot be used for other data types.

When you need to input many different items of data you must use input controls. In this section you will use an input control called *TextBox*.

Text boxes are a special kind of object. The *Text* property of these objects is blank. The object displays a blank space on a form, in which the user can type in new data. The new data that the user types into the text box is assigned to the *Text* property of the text box.

To create a text box, you find the *TextBox* control in the Toolbox. Drag or double-click the control to create a text box on the form. You can make the text box bigger or smaller depending on how much space you think the user will need.

In the example form shown here there are three text boxes and a button. Suggested names for these objects are given. There are also three labels. These have been added so that the user knows what data to type in each box. As these labels are not used in the program code, there is no need to give them special names.

Now you will create this user interface.

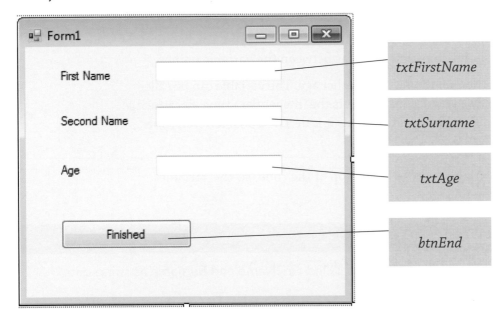

Activity Create a user interface

- Start Visual Basic. Make sure Windows Forms Application is selected.

- Create a new project called User Questionnaire.

- Find the control called *TextBox* in the Toolbar. Drag or double-click this control to add three text boxes to *Form1*.

- Add labels next to the text boxes, and a button. Arrange the objects, and set the text values, so that the form looks like the example given in the screenshot.

- Add a button to the form.

- Give the text boxes and the button names as shown in the screenshot.

- Double-click on *btnEnd*.
- Enter *End* in the code for *btnEnter_Click*.
- Run the program using the Debugging tool to make sure there are no errors.
- Save your work.

Declare variables

You have created three text boxes for user input. The next step is to declare variables to store that input. You have asked the user to input their first name and their surname. Good names for these variables would be *FirstName* and *Surname*. Given that names are made of characters these can be string variables.

Since *FirstName* and *Surname* are both string variables, they can be declared in a single line.

```
Dim FirstName, Surname As String
```

If your program includes two or more variables of the same data type, you can declare them on the same line, as shown here. Put commas between the variable names.

The final piece of data that the user inputs is his or her age. The variable can be called *Age*. Age is a whole number, with no decimals, so it is the integer data type. Because *Age* is a different data type from *FirstName* and *Surname* it is declared on a different line.

```
Dim Age As Integer
```

These lines declaring the variables can go at the top of the code, so the variable scope covers all items on the form.

Activity Declare variables

- At the top of the code, declare two variables called *FirstName* and *Surname* as string data type.
- Declare a variable called *Age* as integer data type.
- Add a comment line above the declarations, to explain what this code does.
- Run the program using the Debugging tool to make sure there are no errors.
- Save your work.

Assign values to variables

Visual Basic is an event-driven language. Computer actions will be carried out in response to an event, such as the user clicking a button. When the user has entered values into the three text boxes, they will click on *btnEnd*, which is marked 'Finished'. When this event happens you want the computer to carry out the final two tasks:

- Assign values to the three variables.
- Output the three variables.

Therefore the code to perform these tasks must be inserted into the code for *btnEnter_click*. In this section you will enter the code to assign values to variables.

You have created three text boxes. Any user input will be stored in the *Text* property of the textbox. So, for example, the first text box on the form is called *txtFirstName*. Whatever the user types in this box will be stored as:

```
txtFirstName.Text
```

This box is where the users types their first name, so whatever value is typed here must be assigned to the *FirstName* variable. Remember that the equals sign is used to assign a value to an item.

So, the code to assign the value from *txtFirstName.Text* to the *FirstName* variable is:

```
FirstName = txtFirstName.Text
```

The value from *txtSurname.Text* will be assigned to the *Surname* variable, and the value from *txtAge.Text* will be assigned to the *Age* variable. The code assigning these values to the three variables must be entered into the sub-procedure *btnEnter_click*.

Initially this sub-procedure contains one line of code, the word *End*. You will enter the new code above this line.

Activity Assign input values to variables

- Move your cursor to the code for *btnEnd_click*.

- Enter the following lines:

```
FirstName = txtFirstName.Text

Surname = txtSurname.Text

Age = txtAge.Text
```

- Add a comment line to explain what this code does.

- Run the program using the Debugging tool to make sure there are no errors.

- Save your work.

Output the variables

In the last section you assigned the input data in the three variables. Now you can add a line of code that will display or output the variables. This line of code will go in the sub-procedure called *btnEnter_click*. It will go below the lines assigning values to the three variables.

You will use the *MsgBox* function, which you learned about in chapter 6. The structure of this command is:

```
MsgBox(…)
```

Inside the brackets you can enter any string, or series of strings. Remember that the & symbol concatenates strings to make a longer message. You will enter the string "Goodbye " plus the first name and surname. The string " " (a space with quote marks around it) can be added to put a space in between *FirstName* and *Surname*.

The code to display this message would look like this:

```
MsgBox("Goodbye " & FirstName & " " & Surname)
```

The third variable is *Age*. *Age* is an integer variable. You cannot mix string and integer variables in the same command, so you need to convert *Age* to a string variable.

Visual Basic has a function that converts a number variable to a string variable.

```
Str(…)
```

Instead of the dots you put the name of a number variable inside the brackets. This turns the number into a string.

The code to display your age in the message box would look like this.

```
MsgBox(" your age is " & Str(Age))
```

Finally, you can put all the variables together in one message box. The full code looks like this:

```
MsgBox("Goodbye " & FirstName & " " & Surname & " your
age is " & Str(Age))
```

Activity Output the variables

- Move the cursor to the *btnEnd_Click* code above the command *End*, which closes the program.

- Type the following code:

```
MsgBox("Goodbye " & FirstName & " " & Surname & " your age is " &
Str(Age))
```

- Debug to check the program is working and save.

Add a simple calculation

When you have completed the program you can make one change and see the effect it has on the program output.

Age is stored as a number value. You can carry out calculations using the number. In this example you add one to the age, to give the user's age next year.

You will learn more about calculations in the rest of this book.

Activity Calculation

- Make sure Visual Basic is open with the User Questionnaire program open on the screen.

- Move the cursor to the *MsgBox* command.

- Amend the code as follows:

```
MsgBox(FirstName & Surname & "Next Year you will be " & Str(Age + 1))
```

- Test that the program works using the Debugging tool.

- If there are errors, correct them. If the program works, save it.

The finished program

The complete code listing for this program is given at the end of this chapter. Check your work against the listing.

■ 7.3 Simple tip calculator

When you pay a bill in a hotel or restaurant and you are very happy with the quality of service, you may want to add a tip or gratuity for the people who served you. Some people leave a tip that is 15 per cent of the total bill. In this section you will create a program where the user inputs a currency value, and the computer calculates 15 per cent of that value.

Remember the basic structure of any computer system (see diagram). All computer programs take this structure.

In this case:

- the input is the amount of the bill
- the processing is calculating 15 per cent of the bill
- the output is the amount of the tip and the total payment required.

The task of writing a program also requires all these elements.

- To enable input you need to create a user interface and declare variables.
- To enable processing you need to assign values to variables, including calculated values.
- To enable output you need to display the results.

In the remainder of this chapter you will go through these steps in order to create a complete program.

Input

↓

Processing

↓

Output

Plan the program

Pseudocode provides a simple way to plan the overall structure of the program.

```
#Input

Bill ← USERINPUT

#Processing

Tip ← Bill * 15%

Total ← Bill + Tip

#Output

OUTPUT Tip

OUTPUT Total
```

Create the user interface and declare variables

A suggested interface design for the tip calculator is shown in the screenshot.

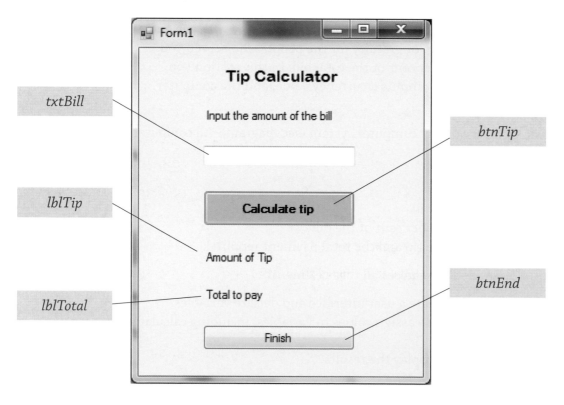

It is quite a complicated interface with four labels, a text box and two buttons. The final button will end the program. The screenshot is annotated with suggested names for the objects.

The program will require three variables:

- the amount of the bill
- the amount of the tip
- the total to pay.

The suggested names for these variables are *Bill*, *Tip* and *Total*. They should all be of the decimal data type. The code that declares the variables should go at the top of the form code, so that the scope of the variables includes all the sub-procedures on the form.

With this information you should be able to create the user interface and declare the three variables.

Activity Create a user interface and declare variables

- Start Visual Basic. Make sure Windows Forms Application is selected. Select New Project.
- Enter the project name Tip calculator.
- Enter labels, buttons and a text box to create a form that looks like the example user interface shown in the screenshot on page 78.
- Add code so that clicking *btnEnd* causes the program to close.
- At the top of *Form1* code, declare the three variables *Bill*, *Tip* and *Total*, as decimal data type.
- Add a comment explaining the purpose of this code.
- Run the program using the Debugging tool to make sure there are no errors.
- Save your work.

Assign values to variables

Next you will assign values to the variables.

The first variable is *Bill*. This variable stores the amount of the restaurant bill. This value is input by the user in *txtBill.Text*. So, the command to assign this value to the variable is as follows.

```
Bill = txtBill.Text
```

The next variable is *Tip*. This variable stores the size of the tip. This value is calculated by multiplying the bill by 15 per cent. In order to carry out calculation you must use an **arithmetic operator**.

Key term

Arithmetic operator A symbol used to create a mathematical formula such as the plus, minus, divide and multiply signs.

There are four main arithmetic operators.

Operator	Action
+	Add
−	Subtract
*	Multiply
/	Divide

The command to multiply the value in the variable *Bill* by 15 per cent is:

```
Bill * 0.15
```

The complete command to assign the result of this calculation to the variable *Tip* is:

```
Tip = Bill * 0.15
```

The final variable is the total to pay. This is calculated by adding the *Bill* and the *Tip*, and assigning the result to the variable *Total*. The command for this is:

```
Total = Tip + Bill
```

Visual Basic is an event-driven language. The event that will cause the computer to carry out this calculation is when the user clicks on *btnTip*, which has the message 'Calculate tip'. So this code must be placed in the sub-procedure *btnTip_click*.

Activity Assign values to variables

- Select the Design tab.

- Double click on *btnTip* to insert a sub-procedure that is linked to this button.

- In the Code Editor tab, add the following code to the *btnTip* sub-procedure.

```
Bill = txtBill.Text

Tip = Bill * 0.15

Total = Tip + Bill
```

- Add one or more comments explaining the purpose of this code.

- Run the program using the Debugging tool to make sure there are no errors.

- Save your work.

Output the results

Finally you will output the results by assigning the values in the variables to the *Text* property of the labels called *lblTip* and *lblTotal*.

- The text of *lblTip* will be the variable *Tip*.
- The text of *lblTotal* will be the variable *Total*.

The code to produce these outputs must go in the *btnTip_click* sub-procedure. It must come after the code that assigns the values to these variables.

Study tip

The order in which sub-procedures are carried out depends on which buttons the user clicks first. It does not matter in what order the different sub-procedures appear in the code window.

This command will show the value of the Tip variable in the label called *lblTip*:

```
lblTip.Text = Tip
```

Instead you might prefer to display the size of the tip together with an explanatory message. The command would look like this:

```
lblTip.Text = "The amount of the tip is £" &
Str(Tip)
```

Using the same method, assign the variable *Total* to *lblTotal.Text*.

Study tip

The variable 'Tip' stores a decimal value. In this command it is converted to a string using the command Str(Tip).

Activity Output variables

- Make sure the cursor is in the sub-procedure *btnTip_click*.
- Add commands to output the variables *Tip* and *Total* as shown above.
- Run the program using the Debugging tool to make sure it works.
- Save your work.

The finished program

The program is now complete. A full code listing is shown at the end of this chapter.

■ Chapter end

Full code listing

You created two programs while working through this chapter.

1 – User Questionnaire

The first program was the user questionnaire that allowed the user to input his or her details (first name, surname and age) and displayed them in a message box.

Here is the full code listing for this program.

```
Public Class Form1

    'Declare variables

    Dim FirstName, Surname As String

    Dim Age As Integer
```

```
Private Sub btnEnd_Click(ByVal sender As System.Object, ByVal …

    'When user clicks 'finished' assign text box values to variables

    FirstName = txtFirstName.Text

    Surname = txtSurname.Text

    Age = txtAge.Text

    'Output the variables

    MsgBox(FirstName & " " & Surname & "Next year you will be " &
    Str(Age + 1))

    'Exit from program

    End

End Sub

End Class
```

2 – Tip calculator

Here is the full code listing for the tip calculator program.

```
Public Class Form1

    'declare variables

    Dim Bill, Tip, Total As Decimal

    Private Sub btnEnd_Click(ByVal sender As System.Object, ByVal …

        End

    End Sub

    Private Sub btnTip_Click(ByVal sender As System.Object, ByVal …

        'assign values to variables

        Bill = txtBill.Text

        Tip = Bill * 0.15

        Total = Tip + Bill

        'output variables

        lblTip.Text = "The amount of the tip is £" & Str(Tip)

        lblTotal.Text = "The total bill is £" & Str(Total)

    End Sub

End Class
```

Overview

In this chapter you learned how to work with string, integer and decimal variables. You learned how to declare variables, assign values to them, and to output the variables as labels on the form.

You learned how to calculate a value and assign it to a variable. You also learned about using the arithmetic operators.

■ Questions

Answer these questions to demonstrate your learning.

1 What data type would you choose for a variable that stored a whole number?
2 What data type would you choose for a variable that stored a yes/no value?
3 Give the command to declare a variable called *Birthday* of the date data type.
4 If the user types a value into a text box called *txtTotal*, what is the name of the property where this value is stored?
5 Give the command that will assign the contents of a text box called *txtAge* to a variable called *Age*.
6 State the four main arithmetic operators. Give the symbol and the action each one performs.
7 Give the command that will multiply the variable *UnitCost* by 10 and assign the value to a variable called *BatchCost*.
8 Give the command that will assign the value of a variable called *BatchCost* to a label called *lblCost*.
9 A form can contain many different buttons. Each button has code attached to it. What tells the computer to carry out the code linked to a button?
10 What are the limitations on the use of *InputBox* to assign user input to a variable?

Further activity

Practice activities can be carried out if you finish the work in this chapter with time to spare. You can also carry out these activities in your own time to help with learning and to improve your skills.

Extension activity: Adapt the tip calculator, so that the user enters not just the size of the bill but also what percentage of the bill to calculate as a tip – for example, 5 per cent, 10 per cent or 15 per cent.

8 Planning, creating and testing a program

■ Introduction

An important skill for a programmer is to understand the problem that the program is designed to solve, and to plan the program to meet the user need. In this section you will learn how to plan and structure a program, and create a program to carry out a calculation.

■ 8.1 Plan and structure

In chapter 3 you learned that a computer is a machine for processing data to create information. A computer takes input, processes it, and produces output. In chapter 7 you created two programs that followed this structure. In each case the program accepted input from the user, processed that input, and the results were output for the user to see on the screen.

The overall purpose of a computer program is to produce useful output. The input and processing are just ways to produce the result that the user wants. When planning a complex computer program the best approach is to work backwards from the required output. This will help you to decide what data the user needs to input and what processing is required to create the output.

Learning content

3.1.1 Constants, variables and data types: understand when to use variables in problem-solving scenarios; understand the different data types available; be able to explain the purpose of data types within code.

3.1.3 Program flow control: understand the need for structure when designing coded solutions to programs; understand and be able to describe the basic building blocks of coded solutions (sequencing); know when to use the different flow control blocks (sequencing) to solve a problem.

In this chapter you will write a program to work out how much profit is made by a small business. The first step is to plan the program, working backwards from the required output.

Case study

At carnivals, festivals and other outdoor events people take photos with their mobile phones or digital cameras. Ts-2-Go is a small company that will print your photo onto a T-shirt while you wait. In this exercise you will create a computer program that will work out how much profit Ts-2-Go can make at an outdoor event, depending on how many T-shirts they sell.

The profit a business makes is calculated by taking away business costs from business income. Therefore the program must calculate costs and income, and take one figure away from the other.

Planning from the output

The first stage of the planning process is to be absolutely clear about what the output of the computer program will be. In this case, the required output is a single figure, which states how much profit the business made from attending a single event, such as a carnival.

Let us plan backwards from that output. How is profit calculated?

- Profit is calculated as **total income** minus **total costs**.

So, to calculate profit you need to know the income and costs of the business.

- The **income** of the business comes from selling T-shirts. The total income from one day of work is calculated by multiplying the price of one shirt by the number of shirts sold.

  Selling price for one shirt * Number of shirts sold

- The **costs** are calculated from the cost of making one T-shirt multiplied by the number of T-shirts made. As the T-shirts are made to request while customers wait, the number of T-shirts made is the same as the number sold.

  Cost of making one shirt * Number of shirts sold

So, this program will need six variables:

- profit
- income
- costs
- selling price of a shirt
- cost of making a shirt
- number of shirts sold.

The selling price, the cost of making a shirt and the number of shirts sold will be input by the user. The other variables can be calculated from these values.

You will need to declare all six variables. For each variable you will need to choose a variable name and a data type. Each variable stores a number value. The number of T-shirts sold is an integer (it must be a whole number). All other values are currency values such as 4.99. A decimal data type is suitable.

The table summarises the result of this analysis. When you analyse a problem like this, a good method is to start with the bottom row, and work upwards.

Data needed	Where from?	Data type	Variable name
Number of T-shirts sold	Input	Integer	NumberSold
Cost of making one T-shirt	Input	Decimal	ShirtCost
Selling price of one T-shirt	Input	Decimal	ShirtPrice
Total costs	Cost of making one T-shirt * Number sold	Decimal	TotalCost
Total income	Selling price * Number sold	Decimal	TotalIncome
Profit	Total income – total costs	Decimal	Profit

When you are planning a program it is helpful to use a table like this to summarise the variables you will need and what data types to use. A table or similar listing which shows the variables and data types used in a project is called a 'Data dictionary'.

It is always better to set out your workings and your decisions. A professional programmer will provide details like this alongside a developing project to document its structure. It is also useful for a beginner to document their programs.

Here are some of the advantages of planning and carefully documenting all the program details such as the variables you need:

- It helps you to structure your thoughts in a methodical way.
- You can use your plan to keep your work on track as you develop your program.
- It helps other people, such as work colleagues, to understand your program.
- It means that in the future your program can be maintained and supported by other programmers during real-life use within the business.

Program structure

The diagram shows the basic structure of a program as explained in chapter 7. By following this structure you will build your program code.

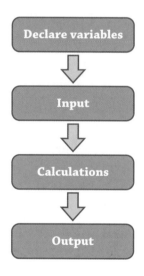

1 Declare variables: all the variables will be declared.
2 Input: the values provided by the user will be input through text boxes and assigned to input variables.
3 Calculations (or processing): code will be added to calculate the remaining variables.
4 Output: the required result will be displayed to the user.

This basic input/processing/output model works for any program.

When a program is very complex, it can be helpful to break it down into parts. Then each part can be analysed in this way. Each part may be called a module or unit. The output from one module is used as the input for the next module.

Pseudocode

Pseudocode provides an easy way to plan the overall structure of a program before coding. Here is the pseudocode for the current program.

```
#Input three variables

    NumberSold ← USERINPUT

    ShirtCost  ← USERINPUT

    ShirtPrice ← USERINPUT
```

```
#Calculate three variables

    TotalCost = ShirtCost * NumberSold

    TotalIncome = ShirtPrice * NumberSold

    Profit = TotalIncome - TotalCost

  #Output

    OUTPUT Profit
```

The three sections of the program are clearly indicated by pseudocode comments. Remember those are the lines that begin with the # mark.

8.2 Write the program

You have planned the variables and the overall structure of the program (see section 8.1). Now you can begin to write the program. This section follows the programming structure that you have already learned.

Input:

- Create a user interface.
- Declare variables.
- Assign input values to variables.

Processing:

- Assign calculated values to variables.

Output:

- Output the result.

At each stage you will see how your original plan helps you to make programming decisions and ensures your work is effective.

The full code listing is provided at the end of the chapter. You can check your finished work against the listing or refer to it if you get stuck.

Create user interface

The user interface controls the input and output to the program. From your plan you know your program will need three input variables:

- number of T shirts sold
- cost of making one T-shirt
- selling price of one T-shirt.

Therefore your interface should have three text boxes, so that the user can input these variables.

The program carries out one task:

- calculate profit

This tells you that the user interface needs one button. When the user clicks that button the program will carry out the task and calculate profit.

Your program uses one output variable:

- profit

Therefore your interface should have one label which will display the output.

Therefore the user interface requires:

- three text boxes
- one button
- one output label.

These objects should have suitable names.

In addition you will need to add further labels. The form needs a title, and instructions to the user, so he or she knows what data to enter in each box.

The next screenshot shows an interface design which has all these requirements. You can design your own interface but make sure it includes all the necessary requirements.

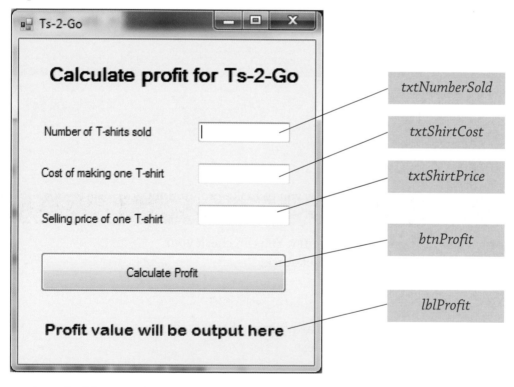

Look at the blue title bar of the form. It has text in it. Instead of saying *Form1* it says Ts-2-Go. You can change the text displayed at the top of a form by clicking on the form. You will see a list of the form properties in the Properties window. Edit the *Text* property of the form. The text you enter will be displayed in the title bar at the top of the form.

Activity Create a user interface

- Start Visual Basic.

- Create a new project called Ts 2 Go.

- Add objects including text boxes, labels and a button to the main form, to create a user interface design.

- Change the *Text* property of *Form1* to 'Ts-2-Go'.

- Debug and save.

Declare variables

You will now start adding code to make the program work as you want it to. The first task is to declare all the variables you will need.

To open the Code Editor tab, right-click anywhere on the form. A short menu appears. The first option on the menus is 'View Code', as shown in the screenshot. Select this option and the Code Editor tab will open. You will see the code for the form.

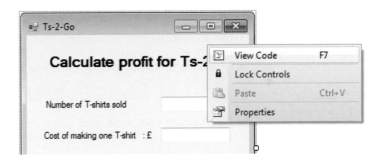

The table on page 85 lists all the variables, with suggested names and data types. You should have the skills to declare all the required variables. Remember that when variables are of the same type they can be declared on the same line. A variable of a different type must be declared on a different line.

Activity Declare variables

- Open the Code Editor tab.

- Add statements at the top of the main code declaring the six variables in your analysis.

- Remember that *NumberSold* is an integer, and the rest are decimal variables.

- Above this section of the code add the comment 'Declare variables'.

- Debug and save.

Assign values to variables

Now the values from the three input boxes will be assigned to the three variables that match these values. This is an action that you want the program to carry out. The action is event-driven. The event that causes this action is the user clicking on the button called *btnProfit*. Therefore the code you write goes within a sub-procedure called *btnProfit_click*.

There is a good match between the names of the text boxes and the names of the variables. This will really help you to write the code quickly and accurately.

For example, there is a variable called *NumberSold*. The value which is assigned is the *Text* property of the text box *txtNumberSold*.

```
NumberSold = txtNumberSold.Text
```

You may notice that while you are typing code, the IntelliSense function will suggest a list of choices. Because you have chosen explanatory names for objects it is easy to find the code you need in the IntelliSense list. If you want you can select code from the IntelliSense list instead of typing out the code in full.

You should be able to complete this coding without any additional help.

Activity Assign input values to input variables

- Looking at the user interface, find *btnProfit*.

- Double click on *btnProfit* to start writing the code for this object.

- Add command lines to assign values to the variables *NumberSold*, *ShirtCost* and *ShirtPrice*.

- At the top of this section of the code add the comment 'Assign input values to variables'.

- Debug and save.

Here is the code so far. The full code listing is at the end of this chapter.

```
Public Class Form1

    'declare variables

    Dim NumberSold As Integer

    Dim ShirtCost, ShirtPrice, TotalCost, TotalIncome, Profit As Decimal

    Private Sub btnProfit_Click(ByVal sender As –

        'assign input values to variables

        NumberSold = txtNumberSold.Text

        ShirtCost = txtShirtCost.Text

        ShirtPrice = txtShirtPrice.Text

    End Sub

End Class
```

Calculate values

The remaining variables must be calculated rather than input by the user. Check back to the table of variables in section 8.1 to see what variables remain, and how they are calculated.

You will now add code to carry out these calculations. The code goes within the *btnProfit_click* sub-procedure.

The first calculated value is total cost. This is calculated by multiplying the cost of making one T-shirt by the number of shirts sold. It is quite easy to write code that carries out this calculation, using the arithmetic operators, which you already know.

```
TotalCost = ShirtCost * NumberSold
```

The table on page 85 will show you what calculation is needed for each variable. The plan you made at the start makes the programming process easier.

Activity Calculate values of variables

- Open the Code Editor window, and move the cursor to the sub-procedure *btnProfit_Click*.

- Enter lines of code to calculate *TotalCost*, *TotalIncome* and *Profit*.

- At the top of this section of the code add the comment 'Calculate values of variables'.

- Debug and save.

Output required result

When you planned the program, you began by thinking about the required final result. The program had to output the amount of profit made. In the final section of the code you will output this value to a label so the user can see it.

The value stored in the variable *Profit* must be assigned to *lblProfit*. That means the label will display that value. The function Str() is used to convert the number variable to a string. A £ sign is added at the start to show it is a money value.

The command is:

```
lblProfit.Text = "£" & Str(Profit)
```

This code belongs within the sub-procedure *btnProfit_Click*. It is the last command in this sub-procedure, and it completes the project.

Activity Output required result

- Open the Code Editor window, and move the cursor to the sub-procedure *btnProfit_Click*.

- Enter a command to assign the value in the variable profit to the *Text* property of *lblprofit*.

- At the top of this section of the code add the comment 'Output result'.

- Debug and save.

Conclusion

Planning the project in advance, and using names for objects, has made the programming task much easier. As you take on more complex work, this type of planning will be essential.

The full coding of the program is given at the end of this chapter.

The development of a programming project requires planning, implementation and finally testing of the program. In the final section of this chapter you will test the program that you made.

■ 8.3 Test the program

To test the program you must run it, and enter test values to see what results you get.

To test a program thoroughly, you need to use a range of test values and track the results. You will learn how to carry out full testing in chapter 26.

The next screenshot shows the Ts-2-Go profit calculator in action. The user has entered test data, and the program has calculated a result.

The user has entered the following data:

> Number of T-shirts: 40
>
> Cost of making one shirt: £2.99
>
> Selling price: £5.99

The program has calculated a total profit of £120.

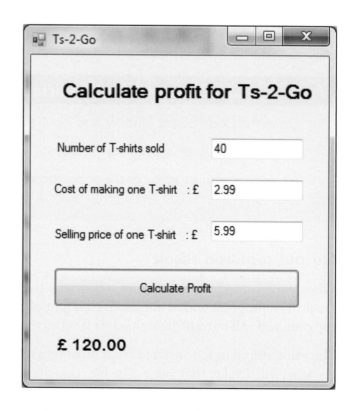

Activity Perform a simple test

- Finish all the stages of program development.

- Run the program using the Debugging tool.

- If you get any error messages, or other problems occur, check your work against the program listing.

- If the code runs without errors, enter test values into the input boxes.

- Note the test data you have used, and the resulting output.

- Save your completed work.

Chapter end

Full code listing

Here is the full listing of the code of the profit calculator for Ts-2-Go.

```
Public Class Form1

    'declare variables

    Dim NumberSold As Integer

    Dim ShirtCost, ShirtPrice, TotalCost, TotalIncome, Profit As Decimal

    Private Sub btnProfit_Click(ByVal sender As -

        'assign input values to variables

        NumberSold = txtNumberSold.Text

        ShirtCost = txtShirtCost.Text

        ShirtPrice = txtShirtPrice.Text

        'calculate values of variables

        TotalCost = ShirtCost * NumberSold

        TotalIncome = ShirtPrice * NumberSold

        Profit = TotalIncome - TotalCost

        'display result

        lblProfit.Text = "£" & Str(Profit)

    End Sub

End Class
```

Overview

In this chapter you learned how to plan a programming project by working backwards from the output. You developed a full listing of the input, calculated and output variables. You created a plan of the variables that would be required. You implemented this plan by creating a program. The program development was structured into the following stages.

1 Create interface.
2 Declare variables.
3 Assign input values to variables.
4 Calculate variables.
5 Output results.

You learned how the development of a program can be greatly simplified by giving variables and programming objects clear and descriptive names.

■ Questions

Answer these questions to demonstrate your learning.

1 Describe three advantages of fully documenting your program plan before you begin work.
2 Give three reasons why giving descriptive names to programming objects helps you to write better code.
3 How do you change the name of an object?
4 An object is called *btnSearch*. What can you guess about this object from its name?
5 When is it OK to declare several variables on the same line?
6 What is the difference between declaring a variable and assigning a value to a variable?
7 The code for a sub-procedure begins like this

```
Private Sub btnQuit_Click
```

What event causes the code in this sub-procedure to be carried out?
8 What does it mean to test a program?
9 What task should you do before you start to write the program code?

Further activity

Practice activities can be carried out if you finish the work in this chapter with time to spare. You can also carry out these activities in your own time to help with learning and to improve your skills.

Practice activity: Create a program that calculates pay by multiplying rate per hour by number of hours worked and deducting tax at 22 per cent.

Extension activity: Add extra code to the program you created in the practice activity.

The code will:

- calculate tax at 22 per cent of pay
- show the amount of total pay, tax and net pay (total minus tax).

9 Catching input errors with *If...Then*

■ Introduction

Errors can occur while a program is in use. In this section you will learn how to catch errors before they cause your program to crash.

You will learn how to use conditional statements in your code. Conditional statements are actions that vary according to the values the user inputs. In this chapter you will use this method to catch input errors before they cause problems in the execution of your program.

■ 9.1 Input errors

Almost all programs use variables. You have seen that variables are used to store input values. The value stored inside a variable can be different every time the program is run.

But sometimes the values that are input can cause problems for the program. For example, this can happen if the person using the program inputs an illogical value, or a value that is impossible for the computer to process. Of course the user should not enter incorrect data like this, but people will make mistakes while using the computer. How does the program cope with input errors like this?

It is important for a computer program to be robust. A robust program does not break down or crash if the user makes a silly mistake. In order to ensure that a computer program is robust it should include methods to deal with input errors.

Here are two common input errors that can cause problems for a program:

- data of the wrong type, which does not match the input variable type
- data that is impossible, such as a negative number where only a positive number makes sense.

In this section you will look at examples of input errors and how the program responds to them.

Input data of the wrong type

In the last chapter you created a program to calculate profit for a small company called Ts-2-Go. The user had to input three values, including the number of T-shirts sold by the company. The number of T-shorts sold was stored as an integer variable.

But what if the user made an error, and entered a character, such as a letter of the alphabet, instead of a number?

An input like this will cause the program to stop while it is running and display an error message.

Here is an example. A user entered the letter 'a' into *txtNumberSold*, instead of a number. Visual Basic stopped the program, and displayed an error message. This is shown in the screenshot.

```
Private Sub btnProfit_Click(ByVal sender As System.Object, ByVal e As System.EventA

    NumberSold = txtNumberSold.Text
    ShirtCost = txtShirtcost.Text
    ShirtPrice = txtShirtPrice.Text

    'Calculate variables
    TotalCost = ShirtCost * NumberSo]
    TotalIncome = ShirtPrice * Number
    Profit = TotalIncome - TotalCost

    'Output result
```

⚠ **InvalidCastException was unhandled**

Conversion from string "a" to type 'Integer' is not valid.

Troubleshooting tips:

When casting from a number, the value must be a number |

Make sure the source type is convertible to the destination t

Get general help for this exception.

The error message is linked to the line that reads:

NumberSold = txtNumberSold.Text

This is the line that assigns the value in *txtNumberSold* to the integer variable. The error message says 'Conversion from string "a" to type 'Integer' is not valid'. In other words, *NumberSold* is an integer variable, but you are trying to assign a string value to it.

An error like this that causes the program to stop working while it is running is called a **run-time error**. In the next activity you will produce this error and see the results.

Key term

Run-time error   A mistake in a computer program that does not prevent it being converted to machine code, but prevents the computer from running the machine code.

Activity Create a data type error

- Start Visual Basic.

- Open the project Ts-2-Go, which you created in chapter 8.

- Click on the Start Debugging button to execute the code.

- Enter values in the text boxes to indicate the shirt cost and shirt price.

- In the top box, labelled 'Number of T-shirts sold', enter the letter 'a'.

- Click on the Calculate profit button.

- Notice the error message that is displayed.

- Click on the Stop Debugging button to halt the program.

Input impossible data

Sometimes a mistake in input data does not cause the program to crash while it is running. The program does not stop or show an error message. Instead the program produces an answer that is incorrect.

For example, a user entered the number of T-shirts sold as –100. In this case the user entered an impossible value. It doesn't make sense to say the company sold –100 shirts, but the program did not spot or trap the error.

There was no mistake with the language syntax, and there was no run-time error to stop the program from executing. But there is a problem with the way the program works, so that it produced an incorrect answer. In the next activity you will produce this error and see the results.

Activity Create a logic error

- Start Visual Basic.

- Open the project Ts-2-Go, which you created in chapter 8.

- Click on the Start Debugging button to execute the code.

- Enter values in the text boxes to indicate the number of T-shirts sold, the costs and the selling price.

- In the top box, labelled 'Number of T-shirts sold', enter the number '–100'.

- Click on the Calculate profit button.

- See what output result you get.

Error trapping

You have seen two examples of input data causing errors to a program. Both these types of error can cause problems for programmers. If the user runs the program and accidentally enters the wrong data or the wrong type of data then the program might go wrong.

It is important to test every program carefully to make sure that it is robust. That means that it can cope with all types of circumstances, including the user entering incorrect data, without breaking down or going wrong. You will learn more about robust systems in section 9.3.

A good way to make a program more robust is to write code that traps input errors. This means that if the user enters a value that will cause problems then the computer displays a warning and stops the program.

In the next section you will see how to use *If...Then* statements to trap errors.

Link

More about debugging your code – chapter 22

■ 9.2 Use an *If...Then* statement to trap an input error

In this section you will learn how to write program code that uses an *If...Then* statement. Using an *If...Then* statement allows you to vary the actions that the program code performs. The program will carry out different actions according to the value of one or more variables.

In this section you will use *If...Then* statements to show a warning message and stop the code if the user enters a negative number of sales.

Structure of *If...Then* statements

The general structure for an *If...Then* statement is shown next. The words in italics will be replaced by extra code to complete the statement.

```
If condition Then

        conditional statement(s)

End If
```

Here is an explanation of the structure:

- The code begins with the word *If*.
- On the same line there is a *condition*. A **condition** means a logical test. A logical test is any test with a yes/no result.
- This line finishes with the word *Then*.
- Next there are some *conditional statements* – in other words one or more lines of code. This code will only be carried out by the computer if the logical test is true.
- On the final line the phrase *End If*. This marks the end of the *If...Then* statement.

Notice that the conditional statements – statements that are only carried out if the logical test is true – are indented from the margin. This makes the code easier to read. The computer will automatically indent the conditional statements when you type the code.

> **Key term**
>
> **Condition**   A logical test that can have the result true or false.

Condition

First you must decide on the condition (the logical test) to include in the statement. The number of T-shirts sold cannot be less than zero. So, an error is made if the value of the variable *NumberSold* is less than zero.

The way to write this in code is

```
NumberSold < 0
```

The symbol < is a **relational operator**. It stands for 'is smaller than'. Relational operators are used to create logical tests to show or test the relation between two values. There are six main relational operators that you need to know about. They are shown in the table.

Relational operator	Meaning	Example of use
<	Smaller than	4 < 9
>	Greater than	100 > 0
=	Equal to	(2*8) = 16
<>	Not equal to	3 <> 4
>=	Greater than or equal to	9 >= 2
<=	Less than or equal to	10 <= (2*5)

If condition is True

What do we want to happen if the condition is true – that is if the user has entered a negative value? We need to show an error message, and then stop the program.

Here are the lines of code to make this happen:

```
MsgBox("Error: Number sold cannot be a negative value.")

End
```

Completed code

So the code for this error trapping will look like this:

```
If NumberSold < 0 Then

        MsgBox("Error: Number sold cannot be a negative value.")

        End

End If
```

This code must be added to the program. It must come after the value is assigned to the variable, but before the variable is used in a calculation.

Activity Trap negative input

- Use your judgement to enter the new lines of code at the correct point in the program.

- Save and test the program.

- If there are any errors in your work, correct them.

- Save the corrected code.

- Run the program using the Start Debugging button and see whether it successfully traps the error if you enter a negative number of shirts sold. You can check your work against the full code listing at the end of this chapter.

■ 9.3 Use an *If...Then* statement to prevent a run-time error

At the start of this chapter you learned about a possible run-time error. This error will be caused if the user enters a string instead of a number into the text box called *txtNumberSold*.

The value input to *txtNumberSold* box is assigned to the integer variable called *NumberSold* in this line of the code.

```
NumberSold = txtNumberSold.Text
```

If a non-numerical value (such as a letter or word) is assigned to the variable *NumberSold* then this will cause a run-time error. The computer cannot assign a character or string to an integer variable. If the value entered into *txtNumberSold* is not a numerical value then there will be a run-time error.

Now you will write code that will stop this error from happening.

IsNumeric()

Luckily Visual Basic provides a ready-made function that will test whether a value is a number or not. It looks like this:

```
IsNumeric(…)
```

Instead of the dots inside the parenthesis you enter the name of any value you want to test. In this case we want to test whether *txtNumberSold.Text* is numeric. So, the code for the condition (the logical test) looks like this:

```
IsNumeric(txtNumberSold.Text)
```

If the value entered in *txtNumberSold* is numeric, then the test gives the result True. If the value entered in *txtNumberSold* is not numeric then the test gives the result False.

Complete the *If...Then* statement

Now you can use that condition in an *If...Then* statement. Remember this is the structure of an *If... Then* statement.

```
If condition Then

    conditional statement(s)

End If
```

The condition to use in this case is the test shown above: whether *txtNumberSold.Text* is numeric. The conditional statement – only carried out if the condition is true – is the code that assigns the value in *txtNumberSold.Text* to the variable *NumberSold*.

The complete code looks like this:

```
If IsNumeric(txtNumberSold.Text) Then

    NumberSold = txtNumberSold.Text

End If
```

This code replaces the single line of code assigning a value to the variable *NumberSold*.

Activity **Prevent a run-time error**

- Find the place in the code that assigns a value to the variable *NumberSold*.

- Delete that line of code and replace it with the three-line conditional statement shown in this section.

- Test the program by entering a non-numeric value in the Number sold text box.

You will see that adding this code has prevented a run-time error.

However, the program does not display an error message if a text value is entered. The program does not stop running if a text value is entered. There is nothing to let the user know that a problem has occurred. You need to add more code, which will be explained in the next section.

■ 9.4 Use *If...Then...Else*

An *If...Then* statement starts with a condition – a logical test. The condition is followed by one or more conditional statements. If the condition is true, then these statements are carried out. If the condition is false, then no statements are carried out.

An alternative to an *If...Then* structure is a longer structure called *If...Then...Else*.

```
If condition Then

    conditional statement(s)

Else

    conditional statement(s)

End If
```

This structure includes two sets of conditional statements:

- If the condition is true then the first set of conditional statements are carried out.
- If the condition is false then the second set of conditional statements are carried out, the ones that follow the word *Else*.

You can use this structure to complete the code. You have already entered the code that will be carried out if the condition is true. Now you will enter the code that will be carried out if the condition is false.

- If the value entered is numeric then it can be assigned to the variable *NumberSold*.
- If the value entered is not numeric then show an error message and close the program.

Here is what the completed *If...Then...Else* statement will look like.

```
If IsNumeric(txtNumberSold.Text) Then

    NumberSold = txtNumberSold.Text

Else

    MsgBox("Error: Number sold must be a numeric value")

    End

End If
```

Activity Use *If...Then...Else* to trap an error

- Adapt the *If...Then* statement to include the additional lines shown here.

- Save and run the program using the Debugging tool.

- Correct any syntax errors.

- Test the program by entering a non-numeric value in the Number sold text box.

You will now see that if the user enters a value that is not a number, the program shows an error message and ends.

■ 9.5 Pseudocode

In previous chapters you have seen how pseudocode is used to set out the structure of a program in a simplified form.

Pseudocode includes the *If...Then* structure. The structure is set out like this

```
IF condition THEN

    Statements

ENDIF
```

Pseudocode also includes the *If...Then...Else* structure. The structure is set out like this:

```
IF condition THEN

        Statements

ELSE

        Statements

ENDIF
```

Of course instead of the word 'condition' you would include a condition, using one of the relational operators. The relational operators are the same in pseudocode as in Visual Basic. The only difference is that in Visual Basic the symbol for 'not equal to' is:

```
<>
```

In pseudocode the symbol for 'not equal to' is:

$$\neq$$

The following pseudocode will display an error message if the user enters a number smaller than 0.

```
Numbersold ← USERINPUT

IF Numbersold < 0 THEN

        OUTPUT "Error: Number sold cannot be a negative
        value"

ENDIF
```

Because pseudocode is never run on a real computer, the issue of data type does not arise. In pseudocode you cannot have a mismatch between data input and the variable type.

■ 9.6 Key concepts

This chapter has introduced several important new concepts. In later chapters of this book you will develop these concepts further.

Validation

The type of error trapping described in this chapter is called validation. Validation is a check that input data is valid. 'Valid' means of the right type or format. Validation is a key check, which is normally built into any computer system that accepts input data.

A program that includes validation of user input is more robust. That means it is less likely to crash due to a run-time error, or produce a bad result due to a **logic error**.

Learn more about robust systems in chapter 10.

Try, try again

In this chapter you have written code that detects errors in input values. In these examples, when the user inputs data that is not valid, an error message is displayed and the program ends.

It is usual in real-life programs to give the user more than one chance to enter data. If the user enters data that is not valid, the computer displays an error message and the user can try again. The code repeats until the data input is valid.

Code that repeats several times is called a loop structure. You will learn to program using loop structures in chapter 11.

Testing

In this chapter you learned that certain types of input data can cause problems for programs, producing run-time and logic errors. It is very important that a computer programmer discovers and corrects all such problems.

The only way to uncover problems due to input data is to test the program with a wide range of inputs. Testing, finding errors and making corrections is a vital part of the process of developing computer solutions.

Find out more about how to test a program in chapter 26.

> **Key term**
>
> **Logic error**   A mistake in a computer program that does not prevent the program from running, but means it does not produce the expected results.

■ Chapter end

Full code listing

Here is the full listing of the code of the Ts-2-Go project, with the additional error-trapping code.

```
Public Class Form1
   'Declare variables
   Dim NumberSold As Integer
   Dim ShirtCost, ShirtPrice, TotalCost, TotalIncome, Profit As
   Decimal
   Private Sub btnProfit_Click(ByVal sender As –
      'assign input values to variables
      If IsNumeric(txtNumberSold.Text) Then
         NumberSold = txtNumberSold.Text
      Else
         MsgBox("Error: Number sold must be a numeric value")
         End
      End If

      ShirtCost = txtShirtCost.Text
      ShirtPrice = txtShirtPrice.Text
      If NumberSold < 0 Then
         MsgBox("Error: Number sold cannot be a negative value")
         End
      End If

      'calculate values of variables
      TotalCost = ShirtCost * NumberSold
      TotalIncome = ShirtPrice * NumberSold
      Profit = TotalIncome – TotalCost

      'Output profit
      lblProfit.Text = "£" & Str(Profit)
   End Sub

End Class
```

Overview

In this chapter you learned how to program using the *If…Then* structure. This structure begins with a condition or logical test. The statements that follow are only carried out if the condition is true.

An alternative to this is the *If…Then…Else* structure. This structure has two sets of statements. The first set of statements is only carried out if the condition is true. The second set of statements is only carried out if the condition is false.

In this chapter you saw the effect that input errors have on a program. User input can cause a program to crash or to produce an incorrect result. Using the *If…Then… Else* structure you can prevent input errors from causing problems. This makes the program more robust.

■ Questions

Answer these questions to demonstrate your learning.

1 What is a run-time error?
2 What does robust mean when used to describe a program?
3 What key words are used to begin and end an *If…Then* statement?
4 List the principle relational operators together with their meanings.
5 A programmer is using the *If…Then…Else* program structure in the code. He or she enters a logical test and some statements that follow the word *Else*. When will these statements be carried out?
6 If an error is detected what should be output for the user to read?
7 What is validation?

Further activity

Further activities can be carried out if you finish the work in this chapter with time to spare. You can also carry out these activities in your own time to help with learning and to improve your skills.

Further activity: In this chapter you have trapped input errors for the first variable of the program – the variable called *NumberSold*. There are two other input variables in the program, and you could write code to catch input errors for all these variables.

- If you have time to practise your coding, create additional error-trapping code for all the variables in the program.

- Remember to test and save your work as you go.

How much of this work you are able to complete depends on how much time you have to spare, but it is good practice at coding. Do as much as you can. When you are doing practical programming you should remember to build error trapping into your code.

10 Computer systems

Introduction

In this chapter there is no programming activity. This chapter gives you an overview of the use of computer systems in everyday life. Computer systems are vital for human life and well-being. That is why it is very important to ensure that systems are tested and developed to be robust and reliable. You will learn about the components of a computer system. You will learn about developments in hardware technology and the impact of changing technology.

10.1 The need for robust and reliable systems

In the last section you looked at how user errors can cause problems for computer software. You looked at ways to adapt a computer program so that the errors were caught before the program could go wrong. This is an example of making a program more **robust**. Robust computer systems can cope with a wide range of inputs without going wrong.

It is also important that computer systems are **reliable**. A reliable system will always react in the same way to the same inputs. That means it is predictable and can be used with confidence.

Computer technology is used for many vital tasks in our society. It is vitally important that these computer systems do not go wrong. For this reason a great deal of work is done to ensure that computer systems are both robust and reliable.

Strengths and weaknesses of computer systems

Computer systems have many positive features. That is why we rely on them for so many important tasks. However, some features of computer systems lead to risks:

- A computer has no additional knowledge or judgement outside of the instructions it is given to perform.
- The computer will not be able to tell if a result is good or bad for people, it will just carry out the instructions in the software.
- Any errors made will quickly spread and multiply because a computer works so fast.

For this reason, computers can cause major problems if they are not well designed.

Learning content

3.1.8.1 Computer systems: understand and be able to discuss the importance of computer systems in the modern world; understand that computer systems must be reliable and robust and be able to discuss the reasons why this is important.

3.1.8.2 Hardware: be able to discuss how developments in different hardware technologies (including memory and processor) are leading to exciting innovative products being created, for example in the mobile and gaming industries.

3.1.16 The use of computer technology in society: be able to evaluate the impact of and issues related to the use of computer technology in society.

Key terms

Robust   Software that will function under a range of different circumstances without failing.

Reliable   Software that produces predictable results.

Significance of computer systems

Computers are used in systems that are vital for human health and well-being or for financial prosperity. If these systems go wrong, there can be very serious consequences. The systems where reliability is most important are called life-critical systems. A life-critical system is a system whose failure may result in death or serious injury to people, or severe environmental harm.

For example, computer technology is used to control safety systems in a nuclear power plant. It can cause a huge environmental disaster if these systems fail to control the temperature of the reactor. This has only happened on a large scale two or three times in history. In each case it was because of some unforeseen circumstance, such as the Japanese tsunami of 2011. Dangerous and unforeseen circumstances can occur without warning . That is why computer systems must be developed and tested to be reliable and robust.

Financial systems throughout the world rely on computer technology. Financial systems control the flow of money between banks, industries and countries. Times of economic hardship put these systems under strain. At such times it is important that computer systems work properly. Failure of financial computer systems can cause severe economic hardship.

On a smaller scale, computer systems can be used to control medical equipment, for example life support systems that help care for seriously ill people in hospital. A computer can tirelessly monitor signals like blood pressure and brain function, all day and night, and raise an alarm if these show danger.

Other examples of critical systems controlled by computers include landing a plane, controlling dangerous machines in a factory, despatching emergency teams to a disaster zone, and controlling electricity networks to prevent power cuts. In all these cases, reliable computer systems literally save lives. But errors in computer systems could lead to large-scale disasters.

Designing computer systems

The systems mentioned here are critical to human well-being. Computer technology is embedded throughout our society. Computers have many important functions. It is important that these systems do not go wrong.

When computer systems are developed it is important to make sure they are robust and reliable. There are two important methods used to ensure this happens:

- error trapping
- testing.

Error trapping

All computer systems need input. Sometimes input may cause problems for the computer. You saw two examples in chapter 9 in which mistakes made by the user caused the software to crash, or to produce incorrect results.

Most problems are caused when input is:

- incorrect due to user error (for example, bad typing)
- extreme or unexpected
- impossible (for example, of the wrong data type).

For this reason, systems are put in place to trap errors and other unusual data.

There are two main ways to capture input errors before they cause problems in computer systems:

- **verification**
- **validation**.

Verification is when important data is input more than once, to check that it has been entered correctly. If you have ever created a password on a computer system you will probably have been asked to enter the password twice. This was to make sure you did not make an error that would have serious consequences and stop you using the computer.

Validation is when input is tested before it is accepted by the computer. Input data must match certain conditions before being used by the software. In chapter 9 you added code to your program so that if the user typed a value that was not a number, the program halted. This is an example of input validation.

> ## Key terms
>
> **Verification** Double-check on data input to make sure it does not contain errors. There are two main forms of verification: to enter the data twice, or to visually check the data against its source.
>
> **Validation** Check input for errors using rules, for example rules about the data type or the size of a number.

Testing

Before any computer system is put into use in real-life situations it must be fully tested. Testing means inputting data and observing the results. To carry out full testing you must try the effect of input that is:

- normal – software must produce good results under normal working conditions
- extreme – software must function when input is unusual or excessive. Sometimes this means giving a warning to the human user. But in any case the software must not break down when input is extreme.
- impossible – the user may accidentally input data that is impossible. An example is if age was shown as a negative number, or if characters were entered instead of numbers. There is a danger that if impossible data is input the computer program will crash. Testing must ensure that error-trapping systems are in place to prevent this.

In this book you will learn how to test your software in full.

10.2 Input devices

All data inside the computer is held in electronic digital form. Input devices are used to convert all types of data into electronic form.

Keyboard

The keyboard is used to convert letters of the alphabet into electronic signals. When you press a key on the keyboard an electronic signal is sent to the computer. The electronic signal is the ASCII code for that letter of the alphabet. As well as letters, the keyboard can be used to input the other symbols you can see on the keys.

Pointing devices

Pointing devices pick up the movements of your hand and turn them into digital signals. You can use a pointing device to move an arrow or other pointer on the screen of the computer. As you move your hand from side to side or backwards and forwards, the pointer on the screen will move. You use pointing devices to work with a graphical user interface, for example to select an icon or open a userwindow.

A mouse is a small device which fits in your hand. You can roll it about on the desk or table. It is attached to a computer by a wire or a wireless signal. The mouse detects the movements you make, and sends electronic signals to the computer. There are one or more buttons on the mouse. By clicking a button you can make a selection on the screen.

A touch pad is an alternative to the mouse. It is a surface across which you move your finger. It picks up the movement of your finger and uses it to control the pointer on the screen. Many laptops have a touch pad. They are convenient when there isn't space to use a mouse, but they can be trickier to use.

Scanner

A scanner is a device that reads an image from a document into the computer. Typically the document is placed face-down on a flat screen, and a light passes over it. This is called a flatbed scanner. Sensors inside the scanner detect light and dark areas of the document. This information is passed to the computer in electronic form. You can also get a hand-held scanner which scans by moving it over a document.

- Advantages: A scanner is the right input device to choose when you need to convert any paper image to a digital file.
- Disadvantages: A scanner cannot be used to create a new picture. It will only read an existing picture into the computer.

Screen input

There are also input devices that let you draw or select items directly onto the screen. A light pen and a touch screen are examples.

A light pen lets you draw directly onto the screen of the computer. Typically it works by picking up the bright point of light that creates the screen image and using it to create an image by drawing onto the screen. You can also use it to move a pointer and select menu items from a graphical user interface.

A touch screen looks like an ordinary computer monitor but it can detect your finger if you touch the screen. By touching the screen you can make choices from the menus on the screen, similar to using a mouse.

Bar code

Nowadays most products for sale in shops have a code number which is printed on the wrapper by the manufacturer. This is a bar code. The numbers are printed in human-readable digits, and as vertical black and white bars. The width of the bars stands for different numbers.

A big advantage of bar codes is that they can be printed using normal ink onto any product wrapper.

Cards

A magnetic stripe holds numbers in magnetic form on a black strip on a plastic card. Magnetic stripe cards are used as credit cards and payment cards by banks. They are also used as ID cards (identity cards), for driving licenses and other secure purposes.

The information on a magnetic stripe is read by swiping the card through a magnetic strip reader

A smart card has more advanced technology than a magnetic stripe card. A smart card has a small computer chip embedded in it. It can store much more data than a magnetic stripe card and it is fairly easy to add new data to the chip. A smart card is also called a chip card, or an Integrated Circuit Card (ICC).

Multimedia input

Microphones, cameras, and video recording devices are available as computer peripherals. These devices allow you to input multimedia content such as images and sounds. Nowadays most smartphones can take pictures and record sound and video.

Sensors

Sensors are devices that detect environmental conditions. An electronic sensor converts an environmental measurement into an electronic signal that can be input to a computer. This means the computer can monitor and record environmental conditions.

A wide range of environmental conditions can be monitored by electronic sensors. Examples of these are:

- heat sensors
- light sensors
- touch sensors
- sensors that detect acidity or dangerous chemicals.

Biometric input

Some security systems use sensors to check identity. Every person has different fingerprints and the lines in the iris (the coloured part of the eye) are also unique. There are sensors that scan fingerprints or eyes to check someone's identity. These are called biometric systems.

Biometric systems are used for security – for example, entry to a bank. They can also be used to approve cash payment. This means you do not need to carry a security card or remember a password. Some schools use biometric systems so that pupils do not need to carry cash.

■ 10.3 Output devices

Information inside the computer is in electronic digital format. People cannot see the data that is inside the computer. Output devices take information from inside the computer and put it into a form that is useful to people.

Monitor

The computer monitor is also called the computer screen or the Visual Display Unit (VDU). A personal computer almost always has a monitor attached to it. The monitor displays output from the computer. The advantage of the monitor is that the user can see output straight away. As soon as you perform an action on the computer, the output appears on the monitor screen. The use of a graphical user interface requires a suitable screen display.

Most desktop computers have a separate monitor which is connected by a wire to the central computer case which contains the processor. The monitor of a laptop or a handheld device, such as a smartphone, is built into the same case as the processor.

Hard copy

Hard copy is the computer term for a permanent output from a computer which you can read. This is usually printing with ink onto paper. A range of different printers and plotters are used to create hard copy. The two most common types of printer are laser printers and inkjet printers. Inkjet printers are less expensive, but not so fast.

Sound output

Sounds can be output from a computer via many different devices, such as speakers and headphones. Sounds can be used to send warnings and signals to the computer user.

All sound output devices take digital electronic signals from the computer and turn them into sounds.

Control systems

A computer signal can be used to turn devices, such as heaters, machines and motors, on and off.

These systems frequently use input devices to detect features of the environment, such as obstacles or temperatures, and then adjust their actions to control the environment. Examples of this include:

- automated production: many factories make use of machines that are controlled by a computer. The machines will perform repetitive production tasks without needing to rest, and without pay.
- robotics: a machine that is run by a computer and carries its own power source and processor so that it can move about, is often called a robot. A robot may be able to carry out many different tasks. However, most robots are not built to look like a metal person – that is just for films!
- automatic steering and piloting: computerised systems are used to control aeroplanes, ships and vehicles. A flying machine with no human pilot is called a 'drone'.

These automated systems have the great advantage of reliable, repeated action. They do not get tired, and they do not need pay or the safety features that human workers require. However, automated systems cannot always deal with unpredictable events, such as accidents and breakages. This means human operators are needed.

■ 10.4 New developments in hardware technology

In chapter 17 you will learn about the way that computer processors work. Changes in technology over the past few years have made processors faster, smaller and more reliable.

Moore's Law

Moore's Law is a prediction that the power of computer processors will double every 18 months. This prediction was first made in 1965 by Gordon Moore of Intel and has proved quite accurate in the roughly fifty years since then.

This means that computer systems are becoming more powerful all the time. This is partly because nowadays people who make computers use Moore's Law to set their targets for improvement.

> **Did you know?**
>
> In 2005, Gordon Moore stated in an interview that his law would be proved false one day. But it hasn't happened yet.

Computers are always improving. People often expect that one day the rate of improvement will slow down, but it hasn't happened yet. Improvements to technology mean that computers:

- are smaller
- are less expensive
- use less energy
- generate less heat
- work more quickly
- process more data.

All of these improvements are linked to the increasing power of computer processors.

Other limitations

At one time the use of computers was mainly limited by the power of computer processors. Many things that used to be impossible can now be done by computers. That is because processors have increased in power.

But nowadays, as processors improve, other factors limit what computers can do. The speed and power of computer systems can be limited by:

- the input and output devices
- communications links
- the design of software
- the human user
- many other factors.

Good software design will help to overcome these problems, and make the most of the power of modern computer systems.

Recent developments

Improvements in the power of computer processors allow improvements to computer systems:

- **Computer games** have become more realistic, with a greater range of activities, and better graphics.
- **Mobile devices** have become smaller and more powerful. Nowadays mobile computer devices are more powerful than large desktop computers were ten years ago.
- **Computer processing power** is built into devices such as phones, so that one device can carry out multiple functions.
- **New technologies** such as satellite positioning systems, street maps and mobile apps give us access to information systems as we go about our everyday business.

Nowadays we take it for granted that we have access to information and computerised services from all locations, through small and relatively inexpensive devices. A few years ago these technologies were new and expensive; now they are widely used by lots of people.

The future

It is very difficult to predict the next stages of development. Some computer scientists have predicted particular new uses for computers in the future:

- Instead of many different types of mobile and laptop system, such as phones, tablets and e-readers, there may come a time in the near future when a single small device, which we can carry with us, will meet all our computing needs.
- Current input and output devices may be replaced by systems that pick up body movements, and project output into the air above a computer console. This means a tiny device could create a large user interface.

- Instead of carrying a mobile computer device, computers might be 'wearable', perhaps incorporated into clothing or even embedded in our bodies.
- Computers might be used to control environmental systems and protect nature against pollution and emissions.

Changes will partly depend on the power of computer processors, and partly on what humans decide to do with that power. If there is strong demand for an item, or a new use for computers, then there is a motive for manufacturers to meet that demand.

Human-like behaviour

In this chapter you have learned that computers have some disadvantages. Many of these are linked to the fact that computers do not react like human beings do. In general, computer systems lack independent judgement and what we sometimes call common sense.

It is possible that in the future computers might be built that behave in more human-like ways. More powerful processors may make this possible. Or it may be that the way that computers are built makes this impossible, no matter how powerful the computers. This is an area where there is disagreement among experts.

The development of human-like thinking by computers is known as artificial intelligence or AI. The goal is to create a computer that can make decisions which are appropriate and useful for human goals and priorities. Currently, computers cannot make complex decisions, or cope with new and unforeseen circumstances. They can only follow instructions given by their software.

Even if computers never behave exactly like humans there are ways that computer systems could become more human-like. More powerful processors may enable these changes.

- Natural language processing means that computers may be able to understand ordinary human speech, and produce output messages that are just like talking to another human being. This is surprisingly difficult for modern computer systems to achieve. Some people doubt whether it will ever be fully achieved.
- Translation: developers hope that computers will be able to translate accurately between all the different languages of the world, so people of different nations can communicate more easily.
- Powerful computer systems may be able to simulate realistic environments and create virtual realities that are just like experiencing new places and experiences. So, for example, you could go on holiday without having to travel.
- Simpler programming interfaces might make it easier for people to write computer software.

The development of new computer systems will be controlled by people who understand computer science. Those who understand computer systems will have more influence over the ways they develop in the future.

■ Chapter end

Overview

In this chapter you learned about computer systems. You learned that computer systems are used for many important uses, including life-critical systems. This means it is important for computer systems to be robust and reliable. Robust means able to cope with many different circumstances without breaking down. Reliable means behaving in predictable ways.

To ensure computer systems are robust and reliable it is important to create error-trapping systems that catch input errors before they cause problems. The two most common types are verification and validation. It is also important to test computer systems. Test data must include normal, extreme and impossible inputs.

Computers are increasing in power all the time, and this will lead to innovations in the way computers are used in everyday life.

■ Questions

Answer these questions to demonstrate your learning.

1 Give two positive and two negative features of computer systems compared to human workers.
2 Describe three life-critical uses of computer systems and explain why it is vital that these systems are robust and reliable.
3 Describe three types of input error and explain why they might cause problems for a computer system.
4 Explain what verification is and how it helps trap input errors.
5 Explain what validation is and give an example of validation of user input.
6 Why is testing a vital part of the development of modern computer systems?
7 Describe three types of input data you would use when testing a computer system.
8 As computer processors get more powerful, what other factors may limit the speed and activity of computer systems?
9 Describe three possible future uses of computers, and explain the advantages these might have for human users.
10 Are there any types of work that you think computers will never be able to do? Explain your answer.

Further activity

Practice activities can be carried out if you finish the work in this chapter with time to spare. You can also carry out these activities in your own time to help with learning and to improve your programming skills.

Write a computer program that verifies an input password.

▪ The user enters a password twice in two different boxes.
▪ The computer compares the two versions of the password.
▪ The computer displays a message saying whether the two versions are the same or not.

11 Loops and algorithms

Introduction

In this chapter you will learn to use loop structures to repeat a block of code.

You will also learn how an algorithm can be used to describe and to plan the structure of program code.

11.1 Program loops

In chapter 9 you learned to use a conditional statement (*If...Then*). You used the conditional structure to trap an error. If the user entered data of the wrong data type, the program stopped. There was no second chance to enter the data.

In this chapter you will create a program where the user enters a password. The program will have a **loop** structure, so that if a user enters incorrect data, the program repeats until the correct data is entered.

Loop commands are found in all programming languages. Another term for a loop structure is an iterating structure. Each repetition of the loop is called an **iteration**.

The commands inside a loop will repeat over and over again. Every loop must have some method of stopping otherwise it will never stop repeating. There are two main types of loop found in almost all programming languages. They use different methods to stop the loop:

- counter-controlled loop
- condition-controlled loop.

Counter-controlled loop

A counter-controlled loop is a loop that repeats a set number of times. This style of loop is most useful when you are working with a group of data items and you know how many items of data there are. You will learn to use counter-controlled loops in chapter 12.

Condition-controlled loop

A condition-controlled loop is a loop that repeats until a particular condition is true. A condition is a logical test that can have the value True or False, just like the condition in an *If...Then* statement.

Key terms

Loop A step in an algorithm that may be repeated one or more times.

Iteration One repetition of a loop.

A condition-controlled loop is the best type to use for the current purpose. The program code allows the user to input data. This code must repeat until the user enters the correct data. Use a condition-controlled loop because:

- you don't know how many times the user will have to try
- you do know the conditions that will make the loop stop.

For this program the condition (the logical test) is whether the user has entered the correct password or not. You will store the correct password as a constant, and the user input as a variable. When the constant and the variable match, that means the user has entered the correct password.

The most flexible and useful conditional loop structure in Visual Basic is the *Do Until...Loop* structure. This is what you will learn in this chapter.

■ 11.2 Write the program without a loop

First you will create a simple program that does not have a loop in it. The user interface should be a simple form with one button on it. When the user clicks on the button an Input Box appears and the user can enter a password.

The program code does not include a loop. That means the user gets one chance to enter the password. If the password is correct, a message box appears that says 'Login successful'. If they enter an incorrect password, a message box appears that says 'Login failed'. The program ends.

Plan the variables

Before you begin to write the code, plan the variables and constants you will need:

- a variable to store the user input
- a constant to store the correct password.

Plan the code

Pseudocode provides a quick and easy way to plan the logic of a program.

Here is a basic structure for a simple password program with no repetition. It uses an *If...Then...Else* structure. In this example the right password is the word 'Orion', but it can be anything.

```
RightPassword = "Orion"

UserPassword ← USERINPUT

IF UserPassword = RightPassword THEN

        OUTPUT "Login Successful"

ELSE

        OUTPUT "Login Failed"

ENDIF
```

You have the skills to write Visual Basic code that matches this structure.

Activity Password input form

- Start a new Visual Basic project.

- Give it a suitable name such as Password Tester.

- Set the *Text* property of *Form1* to 'Password input form'

- Add a single button to the interface and give it a suitable name such as *btnLogin*.

- Set the *Text* property of the button to 'Log in to system'.

- Declare a constant of string data type that stores the correct password. You can choose any word or other text string you like to be the password.

- Declare a variable of string data type that will store the password entered by the user.

- Add code so that when the user clicks the button an Input Box appears. The value entered by the user is assigned to the password variable.

- Add a conditional statement using *If...Then...Else*.

- The logical test is whether the input variable matches the constant.

  - If the logical test is true, the user sees a message box that says 'Login successful'.
  - If the logical test is false, the user sees a message box that says 'Login failed'.

- The program should then end.

- Debug to check the program works properly and save.

It is important that you get this stage of the code right before you add a loop, therefore the program code is shown in full below. You should try to do this task first without looking at the answer. In this example the correct password is 'Orion' but you can use any word you like.

```
Public Class Form1
  'declare constant and variable
  Const RightPassword As String = "Orion"
  Dim UserPassword As String
  Private Sub btnLogIn_Click(ByVal sender As –
    'use input box to allow user to enter password
    UserPassword = InputBox("Enter password")
    'use conditional statement to test password
    'and display a message
    If UserPassword = RightPassword Then
        MsgBox("Login successful")
    Else
        MsgBox("Login failed")
    End If
    'end the program
    End
  End Sub
End Class
```

■ 11.3 Add a loop to the program

Now you will add a loop to the program so that the user can keep entering the password until they get it right. You will use a condition-controlled loop.

Types of condition-controlled loop

Remember that a condition-controlled loop will repeat until a condition (a logical test) tells the loop to stop. There are different types of condition-controlled loop:

- There are loops which will stop when the condition is true. Other loops will stop when the condition is false.
- There are loops where the condition comes at the top of the loop. Other loops have the condition at the end of the loop.

In this chapter you will use the loop where the test comes at the **top** of the loop. The loop will stop when the condition is **true**.

Planning the loop

Before you use a condition-controlled loop in a program, you have to decide:

- which commands will be part of the loop and, therefore, which commands will be repeated
- what condition will make the loop stop.

In this example:

- the commands that will be part of the loop are the commands that allow the user to input a password
- the condition that will make the loop stop is 'correct password entered'.

You can use pseudocode to plan the loop structure. The pseudocode loop structure is called *Repeat...Until*. In a loop like this the condition comes at the end of the loop. The loop stops when the condition is true.

Here is a simple program structure which loops until the user enters the right password.

```
RightPassword = "Orion"

OUTPUT "Enter Password"

REPEAT

        UserPassword ← USERINPUT

        OUTPUT "Login failed"

UNTIL UserPassword = RightPassword
```

There is a problem with this program structure. Because the condition does not come until the end of the loop, the user sees an error message even if the right password has been entered.

The program will work better if the condition comes at the top of the loop.

Do Until...Loop

Visual Basic provides a loop structure with the condition at the top of the loop. The loop will end when the condition is true. It is called a *Do Until* loop. The basic structure of the loop is like this:

```
Do Until condition

        statements

Loop
```

Instead of the word 'condition' you would enter the test that you want the computer to use. Instead of the word 'statements' you would enter the code that you want to repeat until the logical test is true.

What test to use

You want the loop to end when the user enters the correct password.

- The constant that holds the correct password is called *RightPassword*.
- The variable that holds the user input is called *UserPassword*.

So, the test you will use is this:

```
UserPassword = RightPassword
```

The loop begins with the following line.

```
Do Until UserPassword = RightPassword
```

Activity Add a loop to the password entry form

Make sure you are working in Visual Basic with the Password Tester form open. You will amend the code you entered last time.

- Delete the *If…Then…Else* structure from the code.

- Only one line of code remains. This says:

```
UserPassword = InputBox("Enter password")
```

- Below this line add the loop structure:

```
Do Until UserPassword = RightPassword

Loop
```

In the next section you will add commands inside the loop.

■ 11.4 Put commands inside the loop

Next you need to decide what program commands to put into the loop structure. Some of the program commands go before the loop, some inside the loop and some after the loop.

- **Before the loop begins** you must give the user one chance to enter the right password. The logical test at the start of the loop will test if the right password was input. You have already entered this code.
- **Inside the loop** are the commands that you want to repeat if the user gets the password wrong. It will show a message saying 'Login failed'. It will allow the user to enter the password again.
- **After the loop** are the commands that are only carried out when the user enters the right password. This will be a message saying that the login was successful.

The commands that go inside the loop are the error message, and a chance to enter the password again:

```
MsgBox("Login failed")

UserPassword = InputBox("Enter password")
```

The command that goes after the loop is the message saying the login was successful:

```
MsgBox("Login successful")
```

Activity Complete the program

Make sure you are working in Visual Basic with the Password Tester form open.

- Amend the code to include the additional commands described in this section.

- Debug and save.

The code for the completed program, with the loop, is given at the end of this chapter.

■ 11.5 Algorithms

You can use pseudocode before you start writing a program, to plan the structure. You did this in sections 11.2 and 11.3.

Pseudocode is a way of setting out an **algorithm**. An algorithm is a list of instructions to solve a problem. The list of instructions must have a start and an end, and it must be clearly laid out in a logical flow. A successful algorithm will result in the correct answer to the problem. A block of computer code typically follows an algorithm.

Key term

Algorithm A series of steps that will solve a problem. The steps are given in sequence with a clear start and end.

A computer programmer may set out an algorithm, perhaps using pseudocode, before starting work on the program.

Algorithms can also be set out using flowcharts. Learn more about flowcharts in the next section.

■ 11.6 Flowcharts

A **flowchart** is a diagram that shows the structure of a computer program. A flowchart can be used in several different ways:

- to explain or describe the structure of a program that is already written
- to plan the structure of a program before it is written
- to explore different program options.

Key term

Flowchart A diagram that sets out an algorithm using boxes connected by arrows.

In this section you will see how to create a flowchart to describe the program algorithm.

Flowchart symbols

There are five main symbols used when drawing a flowchart.

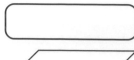 This symbol with round corners is used at the start and end of the flowchart. The word *Stop* or *Start* goes inside the box.

 This symbol is used to represent any input or output. The contents of the input or output are shown inside the box.

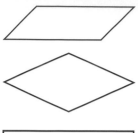 This symbol is used to represent a condition or logical test. The test is shown inside the box. Two arrows come out of the box. One arrow is marked YES (or True) the other arrow is marked NO (or False).

This symbol shows a process such as a calculation. The details of the calculation are shown inside the box. This type of box is not used in the current example.

Arrows are used to connect the boxes. The direction of the arrow shows the flow of the program. In general the flow goes from the top of the page, downwards.

In general one arrow enters a box and one arrow leaves. The exception is the decision box, where there are two arrows. The logical test inside the decision box shows which arrow to choose.

Example flowchart

The next diagram shows how these symbols are combined together to create a complete flowchart.

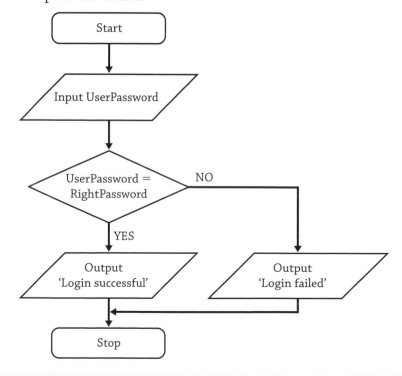

Note the following features that are good practice when making a flowchart:

- The flowchart must have one start and one end point.
- The flowchart arrows point from top to bottom of the page.
- The YES arrow leaves the condition box in a straight line, while the NO arrow branches off to one side.

Loop

The next diagram shows how these symbols are combined together to create a complete flowchart. This flowchart matches the program code you wrote in section 11.4.

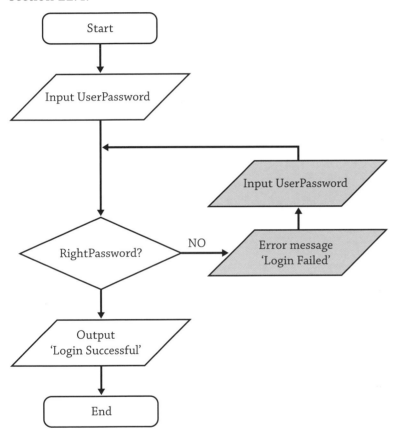

The boxes shaded in blue are the instructions that go inside the loop. Shading is not generally used in flowcharts – this is just to help your learning.

Because the flowchart describes a loop you will see that the arrow turns back up the page and joins the main flow. This structure is always seen in a loop.

■ Chapter end

Full code listing

Here is the full listing of the code of the Password Tester including *Do Until...Loop*.

```
Public Class Form1
    'declare constant and variable
    Const RightPassword As String = "Orion"
    Dim UserPassword As String

    Private Sub btnLogIn_Click(ByVal sender As -
        'input box to allow user to enter password
        UserPassword = InputBox("Enter password")

        'conditional loop with test at the top of the loop
        Do Until UserPassword = RightPassword
            MsgBox("Login failed")
            UserPassword = InputBox("Enter password")
        Loop

        'end the program
        MsgBox("Login successful")
        End
    End Sub

End Class
```

Overview

In this chapter you learned how to write a program that includes a loop or iterating statement. You learned that there are two types of loop: condition-controlled and counter-controlled. You learnt to write condition-controlled loops. The Visual Basic code to create a loop uses the key words *Do Until...Loop*. Other types of loop are available in Visual Basic.

You learned that pseudocode and flowcharts are two ways of setting out the algorithm of a program. They can be used to plan a program in advance, or to set out the logic of a completed program.

■ Questions

Answer these questions to demonstrate your learning.

1 Explain the difference between a counter-controlled loop and a condition-controlled loop.
2 What is the purpose of the condition or logical test in a condition-controlled loop?
3 These Visual Basic commands display a message and accept user input.

```
MsgBox("Do you want to stop this application?")

Reply = InputBox("Type Y or N")
```

Add code so that these commands are repeated until *Reply* = "Y".
4 Draw the five main flowchart symbols and explain their use.
5 How many stop symbols should there be in a flowchart?
6 What is the purpose of a flowchart arrow?
7 Draw a flowchart to show the structure of a program that takes user input, loops, and stops when the user enters a number greater than 6.

Further activity

Further activities can be carried out if you finish the work in this chapter with time to spare. You can also carry out these activities in your own time to help with learning and to improve your skills.

Further activity:

1 In chapter 9 you used this code to catch invalid user input

```
If NumberSold < 0 Then

    MsgBox("Error: Number sold cannot be a negative value")

    End

End If
```

Adapt this program so that the code loops until the user enters a value which is 0 or more.

2 In chapter 9 you used this code to trap invalid user input

```
If IsNumeric(txtNumberSold.Text) Then

    NumberSold = txtNumberSold.Text

Else

    MsgBox("Error: Number sold must be a numeric value")

    End

End If
```

Adapt this program so that the code loops until the user enters a numerical value.

12 Arrays

■ Introduction

In this section you will learn how to create a program that uses a counter-controlled loop. That is a loop that repeats a set number of times. You will use the loop structure to work with an array, which is a group of linked variables used to store a list of data.

■ 12.1 Enter and display a list

In this section you will create a simple program that allows the user to input a series of names and display them on the screen as a list. In this first section you will not use an **array** or a loop. In later sections you will use an array and a **counter-controlled loop** to improve and simplify the program.

Case study

The case study for this program is a teacher who is running a drama club after school. The program will be used to input the name of each pupil in the drama club, and display a list of all the members of the club.

Create user interface

The screenshot opposite shows the user interface for this program. There are four objects – three buttons and a label. You should know how to create an interface like this from prior learning. Notice that the form has a suitable text heading. There are suggested names for the objects. These names will be used in the program code.

Learning content

3.1.1 Constants, variables and data types: understand and be able to program with one- and two-dimensional arrays

3.1.3 Program flow control: understand how problems can be broken down into smaller problems and how these steps can be represented by the use of devices such as flow charts and structure diagrams; understand and be able to describe the basic building blocks of coded solutions (i.e. sequencing, selection and iteration); know when to use the different flow control blocks (i.e. sequencing, selection and iteration) to solve a problem.

3.1.9 Algorithms: be able to create algorithms to solve simple problems; be able to detect and correct errors in simple algorithms.

Key terms

Array   A group of variables of the same data type; the members of an array are called elements; elements have the same variable name; they are distinguished by an item number.

Counter-controlled loop   A loop that repeats a set number of times and then stops.

Activity Start program and create user interface

- Start Visual Basic and begin a new project. Give it a suitable name such as Drama Club.

- Create the user interface shown here. Remember to include the text at the top of the form.

- Give all the objects suitable names.

- Add code so that the 'Quit' button closes the program.

- Debug and save.

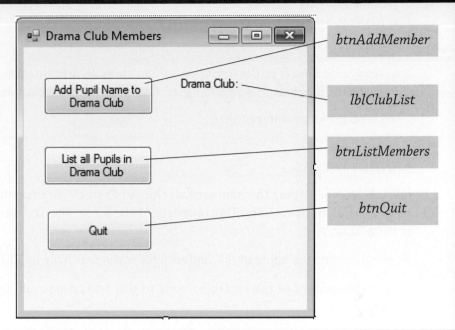

Declare variables and assign values

To keep this task simple assume there are only three pupils in the drama club. In real life there would be more than this. You will need three variables to store their three names. The variables can be called *Pupil1*, *Pupil2* and *Pupil3*. The data type needed to store a name is the string data type.

The command to declare these variables is as follows.

```
Dim Pupil1, Pupil2, Pupil3 As String
```

You have learned two ways to input values to variables: using the *InputBox* command, and using text boxes on the form. The *InputBox* method is the most convenient way to assign input to a string-variable.

You have already learned the command to assign a value to a variable using the *InputBox* function. As a reminder, here is the command to use *InputBox* to assign a value to the variable *Pupil1*:

```
Pupil1 = InputBox("Enter pupil name")
```

The words inside the quotation marks are the text that will appear in the input box. You will need three lines of code, to assign input values to *Pupil1*, *Pupil2* and *Pupil3*.

Activity Declare variables and assign input values

- Make sure the new project is open in Visual Basic.

- Declare the three variables *Pupil1*, *Pupil2* and *Pupil3*.

- Add code linked to *btnAddMember*. You should add three lines of code. Each line uses the *InputBox* function to add a value to one of the three variables.

- Debug and save the program.

Output results

lblClubList will display the names of all the pupils in the drama club. You will add each variable in turn to the *Text* property of the label. The *Text* property of the label is *lblClubList.Text*.

At the moment the value of *lblClubList.Text* is the text 'Drama Club:'.

To add the content of the variable *Pupil1* to this text, you would use the following command:

```
lblClubList.Text = lblClubList.Text & Pupil1
```

Remember that the symbol & is used to concatenate strings, that is, add them together. The new value of the text property is the old value **plus** the value of *Pupil1*.

To add all three pupil names in order you would use these commands:

```
lblClubList.Text = lblClubList.Text & Pupil1

lblClubList.Text = lblClubList.Text & Pupil2

lblClubList.Text = lblClubList.Text & Pupil3
```

There is only one problem with this code. The three names would be added without any space or new line in between them. For example if the names Tom, Jo and Helen were stored in the three variables, the label would look like this:

```
Drama Club:TomJoHelen
```

To make this look like a proper list you need to add line breaks in between the names. The code to add a line break to a label is *vbNewLine*.

If you make this change, the new code now looks like this:

```
lblClubList.Text = lblClubList.Text & vbNewLine & Pupil1

lblClubList.Text = lblClubList.Text & vbNewLine & Pupil2

lblClubList.Text = lblClubList.Text & vbNewLine & Pupil3
```

This starts a new line before each of the pupil names.

You will add this code to *btnListMembers*, so that when the user clicks this button, the list of drama club members is displayed.

Activity Create output

- Make sure the new project is open in Visual Basic.

- Add code linked to *btnListMembers*, so that when the user clicks this button, the list of drama club members is displayed, each name on a new line.

- Debug and save.

Here is the complete code listing for the program you have just created. Try to complete the task on your own before you refer to this code.

```
Public Class Form1

  Private Sub btnAddMember_Click(ByVal sender As –

    Pupil1 = InputBox("Enter pupil name")

    Pupil2 = InputBox("Enter pupil name")

    Pupil3 = InputBox("Enter pupil name")

  End Sub

  Private Sub btnListMembers_Click(ByVal sender As –

    lblClubList.Text = lblClubList.Text & vbNewLine & Pupil1

    lblClubList.Text = lblClubList.Text & vbNewLine & Pupil2

    lblClubList.Text = lblClubList.Text & vbNewLine & Pupil3

  End Sub

  Private Sub btnQuit_Click(ByVal sender As –

    End

  End Sub

End Class
```

This code works, but it is very repetitive. If you wanted to create a program to input a class of 30 pupils it would need a lot of lines of code. In the rest of the chapter you will learn how to simplify the code, by using an array and counter-controlled loops.

■ 12.2 Use an array to simplify the code

In the previous section you used three variables, called *Pupil1*, *Pupil2* and *Pupil3*, to store three pupil names. All three variables stored the same type of data, and were used for the same purpose.

Using an array

Instead of creating a lot of different variables you can use a single variable called an array. An array is a linked group of variables. The different variables in the array are called the elements of the array.

All the elements in the array have the same name, but a different number. The number that tells them apart is called the index number. The index number is shown in brackets after the name of the array.

So, instead of declaring three separate variables, you can declare one array with three elements. Instead of thinking of the three pupil names as three separate pieces of information, think of them as three parts of a single group. An array stores the names of all the members of that group.

In this example we will use an array called *Dramaclub* to store the three pupil names. Instead of using the separate variables *Pupil1*, *Pupil2* and *Pupil3*, we will use the array elements *Dramaclub(1)*, *Dramaclub(2)* and *Dramaclub(3)*.

Element 0

In Visual Basic the first element of every array is called element 0. In this example, in order to simplify the code, we will ignore element 0. We will not use it in the commands. In some programs element 0 is very useful. You should remember that in any array, this extra element exists.

Declare an array

To declare an array you must specify the:

- name of the array
- number of elements
- data type of the elements.

In this case the array is called *Dramaclub*, the number of elements is three and the data type is string. The code to declare this array of three elements is:

```
Dim Dramaclub(3) As String
```

This code means create an array called *Dramaclub* with three elements. Each element is a string variable. You can choose any data type for the elements of an array.

The three elements of this array will be called:

Dramaclub(1)

Dramaclub(2)

Dramaclub(3)

Study tip

Because it includes element 0, the array will have one more element than the value entered for 'club size'. However, as we are not using element 0, this does not affect the code.

Store size of array as a constant

The elements of an array are used throughout a program's code. The number of elements is very important. It is most convenient to store this value as a constant. The value is shown once, in the constant declaration, and from then on the name of the constant is used throughout the program. Then, if the number of elements in the array changes – for example, if the size of the drama club changes, only one line of the program code needs to change.

So, instead of declaring an array with three elements, it is better to follow these steps:

> **Link**
>
> Constants – chapter 5

- Declare a constant called *club_size*, storing the number 3.
- Declare an array with (*club_size*) number of elements.

Therefore the complete code to declare the variable at the top of this program should be:

```
Const club_size As Integer = 3

Dim Dramaclub(club_size) As String
```

Activity Use an array

- Make sure the project is open in Visual Basic.
- Change the declaration section of the code to include a constant *club_size* and an array of that number of elements, as shown above.
- Change all references to *Pupil1* to *Dramaclub(1)*.
- Change *Pupil2* to *Dramaclub(2)*.
- Change *Pupil3* to *Dramaclub(3)*.
- Debug and save.

This change has not simplified the program very much, but you are now ready to use a counter-controlled loop to get rid of the repetition in the code.

■ 12.3 Counter-controlled loop

In chapter 11 you learned how to create a condition-controlled loop. This is a loop that repeats until a particular condition is true. You did not know in advance how many times the loop would repeat, but you did know the condition (the logical test) that would make the loop stop.

In this section you will learn to use a counter-controlled loop. A counter-controlled loop is a loop that repeats a set number of times. You decide in advance how many times the loop will repeat; when it has repeated that many times it will stop.

You have changed the original code so that instead of using three different variables to store the three pupil names, you have used an array with three elements. Now the loop can count through the three elements, using an *Input Box* to add a value to each array element in turn.

Counter-controlled loop

The code for a loop that will repeat exactly three times is as follows:

```
For counter = 1 To 3
        code
Next
```

Instead of the word 'code' you would type whatever commands you want to be repeated inside the loop.

The word *Next* marks the end of the counter-controlled loop.

The counter

counter is an integer variable that is used to count the number of times the loop has repeated. In this example the counter will count up from 1 to 3, so the loop will repeat three times.

- In modern versions of Visual Basic there is no need to declare the counter, because the program will work out what type of variable you need.
- You can use the word *counter* for this variable; it is not a reserved word. Some programmers like to use the word *Index* or the letter *i* (lower case) as the name of the counter variable. Any of these options will work just as well.

The lower and upper limit of the loop

In the example shown above the counter goes from 1 to 3, so the looped commands are carried out three times. Remember that we have stored the size of the drama group as the constant *club_size*, so we can use this constant to set the number of repetitions:

```
For counter = 1 To club_size
        code
Next
```

The input command

The command that goes inside the loop is the command to assign a value to each element of the array. In the previous version of the program there were three input commands that looked like this:

```
Dramaclub(1) = InputBox("Enter pupil name")

Dramaclub(2) = InputBox("Enter pupil name")

Dramaclub(3) = InputBox("Enter pupil name")
```

Instead of entering three commands, we can simplify the code by using just one command and putting it inside a loop which repeats three times:

- Each time the command is carried out, the array index number increases by one.
- Each time the loop repeats, the loop counter increases by one.

> ### Study tip
>
> If you were using element 0 of the array you would change the loop command to say
>
> ```
> For Counter =
>     0 To club_size
> ```
>
> In this example you are not using element 0 of the array.

The loop counter is the same as the array index number. This is the key to using counter-controlled loops to process the elements of an array. Put the input command inside a loop. Use the counter as the array index number.

The full command will look like this:

```
For counter = 1 To club_size

    Dramaclub(counter) = InputBox("Enter pupil name")

Next
```

The code is now much shorter and simpler. And this code is the same whether you need to input values to an array of three elements, or an array of three hundred or three thousand elements. The code is the same.

Assigning values to all the elements of an array like this is called populating the array.

Activity Populate an array

- Make sure the Drama Club program is open in Visual Basic.

- Change the input section of the code. Delete the three lines of input code and replace them with one line of code inside a counter-controlled loop.

- Debug and save.

Using the loop to output the array

A similar method can be used to output the array:

- Put the output command inside a loop.
- Use the loop counter as the array index.

See if you can work out what the code should be.

Activity Output an array

- Make sure the Drama Club program is open in Visual Basic.

- Change the output section of the code. Output the three elements of the array, using a counter-controlled loop.

- Debug and save.

Here is a complete listing for the program so far. Try to complete the work for yourself before looking at the code.

```
Public Class Form1

    Const club_size As Integer = 3

    Dim Dramaclub(club_size) As String

    Private Sub btnAddMember_Click(ByVal sender As —
```

```
        'input values to the array

        For counter = 1 To club_size

            Dramaclub(counter) = InputBox("Enter pupil name")

        Next

    End Sub

    Private Sub btnListMembers_Click(ByVal sender As –

        'output values from the array

        For counter = 1 To club_size

            lblClubList.Text = lblClubList.Text & vbNewLine &
            Dramaclub(counter)

        Next

    End Sub

    Private Sub btnQuit_Click(ByVal sender As –

        End

    End Sub

End Class
```

> **Study tip**
>
> When a line in Visual Basic is too long, it will run over on to the next line. This does not affect the working of the code.

■ 12.4 Make a copy

In chapter 19 you will do more work with the Drama Club project. You will save the *Dramaclub* array to a file, so it is saved even when Visual Basic is closed down.

To make a copy of the project that you will use in chapter 19:

- exit from Visual Basic
- open the storage area where you have saved your Visual Basic work.

The screenshot opposite shows what you will see on the screen. The exact appearance will depend on what files you have saved in this area and how your computer is set up.

- Find the folder called 'Drama Club' as shown in the screenshot.
- Right-click on the folder, and select Copy.
- Put the mouse pointer anywhere within the storage area, right-click and select Paste.
- You will see a folder called 'Drama Club – Copy'.

You will use the copy to complete the work for this chapter.

Activity Make a copy of a project

- Make a copy of the Drama Club project, as shown here.
- For the remainder of chapter 12 work with the copy of the project.

■ 12.5 Pseudocode algorithm

You have learned that pseudocode is a simplified language that you can use to set out program algorithms. Array commands are very similar in pseudocode to the Visual Basic example you have learned. The only differences are:

- like with other variables, there is no need to declare an array in pseudocode
- square brackets are used instead of ordinary brackets to enclose the index number.

Here is the pseudocode for the program you have just written. You will see it is simpler than the Visual Basic code.

```
club_size ← 3

 FOR counter ← 1 to club_size

      Dramaclub[counter] ← USERINPUT

 ENDFOR

 FOR counter ← 1 to club_size

      OUTPUT Dramaclub[counter]

 ENDFOR
```

Activity A simple variant

- To make this algorithm suitable for a class of 15 pupils, only one line of the pseudocode needs to be changed.

- Make this change.

- Write out the full pseudocode.

■ 12.6 Two-dimensional array

A simple array, as you have used up to now in this chapter, is like a list. Each element in the list has a single index number. For example, an array called *Dramaclub* could have the following elements.

Dramaclub	
1	Jay Patel
2	Jo Anderson
3	Janet Miles

Each element of this array has a single index number. So, *Dramaclub(1)* is Jay Patel, *Dramaclub(2)* is Jo Anderson, and so on. This is called a one-dimensional array. A one-dimensional array is like a table with many rows but only one column.

It is possible to create arrays with more than one dimension. For example, the following is a two-dimensional array. A two-dimensional array has more than one row and more than one column.

Dramaclub	1	2
1	Jay	Patel
2	Jo	Anderson
3	Janet	Miles

Each element in a two-dimensional array has two index numbers. The first index number stores the row number. The second index number stores the column number. So, the string 'Jay' is stored in the element *Dramaclub(1,1)* and 'Patel' is stored in the element *Dramaclub(1,2)*. 'Jo' is stored in element *Dramaclub(2,1)* and so on.

You can have arrays with more than two dimensions, but in this book we will only look at one- and two-dimensional arrays. A one-dimensional array has rows. A two-dimensional array has rows and columns.

In this section you will adapt the program to use a two-dimensional array to store the first name and surname of each pupil separately.

Study tip

A two-dimensional array can have more than two columns. 'Two-dimensional' means the array has rows and columns, it does not mean the array has two columns. Some two-dimensional arrays may have lots of columns.

Declare a two-dimensional array

You will remember that the command to declare an array of string variables with three elements is:

```
Dim Dramaclub(3) As String
```

If, instead of a number, you wish to use a constant to determine the size of the array, then the command is:

```
Dim Dramaclub(club_size) As String
```

This creates an array with a row for every pupil in the club. Supposing that you want to enter two items of information (first name and surname) for every pupil in the club, your array declaration must specify number of rows and number of columns. The array declaration would be:

```
Dim Dramaclub(club_size, 2) As String
```

If you imagine an array being like a table, as shown on the previous page, then the first number tells you how many rows in the list, and the second number tells you how many columns. The *Dramaclub* array has three rows and two columns.

Input values to a two-dimensional array

The looped command to input the names of all the pupils in the class to a one-dimensional array is:

```
For counter = 1 To club_size

    Dramaclub(counter) = InputBox("Enter pupil name")

Next
```

In the new array there are two items to input each time the program goes round the loop.

- *Dramaclub(1, 1)* is the first name.
- *Dramaclub(1, 2)* is the surname.

This means there have to be two input commands inside the loop.

```
For counter = 1 To club_size

    Dramaclub(counter, 1) = InputBox("Enter pupil first name")

    Dramaclub(counter, 2) = InputBox("Enter pupil surname")

Next
```

> **Study tip**
>
> A two-dimensional array includes a 0 row and a 0 column. In this chapter we are not using the 0 elements of the array.

Output a two-dimensional array

With a one-dimensional array, the looped command to output the names of the pupils to a label is:

```
For counter = 1 To club_size

    lblClubList.Text = lblClubList.Text & vbNewLine &
    Dramaclub(counter)

Next
```

In order to output the two values (first name and surname) there need to be two output commands inside the loop:

```
For counter = 1 To club_size

    lblClubList.Text = lblClubList.Text & vbNewLine &
    Dramaclub(counter, 1)

    lblClubList.Text = lblClubList.Text & vbNewLine &
    Dramaclub(counter, 2)

Next
```

This code will place each element of the array on a different line. So the list will look like this:

Jay

Patel

Jo

Anderson

Janet

Miles

It would be much better if the first name and surname are shown on the same line, with a space in between. If the code is improved in this way, it will look like this:

```
For counter = 1 To club_size

    lblClubList.Text = lblClubList.Text & vbNewLine &
    Dramaclub(counter, 1)

    lblClubList.Text = lblClubList.Text & " " &
    Dramaclub(counter, 2)

Next
```

Replacing *vbNewLine* with quotation marks around a space, like this " ", adds a space into the label text rather than starting the text on a new line.

Activity Use an array

- Make sure the Drama Club – Copy is open in Visual Basic.

- Change the program coding to use a two-dimensional array. You will need to amend the declaration, the input code and the output code.

- Debug and save.

A full code listing for this program is given at the end of the chapter.

Pseudocode

In pseudocode the two dimensions of the array are shown in separate square brackets. So this line of Visual Basic

```
Dramaclub(counter, 1) = InputBox("Enter pupil first name")
```

Is equivalent to this line of pseudocode

```
Dramaclub[counter] [1] ← USERINPUT
```

The full pseudocode listing is shown at the end of this chapter.

Storing arrays

In chapter 19 you will learn how to store the elements of an array in a text file, so they can be saved after you close the program down.

> **Link**
>
> Save array to file – chapter 19

■ Chapter end

Full code listing

Here is the full listing of the code to enter pupil names into a two-dimensional array and output them using a counter-controlled variable.

```
Public Class Form1

    Const club_size As Integer = 3

    Dim Dramaclub(club_size, 2) As String

    Private Sub btnAddMember_Click(ByVal sender As –

        'input values to the array

        For counter = 1 To club_size

            Dramaclub(counter, 1) = InputBox("Enter pupil first name")

            Dramaclub(counter, 2) = InputBox("Enter pupil surname")

        Next

    End Sub
```

```
Private Sub btnListMembers_Click(ByVal sender As –

    'output values from the array

    For counter = 1 To club_size

        lblClubList.Text = lblClubList.Text & vbNewLine &
        Dramaclub(counter, 1)

        lblClubList.Text = lblClubList.Text & " " &
        Dramaclub(counter, 2)

    Next

End Sub

Private Sub btnQuit_Click(ByVal sender As –

    End

End Sub

End Class
```

Pseudocode

Here is the pseudocode for the program algorithm.

```
club_size ← 3

FOR counter ← 1 to club_size

    Dramaclub[counter] [1] ← USERINPUT

    Dramaclub[counter] [2] ← USERINPUT

ENDFOR

FOR i ← 1 to club_size

    OUTPUT Dramaclub[counter] [1]

    OUTPUT Dramaclub[counter] [2]

ENDFOR
```

Overview

In this section you learned about a type of variable called an array. An array is a collection of linked variables that are called the elements of the array. Each element has the same general name, and a different index number.

In a one-dimensional array each element has a single index number. In a two-dimensional array each element has two numbers, which may be compared to the rows and columns of a table.

The most convenient way to process the elements of an array – for example, to input or output the array contents – is to use a counter-controlled loop. A counter-controlled loop repeats a set number of times.

It is useful to use a constant to store the number of elements in the array. This number can also be used to set the number of loop iterations used to process the array.

■ Questions

Answer these questions to demonstrate your learning.

1 What is the command to declare an array of five string elements called *Customer*?

2 Explain how using a constant to store the number of elements in an array simplifies the programming task.

3 Explain what the effect of this code would be:

```
lblCustomerList = lblCustomerList & vbNewline & "Peter
Smith"
```

4 Describe two differences between pseudocode and Visual Basic code.

5 What is pseudocode used for?

6 An array is declared using the following code. How many elements are there in the array?

```
Dim Client(5,2) As String
```

7 List the elements of the *Client* array.

8 Write the code that would assign the value from the input control *txtClientName* to the first element of the *Client* array.

Further activity

Practice activities can be carried out if you finish the work in this chapter with time to spare. You can also carry out these activities in your own time to help with learning and to improve your skills.

Further activity: A librarian wishes to store a list of book titles. Create a program that allows the librarian to input five book titles, and output these as a list. Use an array to store the five titles. Use the constant *Library_size* to store the number of titles.

Extension activity: Amend the program you just created so that the librarian can store the following information about each book:

- the book title

- the author surname

- the initial letter of the author's first name or names.

You will need to use a two-dimensional array of size (*Library_size*, 3).

13 Data structures

Introduction

In chapter 12 you learned about arrays. An array is a collection of variables, all of the same type. In this chapter you will learn to create new data types, which can combine variables of different types into one complex structure.

Learning content

3.1.2 Structures: be able to explain what a data structure is; be able to produce their own data types that go beyond the built-in structures of the language they are using, such as arrays.

13.1 Combine data elements to make a structure

You have learned how to declare an array and assign values to each element of the array. An array is a collection of elements that are all of the same type. The data type in the example you made was an array of strings. It stored the names of all the pupils in a group.

In this section you will learn to create a new user-defined data type that combines elements of different data types. This is useful when you want to store a range of different items of information. A new data type that the programmer has created by combining different data types is called a structure.

Case study

Computer programs are used in a wide range of businesses. One of the uses of computers is to keep records that the business needs. In this section you will create a new data type to store a record of an animal patient for a vet. This data type will store all the information that the vet needs to know about the animal patient.

You might like to take some time to think about what pieces of information a vet needs to record about each animal patient. There are many different correct answers.

Data elements

In this chapter you will create a data structure that stores the following items of data:

- pet's name
- pet's date of birth
- animal species
- whether the pet has had its injections (Yes/No)
- owner's name.

The program you write in this chapter will create a single variable of this structure and store information about one pet. To store data about more than one pet, you would use a database. You learn about how to program with databases in chapter 20.

Link

Databases – chapter 20

Data types

To declare this structure you have to decide on a suitable data type for each of these elements of information. There may be more than one correct answer in some cases. Here are the data types that you will use in this chapter.

Element	Data type
Pet's name	String
Pet's date of birth	Date
Animal species	String
Has the pet had its injections? (Yes/No)	Boolean
Owner's name	String

Key term

Boolean   A logical value. There are two Boolean values: true and false (sometimes written as yes and no).

As a reminder:

- The **string** data type is used to store any series of characters.
- The **date** data type can store a date in the format day/month/year.
- The **Boolean** data type stores a true/false answer.

Developing a program using this data structure

You will now create a new programming project to store one animal record, using this data structure. As before, you will follow this plan:

1 Create user interface.
2 Declare variables.
3 Input values.
4 Calculate values.
5 Output values.

It will take more than one chapter to complete this work.

■ 13.2 Create the user interface

The user interface will be a form that allows the user to input all of the data elements in the data structure. You will use some new form controls, as well as the familiar text box.

Text box

The string data will be entered using text boxes, which you have used before. Remember that whatever the user types in the text box, it will be stored as the *Text* property of that text box. You can then assign that value to a variable.

You will create two text boxes on the form. They are called *txtName* and *txtOwnerName*.

Check box

The Boolean data type is used to store simple yes/no data. There is one Boolean element in the data structure. This records whether the pet has had its injections or not.

A **check box** is a simple data field that looks like a small box. If the user clicks on the box then the box is 'checked'. This screenshot shows an unchecked and a checked box.

A check box can be used to select a Boolean yes/no answer.

The text property of the check box stores the message (in this example it is 'Tick if had injections'). This property does not change. The check box also has a property called *Checked*. If this value is true then the box has been checked (ticked). If this value is false then the box has not been checked.

You will create one check box on the form. It will have the name *chkInjections*.

Combo box

A combo box is a box that combines two things.

There is a drop-down list of answers from which to pick one.

You can enter an answer that is not on the list by simply typing it in.

> **Key terms**
>
> **Check box** An object on a form that lets the user select a true/false value by clicking on a box. A checked box is marked with a tick and represents the value True.
>
> **Combo box** An object on a form that lets the user select from a drop-down list of options. The user can also enter a new value by typing it in.

In this example, you will use a **combo box** to enter the animal species of the pet. The list will show some of the most common pet species, but the vet can enter a different species if needed. The selected or typed value is stored in the *Text* property of the combo box.

The combo box will be called *cmbSpecies*.

Date/time picker

A date/time picker is a control that lets the user pick any date and time from a drop-down calendar. The screenshot on page 148 shows what a date-time picker looks like when it is in use.

In this example, you will use the date/time picker to select the pet's date of birth. The computer will give the control the name *DateTimePicker1*, and this is a suitable name, so leave it unchanged.

The interface design

As well as the input controls mentioned here you will add two buttons to the form. Call them *btnSave* and *btnQuit*.

You will also have to add labels to explain the information that has to be entered into each input control. There is no need to give these labels special names as they are not used in the program code.

The complete interface design with all the controls is shown in the screenshot.

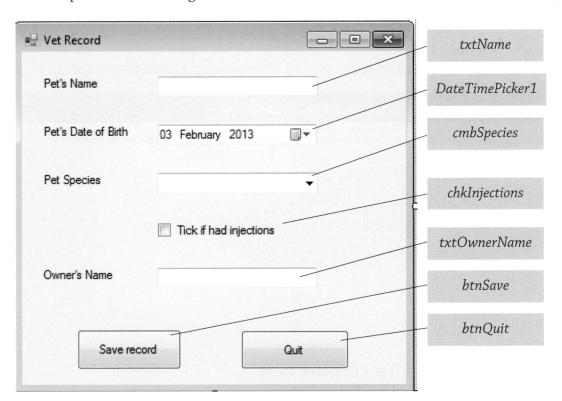

A note on using the date/time picker

When you test this program you will use the date/time picker to pick a date.

- When you click on the arrow at the right of the date/time picker a calendar will open (see the screenshot). You can scroll through day by day.
- At the top of the calendar the month is shown. If you click on this, the calendar will change to show months of the year and you can scroll through those.
- If you click again at the top, the calendar will change to show years and you can scroll through those.

In this way you can pick any day, month or year.

Activity Start program and create user interface

- Start Visual Basic and begin a new program. Give it a suitable name, such as Vet Record.

- Create the user interface shown here.

- Remember to include the text at the top of the form.

- Add text to the buttons and the check box control as shown in the screenshot.

- Give all the objects suitable names, as explained in this section.

- Add code so that the Quit button closes the program.

- Debug and save.

■ 13.3 Add options to the combo box

The combo box will display a drop-down menu of common pet species. In this section you will enter the list of menu items.

The property of the combo box that you need to change is the *Items* property. If you select it you will see that it shows the word 'Collection' in brackets and a button with three small dots on it (an ellipsis).

When you click on the ellipsis button, a small window appears. In this window you can type the items that you want the user to see on the drop-down combo box menu. This list is called the string collection.

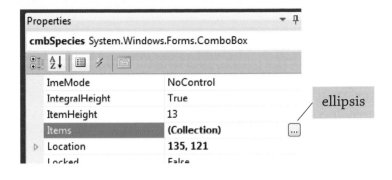

ellipsis

A possible list of pet species is shown in the screenshot but you can decide on your own list.

When you have finished entering the string collection, click on OK to accept it. You can always go back and change it later.

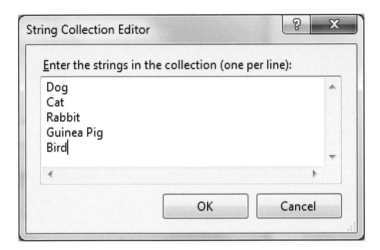

Activity Enter collection of items for combo box

- Make sure the program is open.

- Select the combo box control. Open the string collection.

- Enter a list of species as shown in this section. You can choose any species you like.

- Debug and save.

■ 13.4 Declare the structure

You have created a user interface which allows you to enter a range of pet data. In this section you will add code to the program to declare a new data type. You will then declare a variable of this new data type which will store the pet data.

To declare a data structure you must decide:

- what elements to include in the structure
- whether the structure is public or private
- a name for the data structure.

Elements

We have already chosen the elements of the data structure: the pet's name, the pet's date of birth, the pet's species, whether it has had injections, and the owner's name. You also decided the data type for each element.

Public or private

A data structure, and the elements in it, must be declared as private or public:

- A **private** data structure can only be used in the part of the program in which it is declared.
- A **public** data structure can be used in any part of the program.

This distinction does not matter to you yet, because your project is very simple, with only one form. However, in later chapters you will make the project larger, with more than one form. So it is best to declare the data structure and the elements as **public**.

Structure name

The data structure is a collection of elements that make up the record of a pet. So, a good name for the data structure is *PetRecord*.

Declare the structure

The code to declare the *PetRecord* structure is as follows:

```
Public Structure PetRecord

    Public Name As String

    Public DoB As Date

    Public Species As String

    Public Injections As Boolean

    Public Owner As String

End Structure
```

Here are some points to note:

- Every line except the last one begins with the word *Public*.
- In the first line, you enter *Public Structure* and then the name of the structure, in this case *PetRecord*.
- Each element in the structure is declared on a different line. For each element, choose a name and declare the data type of the element.
- In this example, the abbreviation *DoB* has been used instead of Date of Birth.
- The last line of the declaration is *End Structure*.

Whenever you declare a data structure, use this layout. Of course, the names and data types of the elements in the data structure will vary.

■ 13.5 Declare a variable

Now that you have created the new data structure, you can use it just like any other data type. Just as you can declare a variable of type string or type integer, you can now declare a variable of type *PetRecord*.

The command is a simple one:

```
Dim Pet As PetRecord
```

Note that this line must come below the code where you declare the data type *PetRecord* otherwise your program won't recognise the data type.

■ 13.6 Assign values to all elements of the variable

The user enters the pet data into the form and then clicks on *btnSave*. When the user clicks on this button, all the values on the form will be assigned to the *Pet* variable.

In this section you will write the code that assigns the data from the form to the different elements of the *Pet* variable.

Element names

The different elements of the *Pet* variable are called:

- *Pet.Name*
- *Pet.DoB*
- *Pet.Species*

and so on. The name of an element of a variable is made up of the name of the variable, then a full stop, then a name which identifies the element.

Assign values to the elements

The data from the form is stored as properties of the different objects:

- In text boxes the data is stored as the *Text* property.
- In the date/time picker the data is stored in the *Value* property.
- In the checkbox the data is stored as the *Checked* property (this is a yes/no value).

The next table shows the five elements of the variable *Pet*:

- The first column shows the element name.
- The next column shows the object property where the data is stored.
- The final column shows the code you must add to the program to assign the data from the object to the variable element.

Element name	Object property	Code to add to the program
Pet.Name	*txtPetName.Text*	`Pet.Name = txtName.Text`
Pet.DoB	*DateTimePicker1.Value*	`Pet.DoB = DateTimePicker1.Value`
Pet.Species	*cmbSpecies.Text*	`Pet.Species = cmbSpecies.Text`
Pet.Injection	*chkInjections.Checked*	`Pet.Injection = chkInjections.Checked`
Pet.Owner	*TxtOwnerName.Text*	`Pet.Owner = TxtOwnerName.Text`

Activity Reset input controls and display message

- Make sure the program is open.
- Double-click *btnSave* and begin to add code.
- Enter the five lines of code from the third column of the table above.
- Debug and save.

■ 13.7 Reset input controls and display user message

Finally, all the values have been assigned to the elements of the variable. Now the input controls can be reset ready for new data to be entered. A message to the user will confirm that the record has been saved. This is good practice as it reassures the user that the program has worked

Reset controls

All the controls will be reset to their original empty values, ready for new data.

- To reset the text boxes and the combo box, assign a blank string to each one. A blank string is shown as double quotation marks, with nothing in between them.
- To reset the check box, set the value to False. This will remove the tick from the box.
- To reset the date/time picker, set the value to Today.

The next table summarises the commands you need to enter to reset the controls to empty. The second column shows the code that you will need to enter into the program.

Object property	Code to add to the program
txtPetName.Text	`txtName.Text = " "`
DateTimePicker1.Value	`DateTimePicker1.Value = Today`
cmbSpecies.Text	`cmbSpecies.Text = " "`
chkInjections.Checked	`chkInjections.Checked = False`
TxtOwnerName.Text	`TxtOwnerName.Text = " "`

Display message to the user

Finally, you can use the *MsgBox* function to display a message to the user confirming that the record has been saved.

Here is a suggested format for this message. The pet's name is included in the message.

```
MsgBox(Pet.Name & ": Record saved")
```

All of these commands should go in the code for *btnSave*. These commands must come after the commands that assign values from the input controls to the variables.

Activity   Reset input controls and display user message

- Double-click *btnSave* to add more code.

- Enter code which will reset the input controls and display a message to the user, as shown in this section.

- Debug and save.

More work with the pet record

Make sure the pet record project is saved. You will return to this project in chapter 16. In that chapter you will add a second form to the project, which will display the pet record on the screen, and let you print it out.

■ Chapter end

Full code listing

Here is the full listing of the code to declare the *PetRecord* data type, declare a variable of this data type, and then assign values to this variable.

```
Public Class Form1

    'declare PetRecord data type

    Public Structure PetRecord

        Public Name As String

        Public DoB As Date

        Public Species As String

        Public Injection As Boolean

        Public Owner As String

    End Structure


    'declare variable Pet of the PetRecord data type

    Dim Pet As PetRecord


    Private Sub btnSave_Click(ByVal sender As -

    'assign values from the input controls to the elements of Pet

        Pet.Name = txtName.Text

        Pet.DoB = DateTimePicker1.Value

        Pet.Species = cmbSpecies.Text

        Pet.Injection = chkInjections.Checked

        Pet.Owner = TxtOwnerName.Text

    'clear the data input controls

        txtName.Text = ""

        DateTimePicker1.Value = Today

        cmbSpecies.Text = ""

        chkInjections.Checked = False

        TxtOwnerName.Text = ""

        MsgBox(Pet.Name & " : Record entered")

    End Sub
```

```
Private Sub btnQuit_Click(ByVal sender As –

        End

    End Sub

End Class
```

Overview

In this chapter you declared a new data structure. Then you declared a variable of this new data type.

You learned to use some new input controls, and to assign values from these input controls to elements of the variable:

- combo box
- date/time picker
- check box.

You learned to reset the input controls to a null value after use.

■ Questions

Answer these questions to demonstrate your learning.

1 What is the difference between the elements of an array and the elements of a data structure?
2 What is the difference between entering data using a text box and using a combo box?
3 A data structure has two elements called *Name* and *Code*. A variable of this data type is declared. The name of the variable is *Agent*. What are the full names of the two elements of the variable *Agent*?
4 Write the code to assign a value from the combo box *cmbCode* to the *Code* element of the *Agent* variable.
5 An element of a variable is called *Job.StartDate*. Give the code that assigns the input of a control called *DateTimePicker1* to this variable.
6 What data type is most suitable for storing a value that has been input via a check box?
7 Give the command to reset a check box called *chkCompleted*.
8 Why would you reset the input controls after their values have been copied to variables?
9 When you declare a public data structure, each line (except the last) begins with what word?
10 What is the last line of a data structure declaration?

Further activity

Practice activities can be carried out if you finish the work in this chapter with time to spare. You can also carry out these activities in your own time to help with learning and to improve your skills.

Further activity: A teacher wishes to store records of all of her students.

- Think about the items of data she might wish to store about one student.

- Declare a data structure called *StudentRecord* which contains these elements.

- Declare a variable called *Student* of this data type.

- Create an input form that matches the data structure.

- Add code to assign the value from the input form to the variable *Student*.

- Add code to reset the data controls and display a message to the user.

14 Functions

■ Introduction

A function is a named process that transforms one value into another. Visual Basic includes a range of ready-made functions that help to simplify your code. You can also create your own functions. In this chapter you will learn about some of the functions that are available in Visual Basic.

■ 14.1 What is a function?

Almost all programming languages include functions. A **function** is a named process that produces a value. To make the computer carry out the process you **call** the function. Calling a function means that you enter the name of the function into your code.

Parameters

Most functions take one value, and transform it into a new value.

The value that is transformed by the function is called a **parameter** of the function. Some functions have no parameters, some have one parameter, and some have more than one. The value that is output by the function is called the **return value**. Most functions return a single value. The return value can be assigned to a variable or an object property, or passed to another function.

Example

The function *Len()* has one parameter – a string variable. The return value of the function is the number of characters in the string (the length of the string). The parameter is a string; the output value is an integer.

Here are three examples of the function *Len()*:

Len("London") will return the value 6.

Len("Tokyo") will return the value 5.

Len("New York") will return the value 8.

Learning content

3.1.4 Procedures and functions: understand what functions are in programming terms; know when the use of a function would make sense and would simplify the coded solution; know about and be able to describe common built-in functions in their chosen languages; use common built-in functions in their chosen languages when coding solutions to problems; understand what a parameter is when working with functions; know how to use parameters when creating efficient solutions to problems.

Key terms

Function A series of commands that transforms one value, into another.

Parameter The value which is used by the function.

Return value The value produced by a function.

You can see from these examples that varying the parameter changes the return value of the function.

"London" → Len("London") → 6

How to call a function

To use a function in your code, you type the name of the function. This is known as calling the function.

- The parameter is shown in brackets after the function name. You can say that the function accepts, or takes, the parameter that is passed to it.
- If there is more than one parameter, they are separated by commas.

Every function returns a value. When you call a function it must be as part of a command that assigns the return value to something, for example a variable. The following command will assign the value returned by the *Len()* function to an integer variable called *stringlength*:

```
stringlength = Len("London")
```

The result of this command will be to assign the integer value 6 to the variable *stringlength*.

Functions you have used already

You have already used several functions as you worked through the activities in this book:

- **InputBox**: This function returns a string value that can be assigned to any variable (see section 6.4 for more detail).
- **MsgBox**: This function displays a message on the screen, and leaves it there until the user clicks on a button (see section 5.5).
- **IsNumeric**: This function accepts as an parameter any value, and tests it to see if it is numeric. If the value is numeric this function returns the value True. If it is not numeric it returns the value False (see section 9.3).
- **Today**: This function returns today's date (see section 13.7). It does not use any parameters. It takes the data it needs from the computer's own clock.

For each of these examples, work out what data type the return value is.

Type conversion functions

Some features of Visual Basic will only work with string data type. For example, *InputBox* will only return a string value, and *MsgBox* will only display a string value. On the other hand, most calculations use number values. For this reason, data type conversion functions are very useful. You can input a value as a string, convert it to a number value, perform calculations, and then convert it back to a string again

There are conversion functions to convert between all the Visual Basic data types. In this section you will learn about two of these.

- The function *Val()* accepts a string and converts it into a number value. This will only work if the string has numbers in it that the computer can recognise and turn into a number value.

- The function *Str()* accepts a number value and turns it into a string. The string can then be output, for example in a message box.

In each case you take the variable or other value that you want to convert. This variable becomes the parameter of the function. You put this value into the brackets following the function name. The function will return a value of a different data type.

Activity Test the *Len()* and *Str()* functions

- Start Visual Basic and begin a new project. Give it a suitable name such as String Length Test.

- Create a simple user interface with one text box and one button. The button should display the text 'Show length of input string'.

- Declare an integer variable called *stringlength*.

- The following code will find the length of the text input to *TextBox1* and assign it to the variable called *stringlength*.

```
stringlength = Len(TextBox1.Text)
```

- The following code will output the variable length in a message box. Notice that the *Str()* function is used to convert the integer variable into a string.

```
MsgBox("The string has " & Str(stringlength) & " characters")
```

- Create code so that the user can type text in the text box and, when the user clicks on the button, the length of the string is displayed as a message in a message box.

- Debug and save.

- Test the program by entering different words and phrases in the text box. When you have finished, close the program.

■ 14.2 Why use functions?

There isn't space in a book like this to list all of the functions that are available to use within Visual Basic. When you are programming, it is often worth checking whether there is a function in Visual Basic that will help with the task as it may save you time.

Some of the most useful functions are used to work with strings. Two examples are given here although there are many more.

Example: *UCase()*

The *UCase* function converts a string into all UPPER CASE.

So, supposing *UserMessage* is a string variable storing the string 'Warning, wrong password', this code:

```
UserMessage = UCase(UserMessage)
```

would convert *UserMessage* to 'WARNING, WRONG PASSWORD'.

There is also a *LCase* function, which converts a string to all lower case characters.

Example: *Left()*

The *Left()* function has two parameters: a string and a number. The function returns that number of characters from the left of the string. So if the number is 9, the function returns the first 9 characters. If the number is 6, the function returns the first 6 characters, and so on.

So, if *UserMessage* is a string variable that stores the string 'WARNING, WRONG PASSWORD' then this code:

```
UserMessage = Left(UserMessage, 7)
```

would convert the string to 'WARNING'.

Benefits of using functions

Functions simplify your code. A function will carry out a processing task and return a value. All you need to include in your code is the name of the function, and any parameters.

Most functions have a name that describes the job that the function does. As you read back through your code, it is easier to understand what the code does because the names of the functions are (usually) fairly easy to understand.

Writing your own functions

You can also create new functions that you can use in your own programs. If there is a complex task you need to carry out, you can create a function to perform the task. You will learn more about creating your own functions in chapter 15.

Activity Assign data to variables

- Continue to work on the Vet Record program.

- Add a function to convert *Pet.Name* to an upper case string.

- Debug and save.

■ Chapter end

Full code listing

Here is the code listing for the first activity in this chapter, 'Test the *Len()* and *Str()* functions'.

```
Public Class Form1

    Dim stringlength As Integer

    Private Sub Button1_Click(ByVal sender As –
        stringlength = Len(TextBox1.Text)
        MsgBox("The string has " & Str(stringlength) & " characters")
    End Sub

End Class
```

Overview

In this section you learned to use functions. A function accepts a value and transforms it, producing a new value. The value that is accepted by the function is called the function parameter. The new value is called the return value.

A function can have one parameter, more than one parameter, or no parameters. A function always returns a single value.

Using a function in your code is known as 'calling' the function. To call a function, you type the name of the function followed by the value of any parameters in brackets.

A function will always return values of a particular data type. The data type it produces will depend on the function.

A range of useful functions is available for Visual Basic programmers.

■ Questions

Answer these questions to demonstrate your learning.

1 Give an example of a function that accepts a string value and returns an integer value.
2 The function *IsNumeric* accepts a value and tests whether it is a numeric value. What is the data type of the return value?
3 Give the command to use the *IsNumeric* function to test the variable *CodeNumber* to see if it is a numeric value.
4 Expand this command to assign the return value to the variable *TestResult*.
5 What does the *Val()* function do?
6 Give two reasons why using functions improves your code.
7 Why would you use a conversion function when you want to display an integer in a message box? What function would you use?

Further activity

Practice activities can be carried out if you finish the work in this chapter with time to spare. You can also carry out these activities in your own time to help with learning and to improve your skills.

Further activity: Create a program with a text box, a button and a label. The user enters a value in the text box and clicks a button.

■ If the value is numeric, it is displayed in the label.

■ If the value is not numeric, the length of the string is displayed in the label.

15 Creating your own functions

■ Introduction

In chapter 14 you used functions to transform values. You used a range of functions that are provided as part of Visual Basic code. In this chapter you will learn to create your own functions that are tailor-made to your needs.

Learning content

3.1.4 Procedures and functions: understand what functions are in programming terms; know when the use of a function would make sense and would simplify the coded solution; know how to write and use their own simple functions; understand what a parameter is when working with functions; know how to use parameters when creating efficient solutions to problems.

■ 15.1 Convert miles to kilometres

Remember that a function is a named piece of code that accepts one or more values called parameters and produces a new value called the return value.

In chapter 14 you looked at some of the functions that are provided as part of Visual Basic. In this chapter you will write a new function. It will convert any distance in miles to the equivalent distance in kilometres. This function is not provided by Visual Basic. You will have to write the function from scratch.

Background information

1 mile is equivalent to 1.609344 kilometres. To convert a distance in miles to a distance in kilometres, you have to multiply the number of miles by 1.609344.

In this example the number of miles will be the parameter of the function. The number of kilometres will be the return value of the function.

Miles (parameter) → Convert (function) → Kilometres (return value)

Design the interface

The user interface will have to have a text box for the user to enter the number of miles and a label to display the number of kilometres. The user clicks a button to make the conversion.

The screenshot on page 164 shows a design for the interface with suggested names for the key objects on the form.

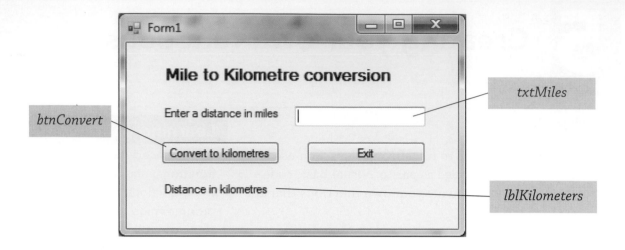

Activity Create user interface

- Start a new program called Miles to Kilometres.
- Create a user interface as shown here, naming the objects as shown.
- Add code so that the Exit button ends the app.
- Debug and save.

■ 15.2 Declare the function

Before it can be used in your code the function must be declared. The function declaration goes at the top of the code for the form. Typically, functions are declared below variables but before the main code of the form.

A function declaration begins with the word *Function* and ends with *End Function*.

The general structure of a function declaration is:

```
Function name(parameter) As datatype

            code

End Function
```

Function name, parameter and data type

In order to complete the function declaration, you must choose:

- a function name
- a parameter name
- a data type for the returned value.

As always, choose names that help people to understand your code. Look back at the diagram in 15.1. That shows good names for the function and parameter.

In this example the function is called *Convert* because it converts miles to kilometres. The parameter is called *Miles* because the value which goes into the function is the number of miles. The returned value will be a number in kilometres. A suitable data type for this is *Decimal*, because the result will not be a whole number.

How the code appears

Here is the first line of the function. It shows the function name, the parameter name and the data type.

```
Function Convert(Miles) As Decimal
```

If you type this code and press enter, you will see several changes. The computer adds some extra code.

- The computer adds a line:

```
End Function
```

This marks the end of the function code.

- The *End Function* statement is underlined with a green line and there is a warning remark. The warning says 'This function is not used in the rest of the program'. This is because your coding is not completed yet.
- The computer automatically adds the text *ByVal* in front of *Miles* (the parameter). The expression *ByVal* refers to the way that a parameter is passed to a function. You don't need to worry about this.

With the new text added by the computer, the function will look like this:

```
Function Convert(ByVal Miles) As Decimal

End Function
```

Activity Declare a function

- Declare a function called *Convert* at the top of the code as shown here.
- Note any extra text added by the computer.
- Debug and save.

■ 15.3 Adding code to the function declaration

In this section you will add code to produce the return value of the function.

The calculation is quite simple. Kilometres are calculated by multiplying the number of miles by 1.609344. To do this calculation in Visual Basic, use the arithmetic operator *.

```
Miles * 1.609344
```

The result of any calculation generates a value. In this case it is the return value of the function.

To make a complete Visual Basic code line you have to assign the value to something. Usually you assign the result of a calculation to a variable or the property of an object.

When you make a function, you assign the value to the name of the function. This function is called *Convert*, so the completed line is:

```
Convert = Miles * 1.609344
```

Putting this line into the function declaration gives completed code that looks like this:

```
Function Convert(ByVal Miles) As Decimal

        Convert = Miles * 1.609344

End Function
```

Activity Add code to a function

- Make sure the Miles to Kilometres program is open.

- Complete the code of the Convert function using the code given here.

- Debug and save.

15.4 Call the function

Now you have created the function *Convert*, you can use the function in your code. This means that you use the name of the function in the main body of your code. This is known as 'calling' the function.

Where to call the function

Here is a reminder about how this app works. When the user clicks *btnConvert* the number in *txtMiles* will be converted into kilometres. The result will be displayed in *lblKilometres*. With this information you can complete the task.

The *Convert* function is carried out when the user clicks on *btnConvert*. You therefore have to start adding code to *btnConvert*.

You call the function by typing its name. The line is not finished yet.

Enter a parameter

To call a function you enter the function name in your code. You must also enter the parameter in brackets after the function name.

The parameter for this function is the number of miles to convert into kilometres. The user entered this value in the text box *txtMiles*. It is stored as the *Text* property of that object. Therefore the parameter for the function is *txtMiles.Text*.

The parameter is shown in brackets after the function name.

```
Convert(txtMiles.Text)
```

The line is not finished yet.

Assign the return value

The function will return a new value. The return value must be assigned to something, for example assigned to a variable or the property of an object.

In this example the number of kilometres will be displayed on the screen as *lblKilometres*. That means the value returned the function will be assigned to the *Text* property of that label.

So the completed line of code is:

```
lblKilometres.Text = Convert(txtMiles.Text)
```

The meaning of this line of code is 'Convert the number of miles entered in *txtMiles*, and display the result in *lblKilometres*'.

The line of code is now completed. But you can add a little explanatory text to help the user to understand the result.

Add explanatory text

To make the result easier for the user to understand, you can add explanatory text to the line.

In this example the & sign is used to concatenate the number of kilometres with a string that says 'kilometres'.

```
lblKilometres.Text = Convert(txtMiles.Text) & " kilometres"
```

This is the finished line of code.

Activity Call the function

- Double-click on *btnConvert* to begin entering code.

- Enter the single line function call as shown in this section.

- Debug and save.

- You can now run the program a few times, entering different values into the app, and seeing what the results are.

15.5 Advantages of using functions

A function holds one or more lines of code. Wherever the name of the function is given in the code, the function will be carried out. This applies both to functions that are provided with Visual Basic and to functions that you have written yourself.

There are several advantages to using functions:

- A function shortens your code. The function name is shorter than the lines of code that it replaces.
- A function makes your code easier to read. If the function name is well chosen it will tell you what the function does. If the function is well named and used sensibly then the code will be easier to read and understand.
- A function can be used more than once in your program. That means the lines of code in the function declaration only need to be typed once instead of in several places. There is less chance of error, and the code is shorter.

The complete listing of the Miles to Kilometres program showing the use of the *Conversion* function is given at the end of this chapter.

Chapter end

Full code listing

Here is the full listing of the Miles to Kilometres program.

```
Public Class Form1

    Function Convert(ByVal Miles) As Decimal
        Convert = Miles * 1.609344
    End Function

    Private Sub btnConvert_Click(ByVal sender As -
        lblKilometres.Text = Convert(txtMiles.Text) & " kilometres"
    End Sub

    Private Sub Button1_Click(ByVal sender As -
        End
    End Sub

End Class
```

Overview

In this section you learned to create your own functions.

- A function is declared at the top of the code where it is used.
- A parameter is the value that is used within the function. Some functions have more than one parameter.
- The value that is created by the function is called the return value.
- The function is called in the main code of a program by entering the name of the function.
- The returned value can be assigned to an object or variable.

■ Questions

Answer these questions to demonstrate your learning.

The questions relate to this function declaration.

```
Function Longest(ByVal string1, ByVal string2) As String

      If Len(string1) > Len(string2) Then

          Longest = string1

      Else

          Longest = string2

      End If

   End Function
```

1 What is the name of this function?
2 How many parameters does it use?
3 What is the data type of the return value?
4 Describe in your own words what this function does.
5 What value is returned by this function if string1 and string 2 are the same length?
6 Write a line of code that calls this function. Use variables called *FirstName* and *Surname* as parameters. Assign the return value to the variable *Result*.
7 Adapt the function declaration so that it returns the length of the longest string as an integer value.

Further activity

Practice activities can be carried out if you finish the work in this chapter with time to spare. You can also carry out these activities in your own time to help with learning and to improve your skills.

Further activity: Use the function *Longest*, shown above, to create a program that accepts two names from the user in text boxes, and displays the longest name in a message box.

Extension activity: Extend the Miles to Kilometres program so that it offers both miles-to-kilometres and kilometres-to-miles conversion.

16 Using more than one form

■ Introduction

Up until now all of the programs you have created have been based on a single form, with input and output functions contained within that form. In this chapter you will amend the Vet Record program so that it extends over more than one form. It will become a multiform project.

This is a long chapter, and you may need to use several sessions to complete all of the work given here.

Learning content

3.1.3 Program flow control: understand how problems can be broken down into smaller problems; understand and be able to describe the basic building blocks of coded solutions.

3.1.5 Scope of variables, constants, functions and procedures: know what is meant by the scope of a variable, constant, function or procedure.

■ 16.1 Program, project or app?

In chapter 13 you created a Visual Basic form to input information about pets for a vet's record system. In this chapter you will extend the Vet Record project to include a second form that will display the record. You will also add code to print out the record.

Link

Pet record project – chapter 13

In chapters 1–15 you created code that linked to a single form. Up until now, for simplicity, the code you have written has generally been called your Visual Basic program. But from now on all of your work will involve several forms that work together to carry out a task. Each form will have its own set of code. A group of linked forms and other modules is called a Visual Basic project.

When you open your project all of the forms and modules will open. When you click on Save All, this will save all of the items in the project.

For this reason we will talk from now on about opening and saving your project.

In chapter 27 you will compile Visual Basic projects to create software that can run independently of Visual Basic. The compiled stand-alone software will be called an application or app.

■ 16.2 Add a new form to the project

You will add a new form to the Vet Record project alongside the form you have already created. The two forms will work together to allow you to input and output the elements of a record.

Make sure the Vet Record project is open on your screen. At the top of the Visual Basic window is a menu bar. If you click on Project on the menu bar the project menu will open. From this menu select 'Add Windows Form…'

The Add New Item window will open. The Windows Form option is selected. At the bottom of the screen there is a box where you can enter a name for the new form.

In this book we recommend that you begin the name of any Visual Basic object with a three-letter extension. The extension will remind you of the type of object. For example, the names of buttons begin btn, and the names of text boxes begin txt. This naming convention makes it easier for you to remember which names go with which objects. You do not have to name Visual Basic objects in this way, but it has some advantages when you are writing code.

For this reason it is recommended that you begin the name of a form with the three-letter extension frm. So a good name for this form would be *frmOutput*. Enter this name in the box and click on the Add button at the bottom right of the window.

Create user interface

You can now add objects to *frmOutput* to create a suitable user interface. A suggested design is shown in the screenshot below. The form has a title, and it contains two buttons and eight labels.

- Change the *Text* property of the form to a suitable title such as Vet Output.
- Add two buttons to the form. Set the text properties of these buttons as shown in the screenshot. Give the buttons suitable names such as *btnPrint* and *btnClose*.

- Four of the labels on the form are shown in bold. The content of these labels will not be changed by the project code. There is no need to name these labels. Simply add them to the form and set the text and font properties as shown here.
- The other four labels (such as *lblName* and *lblSpecies*) will be used to display the content of the pet record. Add these five labels in the positions shown. Change the titles of these labels to the names given in the screenshot. These labels will be used in the project code.

Rename Form1

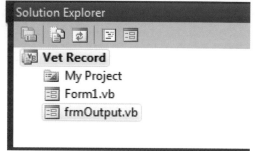

Up until now you have not made any use of the window called Solution Explorer. You will find this in the top right-hand corner of the Visual Basic development environment. The screenshot shows the appearance of Solution Explorer window.

The Solution Explorer window shows all of the forms in the current project. You will see that there are two forms, called Form1.vb and frmOutput.vb. The letters vb tell you these are Visual Basic files.

Now you will rename *Form1*. It is suggested that you call this form *frmInput*. Right-click on this name. Select Rename from the short menu that appears, and then type a new name. Remember to include .vb at the end of the name.

Activity Create an output form

- Open the Vet Record project you made in chapter 13.
- Add a new form to the project, called *frmOutput*.
- Add labels and buttons to create the user interface shown in this section, and save the project.
- Rename *Form1* to *frmInput*.
- Debug and save.

■ 16.3 Switching between forms

The project now has two forms. In this section you will add code to each form so that the user can switch between the two forms at the click of a button.

Select which form to work with during coding

Your Visual Basic project now consists of two forms – *frmInput* and *frmOutput*. When you add code and change the form designs you will need to be able to switch between the two forms as you work on your project.

If you look at the top of the Visual Basic development environment you will see there are tabs for all of the forms in the project. Clicking on a tab will open that form, so you can change the design or the code.

For each form there are two tabs. For example, for the *frmInput*:

- frmInput.vb [Design] shows the design of the form
- frmInput.vb shows the code linked to the form.

When you are working on any project you can use the tabs to swap between forms.

Swapping between two forms while the program is running

The project has two forms. When the project is running the user will only see one form at a time. The user will swap between forms. Swapping between forms is called navigation.

Each form will have a navigation button on it. When the user clicks on the navigation button the current form will disappear and the other form will appear.

There are two commands which make a form disappear from the screen when the program is running. They are *Hide()* and *Close()*.

- *Hide()*: when you hide a form it stays open in computer memory. All the code keeps running but the form becomes invisible. The user cannot see it. You will use this code on *frmInput*.

- *Close()*: When you close a form it is wiped from the computer memory. All the code on the form stops running. If you close the main form of a multi-form project, the whole project will end. You will use this code on *frmOutput*, as it is not the main form of the project.

If a form is either closed or hidden you can show the form again using the command *Show()*.

frmInput

You will add a button to *frmInput*. When the user clicks the button, *frmInput* will hide and *frmOutput* will show.

The code to hide *frmInput* is

```
Me.Hide()
```

In general, *Me* in Visual Basic refers to the currently active form or object. So this line of code tells the computer to 'hide this form'.

The code to show *frmOutput* is:

```
frmOutput.Show()
```

frmOutput

You will add code to the OK button on *frmOutput*. This code will close *frmOutput* and show *frmInput*.

The code to close *frmOutput* and show *frmInput* is

```
Me.Close()
frmInput.Show()
```

Activity Control movement between forms

- Make sure the Vet Record program is open.

- Edit *frmInput*. Add a new button called *btnOutput*. The text on this button should read 'Output the record'. Add code to this button so that clicking it hides *frmInput* and shows *frmOutput*.

- Edit *frmOutput*. Add code to *btnClose* so that clicking on this button closes *frmOutput* and shows *frmInput*.

■ 16.4 Change the scope of the variable

Every variable has a scope. The scope of a variable tells you where the variable name will be recognised by the computer. The place where the variable is declared tells you what its scope is.

You already know that:

- if a variable is declared within a sub-procedure, then the variable can only be used in that sub-procedure
- if the variable is declared at the top of the code for a form, then the variable can be used anywhere in the code for that form.

But if you want to use a variable in more than one form of a project, then the variable has to be declared in a separate project module.

Scope of the *Pet* variable

The information used in this project is stored in the elements of a variable called *Pet*. This is of the *PetRecord* data type. The *PetRecord* data type, and the variable *Pet*, are both declared in the code at the top of *frmInput*. This means that data type and record can only be used within that form.

You have now added a second form to the project. This form will display the contents of the *Pet* variable. So clearly the *Pet* variable must be used by both forms in the project. The scope of the variable must cover both forms.

That means the declaration of the data type and the variable must be moved from *frmInput* to a separate project module.

Lifetime of a variable

The scope of a variable tells you where the variable can be used.

The lifetime of a variable tells you how long the variable exists. In general, a variable exists for as long as the code where it is declared is open. So the *Pet* variable will be open, storing data, for as long as the Vet Record project is open. When you close the project the data in this variable will be lost. Next time you use the project you will need to add new information to the *Pet* variable.

You have learned how to close a form. When a form is closed, any variables declared within that form will be lost.

Create a project module

A project module is a place to declare any items – variables, data types, functions or procedures – that will be used by more than one form in your project. The scope of any variable or other item included in the project module will extend over all of the forms in the project. The lifetime of a variable declared in the project module will last as long as the project is open. The variable will not be lost when any particular form is closed.

For these reasons it is often very convenient to declare variables in the project module instead of in the code linked to a project form.

To create a project module, open the Project menu and select Add Module. The module is added to the project just like a form. You don't need to give it a special name – just use the name *Module1*, which is given to it by the computer.

A project can include more than one module, but here we will only use one module per project.

Copy variable declaration to the project module

You may be used to using cut and paste to move text around in a word-processed document. You can use this method to cut the code that declares the data type and the variable in frmInput and paste it into the new *Module1*.

At the moment *Pet* is a local variable. It is a variable that is local to one form, and it is only used in that form. You need to change it to a public variable, which can be used in any part of the project.

> ### Study tip
> Use Ctrl+X and Crt+V to cut and paste selected text. You can also pick Cut and Paste options from the Edit menu.

Change the code that reads:

```
Dim Pet As PetRecord
```

to:

```
Public Pet As PetRecord
```

This declares the variable *Pet* as a public variable. After you have done this, you can use the *Pet* variable in any of the forms of this project.

Activity Change scope of variable

- Make sure the Vet Record program is open.

- Create a new project module.

- Move the declaration of the *PetRecord* data type and the declaration of the *Pet* variable from *frmInput* to *Module1*.

- Change *Pet* from a local to a public variable by changing the word *Dim* to the word *Public*.

- Debug and save.

Here is the full code listing for Module1:

```
Module Module1

    Public Structure PetRecord

        Public Name As String

        Public DoB As Date

        Public Species As String

        Public Injection As Boolean

        Public Owner As String

    End Structure

    Public Pet As PetRecord

End Module
```

■ 16.5 Display values in *frmOutput*

The *Pet* variable has five elements. The five elements of the *Pet* variable will be displyed as five labels on *frmOutput*.

In this section you will adapt the code of *frmOutput* so that the elements of the variable are assigned to the different labels on the form.

As soon as the user sees *frmOutput* it must show the elements of the *Pet* variable. When *frmOutput* is opened (or loaded) the different values are immediately assigned to the *Text* properties of the labels on the form.

Load *frmOutput*

A form is an object. Like a button or any other object, the form has properties, and it can have associated events. The typical event for a button is the click event; that event happens when the user clicks on the button.

The typical event for a form is the load event; that happens when the form is opened or loaded. Now you will add code that will be carried out when *frmOutput* is opened or loaded.

Look at the design of *frmOutput*. Put the mouse pointer anywhere on *frmOutput*, away from the buttons and labels that are on the form. Then double-click the form.

The code window for *frmOutput* will open. The code looks like this:

```
        Private Sub frmOutput_Load(ByVal sender As –

        End Sub
```

The event is *frmOutput_Load*. That means the code will be carried out when *frmOutput* loads. At the moment this event has no code associated with it. Now you will add that code.

Assign string values to labels

Three elements of the pet variable store string values. These are:

- *Pet.Name*
- *Pet.Species*
- *Pet.Owner*.

These string values can be directly assigned to the matching labels on *frmOutput*. Here is what the code will look like:

```
Private Sub frmOutput_Load(ByVal sender As —

        lblName.Text = Pet.Name

        lblSpecies.Text = Pet.Species

        lblOwner.Text = Pet.Owner

End Sub
```

This code assigns the string values in the Pet record to the text property of each of the three labels.

Use a Boolean value to change a label

The final value in the pet record is the value *Pet.Injection*. This is a Boolean variable. Remember that a Boolean variable stores a true/false value. You can use this yes/no value in an *If…Then…Else* statement to select the correct output label.

```
If Pet.Injection Then

    lblInjections.Text = "Has had all injections"

Else

    lblInjections.Text = "Has not had injections"

End If
```

This code assesses the truth value of the value *Pet.Injection*.

If *Pet.Injection* is True then the label will show the text: 'Has had all injections'.

If *Pet.Injection* is False then the label will show the text: 'Has not had injections'.

There are only two possible values, and the label reflects which has been selected.

Activity Display output

- Make sure the Vet Record program is open.
- Add code to *frmOutput* so that when the form is loaded the labels on the form display the various elements of the *Pet* variable.
- Debug and save.

Here is the completed code for the output form:

```
Private Sub frmOutput_Load(ByVal sender As –
    lblName.Text = Pet.Name
    lblOwner.Text = Pet.Owner
    lblSpecies.Text = Pet.Species
    If Pet.Injection Then
        lblInjections.Text = "Has had all injections"
    Else
        lblInjections.Text = "Has not had injections"
    End If
End Sub
```

■ 16.6 Add a main menu form

Many multiform projects have a main menu or home page with links to the other forms that make up the project. This is a good structure for a project, and it gives the user maximum control over the different forms that make up the project.

A suggested main menu form for the vet project is shown in the screenshot.

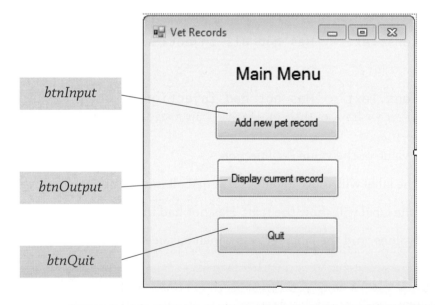

Activity Add a main menu form

- Add a new form to the Pet Record program which will serve as a main menu.
- Name it *frmMain*.

■ 16.7 Add navigation buttons

Now you need to work with the different forms and modules of the project, making changes to the code. You have already seen that the tab bar at the top of the development area includes tabs for the different forms (see section 16.3). You can swap between forms using these tabs.

As your project gets larger there may not be room to show every tab on the tab bar. In this case click on the down arrow at the right of the tab bar. This will open a drop-down menu that shows all of the forms and modules in the project so that you can choose which one you want to edit.

	frmInput.vb
	frmInput.vb [Design]
	frmMain.vb
	frmMain.vb [Design]
	frmOutput.vb
	frmOutput.vb [Design]
	Module1.vb
	Vet Record

Links between the three forms

There should be active links between the three forms, so that clicking on the buttons will allow the user to move between the different forms.

- By clicking on the buttons on the main menu the user will be able to open either *frmInput* or *frmOutput*.
- By clicking on Main Menu buttons on the input and output forms the user will be able to return to the main menu.
- By clicking on *btnOutput* on the input form the user will be able to open the output form.

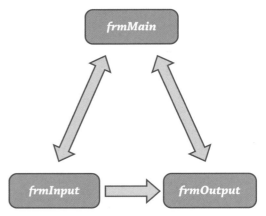

Structure of the vet record project

The buttons which let the user move between forms are called navigation buttons. In a project with more than one form you must have navigation buttons.

When you are planning a project with more than one form, draw a structure diagram showing the links between forms.

Navigation buttons

Looking at the diagram will help you to decide what navigation buttons you need. In this project:

- *frmMain* has three navigation buttons: *btnInput*, *btnOutput* and *btnQuit*. You will need to add code to these buttons to make them work.
- *frmInput* has one navigation button. It is called *btnOutput* and it opens *frmOutput*. You will need to add another navigation button which opens the Main Menu.
- *frmOutput* has one navigation button. It is called *btnClose*. At the moment it opens *frmInput*. You will need to change the code on this button so that it opens *frmMain*.

Set frmMain as the project Startup form

Finally, you must ensure that *frmMain* is the first form which opens when the Vet Record project starts up. To make this happen you must make *frmMain* the project Startup form.

Look at the Solution Explorer window. It now shows the three forms and the module, which together make up the project. It also shows something called My Project.

If you double-click on My Project a project window opens that shows key facts about the project.

In the centre of this window you can select which form should be the Startup form for the project. Use the drop-down menu to select *frmMain*.

Set *frmMain* as the Startup form for the project

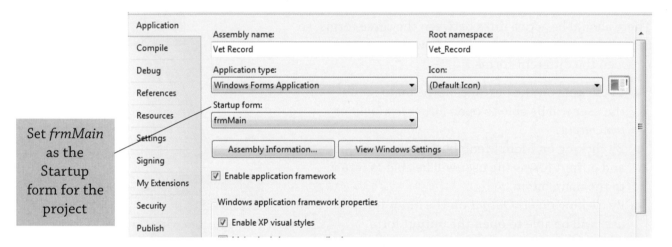

Activity Navigation buttons

- **Edit *frmMain*:** Add code to the three buttons on *frmMain* so they work as navigation buttons.

- **Edit *frmInput*:** Add a button called *btnMain* which closes *frmInput* and opens *frmMain*.

- **Edit *frmOutput*:** Edit the code on *btnClose* so that it closes *frmOutput* and opens *frmMain*.

- **Startup form:** Set *frmMain* as the Startup form for the project.

- Debug and save.

The full code listing is shown at the end of this chapter.

■ 16.8 Print the output

There is a button on *frmOutput* called *btnPrint*. Now you will add code to that button so that when the user clicks the button the contents of *frmOutput* will be sent to the printer.

For this you will have to use a new and more complex control called the PrintForm PowerPack. The Visual Basic PrintForm PowerPack lets the user print out an image of the active Windows Form when the program is running.

Open the PowerPacks toolbox

You have used the Toolbox on the left of the Visual Basic screen to add controls to the forms. For example, you used the Toolbox to add a button or a text box to a form. The PrintForm control is in another part of the Toolbox that you have not used before. This area is called Visual Basic PowerPacks.

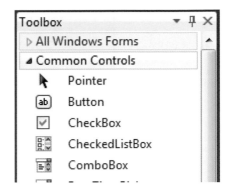

The Toolbox is divided into sections. The first section is called All Windows Forms. The second section is called Common Controls. The Common Controls section is open, and this is the section that you normally use.

You can open and close the sections of the Toolbox by clicking on the arrow shape next to the section name.

When all of the sections are closed, the Toolbox looks like the screenshot shown here. At the bottom of the Toolbox is a section called Visual Basic PowerPacks. Click on this section to open it and see the controls it contains.

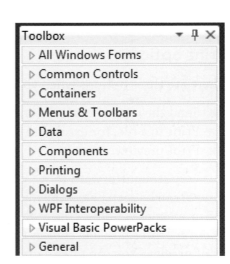

Add the PrintForm control to the form

The PowerPacks section contains a number of controls. One of the controls is called PrintForm. To allow you to print from *frmOutput* you need to drag the PrintForm control onto the form.

But notice that when you do this the PrintForm control does not appear on the form. Instead you will see a new object in an area underneath *frmOutput*. The object is called *PrintForm1*.

PrintForm1 is linked to *frmOutput*, but it appears below the form instead of on the form. Because *PrintForm1* is now linked to *frmOutput*, printing commands will work for this form.

Print options

There are three options when you print out a form:

- Send the output to a printer.
- Print to a file, for example a PDF file.
- Print preview.

It is very straightforward to swap between these print options. The PrintForm1 control can be seen below the form design. Click on this object to select it, and look in the properties window. One of the properties of the object PrintForm1 is *PrintAction*. There are three possible choices for this property: print to file, print to printer and print preview. You can open a drop-down menu of choices or click between them. Select whichever of the three print options is best for your current needs.

Code which prints the form

You need to add code to *btnPrint* so that when the user clicks this button, the output form is printed.

The code which makes this happen is:

```
PrintForm1.Print()
```

Other ways of printing

The method you have used in this section is the simplest type of printing in Visual Basic. There is no additional formatting or other changes to the printed output. Your printed copy is exactly the same as the form design.

There are other ways of printing from the Visual Basic environment. In general they require a lot more coding. For this reason, when your project requires printed output stick to the method given in this section:

- Create an output form that matches whatever you want to print.
- Use PrintForm to print out the form.

As you develop as a programmer you may want to learn other ways of printing from Visual Basic, but they are beyond the scope of this book.

Activity Print form content

- Make sure the Vet Record program is open.

- Add the PrintForm control to *frmOutput*.

- Set the print option to your preference: print preview, printer or PDF.

- Add code to *btnPrint* so that clicking this button prints out the form.

- Debug and save.

The complete code listing for all forms in the Vet Record project is shown at the end of this chapter.

■ 16.9 Overview of the Vet Record project

You have created a fairly complex project. It has three forms: a main menu, an input form and an output form. This is a good basic overall structure to use for any programming project in Visual Basic.

The full code listing for this project is given at the end of the chapter. Note that the full code listing includes comments. You should include comments in your project code. Comments explain the purpose of each section of code. They will help you to read your own program code, and they will help colleagues to understand your work,

You have learned about the scope and lifetime of a variable. A variable only exists and retains its content while the code that declared the variable is open. That means that the *Pet* record used in this project will cease to exist when the project is closed.

■ Chapter end

Full code listing

Here is the full listing of the code for the three forms that make up the Vet Record project, plus the code module.

frmMain

```
Public Class frmMain

    Private Sub btnInput_Click(ByVal sender As -

        'Hide main menu and open input form

        Me.Hide()

        frmInput.Show()

    End Sub

    Private Sub btnOutput_Click(ByVal sender As -

        'Hide main menu and open output form

        Me.Hide()

        frmOutput.Show()

    End Sub

    Private Sub btnQuit_Click(ByVal sender As -

        'End application

        End

    End Sub

End Class
```

frmInput

```
Public Class frmInput
    Private Sub btnSave_Click(ByVal sender As -

        'assign values from the input controls to the elements of
        Pet

        Pet.Name = txtName.Text

        Pet.DoB = DateTimePicker1.Value

        Pet.Species = cmbSpecies.Text

        Pet.Injection = chkInjections.Checked
```

```
        Pet.Owner = TxtOwnerName.Text

        'Clears the input fields ready for next use
        txtName.Text = ""
        DateTimePicker1.Value = Today
        cmbSpecies.Text = ""
        chkInjections.Checked = False
        TxtOwnerName.Text = ""
        MsgBox(Pet.Name & : "Record added")
    End Sub

    Private Sub btnOutput_Click(ByVal sender As -
        'Hides this form and opens output form
        Me.Hide()
        frmOutput.Show()
    End Sub

    Private Sub btnMain_Click(ByVal sender As -
        'Closes this form and opens main menu
        Me.Close()
        frmMain.Show()
    End Sub

End Class
```

frmOutput

```
Public Class frmOutput

    Private Sub frmOutput_Load(ByVal sender As -
        'When the form is loaded the elements of the pet record
        'are assigned to the form labels
        lblName.Text = Pet.Name
        lblOwner.Text = Pet.Owner
        lblSpecies.Text = Pet.Species
        lblDoB.Text = Pet.DoB
```

```
        If Pet.Injection Then
            lblInjections.Text = "Has had all injections"
        Else
            lblInjections.Text = "Has not had injections"
        End If
    End Sub

    Private Sub btnPrint_Click(ByVal sender As -
        'Prints the output form
        PrintForm1.Print()
    End Sub

    Private Sub btnClose_Click(ByVal sender As -
        'Closes this form and opens the main menu
        Me.Close()
        frmMain.Show()
    End Sub

End Class
```

Module1

```
Module Module1
    'declare PetRecord data type

    Public Structure PetRecord
        Public Name As String
        Public DoB As Date
        Public Species As String
        Public Injection As Boolean
        Public Owner As String
    End Structure

    'declare variablePet of the PetRecord data type
    Public Pet As PetRecord

End Module
```

Overview

In this section you learned to create a multiform project.

- You saw how to work with a group of forms and a module.
- You learned how to add code to a button that closes the form and opens another form.
- You learned how to declare public variables in modules. These variables can be used by any form in a project.
- You also learned how to use the PrintForm control to allow the user to print out the contents of a form while the project is running.

■ Questions

Answer these questions to demonstrate your learning.

1. What is the effect of the code *Me.Close()*?
2. If your project has a form called *frmDataEntry*, what code would you use to open this form so the user can see it on the screen?
3. What is the difference in scope between a local variable declared on a form and a public variable declared in a module?
4. What is meant by the lifetime of a variable, and what is the lifetime of a variable declared in a project module?
5. A Boolean variable called *Homework* is set to True if a student has handed in his or her homework and False if a student has not handed in his or her homework. Write the code that you would use to display this information on an output form.
6. Describe the actions you would take to ensure that a form called *frmHome* is the first form that the user sees when a project starts up.
7. Describe all of the actions you would take to add a functioning Print button to a form called *frmPrintRecord*.

Further activity

Practice activities can be carried out if you finish the work in this chapter with time to spare. You can also carry out these activities in your own time to help with learning and to improve your skills.

Practice activity: Open the Ts-2-Go project (chapter 8). Alter this project so that there is an input form, an output form and a main menu. Add a Print button to the output form.

Practice activity: Open the project that allows a teacher to input the names of all of the pupils in the drama club and output the club list (chapter 12). Alter this project so that there is an input form, an output form and a main menu. Add a Print button to the output form.

17 The computer processor

Introduction

In this chapter there is no programming activity. You will learn about the technology of the processor. This is the part of the computer where all processing activity is carried out. This component enables computers to work.

17.1 The central processing unit

You have learned that the standard basic model of a computer system is Input → Processing → Output. Data is input to the computer via input devices. It is altered or transformed in some way – this is processing. The resulting information is output from the computer.

In this chapter you will learn about the processor: the part of the computer that carries out the processing work which converts input to output. Another term for the processor is the **CPU**, which stands for central processing unit.

Digital data

All data within the computer is stored as electronic signals in micro-circuits. Only two types of electronic signal are used in the computer system – on and off. A micro-circuit can either carry an electric signal, or not.

All of the items of data inside the computer are stored in the form of on/off electronic signals. Data stored in this form is known as digital data.

In chapter 4 you learned about the binary number system. This is a way of representing numerical values using 1s and 0s. These 1s and 0s represent the on and off signals of digital data.

Obviously there are not literally 1s and 0s inside the computer. Instead there are constantly changing on/off electronic signals, which represent the data in electronic digital form.

Remember that all data must be converted into digital form:

- Text is represented by ASCII code.
- Software instructions are represented by machine code.
- Sounds, images and other types of data are all converted into digital form.

Learning content

3.1.8.2 Hardware: categorise devices as input or output depending on their function.

3.1.8.3 The CPU: describe the purpose of the processor (CPU); understand how different components link to a processor (ROM, RAM, I/O, storage, etc.); explain the effect of common CPU characteristics on the performance of the processor (these should include clock speed, number of cores and cache size/types).

3.1.8.4 Memory: explain the purpose of virtual memory and cache memory; explain the concept that data and instructions are stored in memory and processed by the CPU.

Key term

CPU The central processing unit of a computer. This is where values are combined and transformed into new values.

Link

Storing different types of data – chapter 4

Electronic data

The data inside the CPU is electronic. The only data that the CPU holds is the current data relating to the activity the CPU is currently carrying out.

The electronic memory inside the CPU is volatile, which means it only exists when the computer is powered up. When the computer is switched off all of the data in the CPU is wiped. This means that any data you want to keep needs to be copied to storage. You learned about storage in chapter 4.

The structure of the CPU

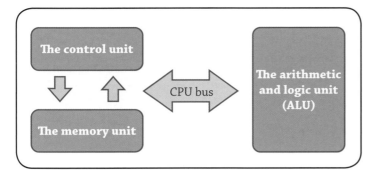

The CPU consists of three major components. These are the arithmetic and logic unit, also called the **ALU**, the control unit and the memory unit. The components are connected by a very fast electronic connection called a bus.

The diagram shows the relationship between the components of the CPU.

> ### Key term
>
> **ALU**   The arithmetic and logic unit. This is the part of the CPU where data transformation occurs. It operates electronically.

The ALU

The ALU is the part of the processor that can transform data. The ALU can carry out mathematical transformations very rapidly. All of the processing of the computer is carried out mathematically. The ALU receives two items:

- a machine code instruction, in digital form
- the data that needs to be processed, also in digital form.

The ALU transforms the digital data, following the machine code instructions, and outputs the resulting value.

The memory unit

The memory unit within the CPU consists of a small number of memory registers. Each register can store an item of data or a software instruction. The memory unit stores the data and instructions before they are sent to the ALU, and the result of the ALU processing is copied back to the memory unit.

The memory unit can also be called the Immediate Access Store (IAS).

The control unit

The control unit is in charge of processing. The control unit takes a software instruction and an item of data from the memory unit and sends them to the ALU. It accepts the result of the processing from the ALU and sends it back to the memory unit.

The control unit keeps track of the sequence of instructions and the location of each item of data and software instruction in the memory unit.

The fetch–execute cycle

When all of these components work together the result is the processing cycle of the computer. This is called the **fetch–execute cycle**.

In the processing cycle:

1 The control unit **fetches** a single instruction from the memory unit, as a digital code. The control unit sends the digital code to the ALU together with some data.
2 The instruction is decoded.
3 The ALU **executes** the instruction (that means it carries out the instruction).
4 The ALU sends the result of the processing back to the control unit, and the control unit stores it in the memory unit.

The cycle then repeats again and again until all of the instructions have been **fetched** by the control unit and **executed** by the ALU.

The diagram illustrates the fetch–execute cycle. A key feature of every computer system is that the CPU can only execute one instruction at a time.

> **Key term**
>
> **Fetch–execute cycle** A single operation of the CPU: a stored instruction is taken from memory, carried out and the resulting value stored to memory.

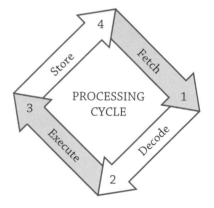

How RAM links to the CPU

In chapter 4 you learned about RAM and ROM. These are areas of memory that are closely connected to the CPU. They can communicate rapidly with the CPU. They store more information than the memory unit.

RAM is the active memory of the computer. The contents of all open software applications and data files are held in RAM. The particular instructions and data needed at that moment are sent from the RAM to the CPU and stored in the memory register.

> **Link**
>
> Primary storage – section 4.1

Peripherals

The key fact about the processor is that it can only handle data if it is converted to digital form. This means that all input and output to the CPU must be converted into digital form. This is carried out by input and output devices. For example, the keyboard is used by the computer user to enter text data. The user presses particular keys to represent text selection. The keyboard sends electronic digital signals to the CPU. These signals represent the keys that the user has pressed.

You learned about storage devices in chapter 4. Secondary storage holds data in a digital form, which can be easily converted back into the signals used by the CPU. Secondary storage has greater capacity than RAM, and it is not volatile, so it is retained when the computer is switched off. However, it takes longer for data to go from storage to the CPU.

Link

Secondary storage – section 4.2

Input, output and storage devices that are connected to the processor are called peripherals.

■ 17.2 Processing power and speed

In this section you will learn about the characteristics of the CPU that make some computers faster and more powerful than others. The power and speed of a computer is limited by the speed with which the computer can carry out the fetch–execute cycle. This is because the CPU can only carry out one instruction at a time.

Clock speed

The control unit of the CPU includes a system clock. This clock sets the speed of the fetch–execute cycle. The CPU fetches instructions and data from the memory registers and sends them to the ALU according to the speed set by the system clock.

A computer that has a fast clock speed carries out each fetch–execute cycle in less time. This means it can perform more calculations in one second of processing. So the computer can process more data and produce results more quickly.

Clock speed is measured in hertz (Hz), which is a general measurement of the speed of any cycle. This tells you how often the cycle repeats in one second. Computer clock rate is expressed in megahertz (MHz) or gigahertz (GHz). This number refers to the frequency of the CPU's master clock signal. One megahertz is one million cycles per second. One gigahertz is one thousand million cycles per second.

In the 1970s the typical speed of a personal computer was 1 MHz. Nowadays modern computer processors have a speed of up to 6 GHz.

Cache memory

Cache memory acts as a buffer between main memory and the CPU.

Cache memory is memory that can be accessed rapidly by the processor. Cache memory holds a copy of data that is stored elsewhere. The data that the computer needs right away is taken from storage before processing begins, and kept in cache memory while it is in use.

Study tip

Cache is pronounced 'cash'.

The larger the cache, the more likely the processor is to find what it needs in there. If it can find what it needs it does not have to go to other less convenient, slower storage. So, the larger the cache, the quicker the processor can work. If the cache is large the processor can use the data in cache, and it does not need to slow down to access other types of memory such as RAM and secondary storage.

There are several types of cache:

- **The memory register** is a very small cache. It only holds the current instructions.
- **L1 cache** is inside the processor chip. This is a small memory cache, but it is quick and easy for the CPU to use.
- **L2 cache** is outside the chip, but it is connected very closely to it. It is larger than L1 cache. Advanced Transfer Cache (ATC) is a type of L2 cache that is positioned directly on the processor chip. Processors that use ATC can work at faster speeds.

Some computers also have L3 cache. This sits between the CPU and the RAM, and can speed up communications between them.

The next table compares the storage capacity of the various kinds of memory.

Memory	Typical capacity
Memory register	A few bytes
L1 cache	64 KB
L2 cache	1 MB
Main memory	10 GB

The memory register is the fastest memory for the CPU to access, but it has the smallest capacity. The main memory has the largest capacity but it takes longer for the data in the main memory to reach the CPU.

■ 17.3 Multi-processor computers

You have looked at ways that computer systems can be made faster and more powerful. This includes faster clock speed and larger memory cache.

However, there is another way that computers can be designed to increase their power. That is to include more than one processor within the computer system.

Distributed processing

A distributed computer system can take advantage of multiple processors. In this case the system might be made of many different computers, all doing different work, but sharing a lot of

Link
Networking – chapter 24

data. A network within an organisation may operate in this way, with different users working at different computers, but taking advantage of good communications to pass data rapidly between the processors.

Multi-core processing

Some modern computer systems include more than one physical processor inside the same computer. The different processors share the same memory and peripherals. These computers are called multi-core or multiprocessor systems.

If you need a lot of processing power, then there are some advantages to joining up several smaller processors instead of creating one big processor:

- You can use processors that have already been tested and are reliable in use. This is less risky than trying to develop a completely new super-size processor.
- A processor generates heat in proportion to its size. A very large processor can be difficult to keep cool, and if it overheats it will stop working.
- Each processor can only carry out one instruction at a time. By using several processors, several instructions can be carried out at the same time. This is called parallel computing.

The most common types of multi-core processor are dual-core (with two processors) and quad-core (with four processors).

Parallel computing

Parallel computing is a way of making use of multiple processors. A large computing problem is divided into many small operations. Several different operations can be carried out at the same time, each one using a different processor.

For example, a computer with a quad-core can carry out up to four operations at the same time.

Parallel processing is becoming more common as a way of increasing computer power. However, to make full use of parallel computing, carefully designed software is required. Not all software is suitable for parallel computing.

> **Key term**
>
> **Parallel processing**   A type of computer operation where more than one operation is carried out at the same time. This is possible if more than one CPU is employed.

■ 17.4 Computer power and limiting factors

The major factors which limit or increase the power and speed of computers are:

- the clock speed
- the cache size
- the number of processors.

However, there are other factors that can limit how quickly a computer works. In recent years processors have become increasingly powerful, and now other factors can be more important than processor speed.

Some important factors that can limit the speed and power of a computer include:

- the software in use
- the speed of other items of hardware, such as input and output devices
- the design and organisation of the computer system, and how the parts relate to each other
- data communications with other computers
- the speed, skill and accuracy of the human user.

A computer that is poorly designed or badly used, or one with a slow broadband connection, can be forced to go much slower than its top speed.

Effects of computer power and speed

Many of the tasks that people want to carry out using computers require a lot of data to be processed very rapidly. An example would be a computer used to fly an aeroplane. The computer must react very quickly to the data that sets out the flying conditions and position of the aeroplane. There can be no delay in sending instructions to the steering and power controls of the aeroplane.

A computer system that must respond immediately to real-life events is called a real-time system. Real-time systems require fast and powerful computer processors.

Other examples of modern computer applications that require a fast processor include:

- searching through large amounts of data to find the answer to a question (for example, searching the Internet)
- translating or producing human language in a natural way
- encrypting and decrypting coded messages
- processing the results of scientific experiments
- producing large or moving images that look realistic.

Processor size

Another key feature of a modern computer system is that computer processors are getting smaller all the time. This means that powerful processors can be small and light. These small processors can be used in handy mobile devices. People make more use of computers nowadays because they are easy to carry around with them.

Smaller processors use less energy, and this means they can run off small batteries. This is another way that modern technology improves the portability of computer devices.

■ Chapter end

Overview

In this chapter you learned about the structure and action of the CPU.

- The CPU consists of the memory unit, control unit and ALU. The interaction of these units when the computer is in operation is called the fetch–execute cycle or the processor cycle.
- Modern computing requires fast processing of large amounts of data. The speed and power of the processor is limited by clock speed and cache size.
- One solution to the problem of processor speed and power is to include more than one processor inside the computer system. This can increase the power of the computer and allow parallel processing where more than one instruction is carried out at the same time.

■ Questions

Answer these questions to demonstrate your learning.

1 Draw a diagram of the main components of the CPU. Label each component.
2 Explain the purpose of each component within the CPU.
3 Draw a diagram of the fetch–execute cycle.
4 Explain the relationship between the clock speed of a processor and the fetch–execute cycle.
5 What is cache size and why does it have an effect on the speed of a processor?
6 Describe two types of cache and how they are used by the computer processor.
7 Explain three factors besides clock speed and cache size that might limit the speed at which a computer carries out a task.
8 Describe three modern uses of computers that depend on fast processing.
9 Explain what a dual-core processor is.
10 Give three advantages that a multi-core processor has over a single large processor.

Further activity

Practice activities can be carried out if you finish the work in this chapter with time to spare. You can also carry out these activities in your own time to help with learning and to improve your skills.

Practice activity: Manufacturers are always improving the specifications of computer systems. Investigate two or more modern computer systems. Describe the key technical features of the computers as described by the manufacturer, including clock speed and cache size. What other features do the manufacturers choose to emphasise in their advertising?

18 Using procedures

■ Introduction

In chapter 14 you learned what a function is. In chapter 15 you learned to write and use your own functions. In this chapter you will learn about procedures. A procedure is similar to a function, but it does not return a value, and so it is used in a slightly different way in coding.

In this chapter you will create a simple game of noughts and crosses. Procedures will make this task easier.

■ 18.1 What is a procedure?

A **procedure** is a set of commands that are collected together and given a name. When you enter the name of the procedure the commands stored in the procedure are carried out.

Procedure or function?

A procedure is similar to a function. However, a procedure does not return a value. Instead it just carries out a series of actions.

Procedure or sub-procedure?

The programming convention is to refer to functions and procedures. Functions return a value and procedures do not. Visual Basic uses slightly different terms. In Visual Basic the two are called function procedures and sub-procedures.

For simplicity this book uses the term 'procedure', but be aware that the term 'sub-procedure' means the same thing. In Visual Basic it is abbreviated to 'sub'.

Declaring a procedure

A procedure is declared at the top of the code, like a function is. The general structure for a procedure declaration is:

```
Private Sub Name (parameters)

        code

End Sub
```

Learning content

3.1.4 Procedures: understand what procedures are; know when the use of a procedure would make sense and simplify the coded solution; know how to write and use your own simple procedures; understand what a parameter is; know how to use parameters.

Key term

Procedure A collection of program commands that are grouped together and given a name. Whenever the name of the procedure is entered into your code, all of the commands are carried out.

Each of these terms helps to define the procedure:

- The first word is *Private*. This procedure is private, which means it is only used within one form. A procedure can also be declared as *Public* in the project module.
- The next word is *Sub*, which stands for sub-procedure.
- Instead of 'Name', 'parameters' and 'code', you would enter the name of the procedure, the parameters and the code to make the procedure carry out an action.
- The code ends with the line *End Sub*, which marks the end of the procedure.

Scope

A procedure has a scope. The scope of a procedure is the same as the scope of a function. If a procedure is declared within the code for a single form it can only be used in that form. If you need to use a procedure throughout a project, you should declare the procedure in the project module. You learned about the project module in chapter 16.

> **Link**
>
> Create a project module – chapter 16

Parameters

Like a function, a procedure can have one or more parameters. The parameters of a procedure are values which can change. As the parameters vary, the action of the procedure will change. If a procedure has a parameter it is included inside the brackets following the procedure name.

If the procedure has several parameters they are included one after the other, with a comma between them.

If the procedure has no parameters, you still include the brackets, but with nothing inside them.

Calling the procedure

Once a procedure is declared it can be used anywhere in your code. This is known as calling the procedure. A procedure can be called in more than one place in your code.

To call a procedure you include the name of the procedure in the code. Where the name of the procedure is shown, all of the code within the procedure declaration will be carried out.

If the procedure has parameters they are given in brackets following the name of the procedure. The number and order of the parameters must match the procedure declaration.

A procedure does not return a value.

Advantages of using a procedure

There are two major advantages of using a procedure:

- It simplifies your main code. One or more lines of code can be replaced by a single procedure name. The name of the procedure should be explanatory. This makes your main code shorter and easier to understand.

- A procedure can be used in more than one place in your code. This reduces the amount of coding you have to do. It also reduces the chance of making a mistake. Once you have written a procedure you can call the procedure at several points throughout your code. This shortens your coding task and avoids repetition.

Once you have developed a procedure you can copy and paste it into other programs wherever it will be useful.

■ 18.2 Noughts and crosses

In this chapter you will create a simple noughts and crosses game. The application will display the playing grid. By clicking on the squares of the grid you will display the noughts and crosses. You can use this to play against a partner.

The first step is to create the user interface. The screenshot opposite shows the user interface for noughts and crosses.

The Visual Basic tool that lets you draw lines on the grid is in the PowerPacks section of the Toolbox. The tool is called LineShape. This is shown in the screenshot below.

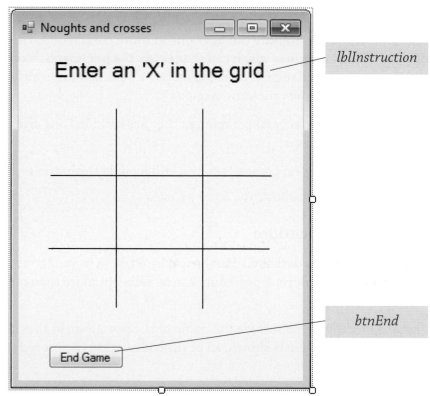

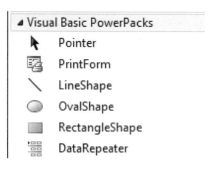

To draw a line on the form:

- open Visual Basic PowerPacks
- select LineShape
- drag the LineShape marker on the form to draw a line.

Activity Create the user interface

- Start a new Visual Basic project. Call it Noughts and crosses.

- Change the *Text* property of the form to Noughts and crosses.

- Using the LineShape tool draw a noughts and crosses grid on the form as shown on the previous page.

- Add *lblInstruction* and *btnEnd* as shown in the screenshot.

- Add code to *btnEnd* so that it closes the app.

- Save the application and run it using Debug to make sure it works properly.

■ 18.3 Add crosses to the grid

You now need to amend the project so that if you click on any square of the grid a cross will appear. The crosses will be shown using labels. The *Text* property of the label is a letter X, and a large font size is used.

The next screenshot shows the form with the crosses added.

If the *Visible* property of the labels is set to False, the crosses will be invisible when the application runs.

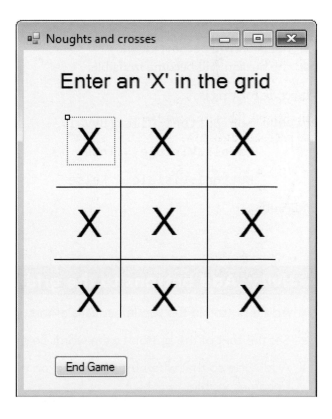

Activity Add labels to the grid

- Add a label in the top left square of the grid.
- Set the *Text* property of the label to X.
- Set the font size to 36.
- Set the *Visible* property to False.
- Copy and paste this label into every square of the grid, so that it looks like the screenshot on this page.
- Save and run the program.

■ 18.4 Select and show

Now you will add a button to the top left-hand square of the grid which will make the X in that square visible.

Add a button to the top left-hand corner. The button can cover the X completely. The screenshot shows what it might look like. This button is called *Button1*.

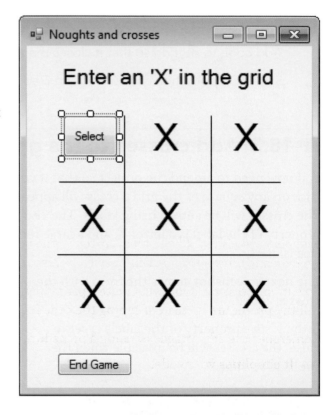

When the user clicks on the button:

- the label will become visible
- the button will become invisible.

The code for this is:

```
Private Sub Button1_Click(ByVal −

        Label1.Visible = True

        Button1.Visible = False

End Sub
```

Activity Add buttons to the grid

- Add a button in the top left square of the grid.
- Set the text of the button to the word 'Select'.
- Add code so that when the user clicks on the button it becomes invisible, and the X becomes visible.
- Save and run the code. Test the button to make sure that it works.

You can make the button blend into the background by altering some of the object properties. Select *Button1* and look in the Properties window:

- Find the property *FlatStyle*. Set this property to Flat.
- Find the property *FlatAppearance*. When you select this property a range of options will open up. This is shown in the screenshot.
- Find the property *BorderSize* and set it to 0.

These changes are shown in the screenshot on the next page.

Activity (optional): Improve the appearance of the interface

Alter the properties of the button as shown here and see how this alters the appearance of the button on the screen.

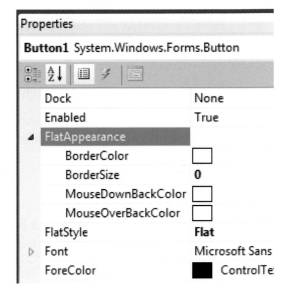

■ 18.5 Create a procedure

The next step is to add a similar button with similar code to every square in the grid. This means the same code will have to be repeated over and over again.

To simplify this task you will create a procedure that stores the code. You can then call the procedure instead of typing the code for every button.

Remember the advantages of using a procedure:

- It simplifies your code.
- It reduces the amount of work you have to do.
- It reduces the chances of making a mistake.
- It makes your code easier to read.

Later in this chapter you will make changes to the code. Because you have used a procedure you will only need to make the change in one place – in the procedure declaration.

What does the procedure do?

The code linked to the button does two things:

- It makes the label visible.
- It makes the button invisible.

Each button on the screen will do the same thing, but the name of the label and the button will vary. That means the button name and the label name are the parameters of the procedure: they are the values that will change each time the procedure is called.

Decide on procedure name and parameters

Before you can write a procedure you must decide on a suitable name for the procedure, and for the parameters. This should be based on the action of the procedure.

In this case the procedure:

- is used to show that the player has chosen one square of the grid
- shows the label in this square
- hides the button in this square.

That helps to decide on the name and the parameters:

- The procedure can be called *Choose*.
- The parameters can be called *thislabel* and *thisbutton*.

Declare the procedure

A procedure is declared at the top of the code, below any variable declarations but before the main body of the code. To declare a procedure enter the words `Private Sub`, then the name of the procedure, then the parameters in brackets.

```
Private Sub Choose(thislabel, thisbutton)
```

The computer will automatically add the code 'End Sub' to mark the end of the procedure. In some versions of Visual Basic the computer will also add the words 'By Val' before each parameter. The code will now look something like this (if you do not see the words 'By Val' that is OK).

```
Private Sub Choose(ByVal thislabel, ByVal thisbutton)

End Sub
```

Now you enter code within the body of the procedure. The code has to do two things:

- make *thislabel* visible
- make *thisbutton* invisible.

So the completed code is:

```
Private Sub Choose(ByVal thislabel, ByVal thisbutton)

    thislabel.Visible = True

    thisbutton.Visible = False

End Sub
```

Activity Create a procedure

- Open the Noughts and crosses project.
- Declare a procedure *Choose* as shown here.

18.6 Call the procedure

Now that you have defined a procedure you can call it from within your code. To do this you enter the name of the procedure and the two parameters that you want to use with the procedure.

In this example the code looks like this:

```
Private Sub Button1_Click(ByVal –

        Choose(Label1, Button1)

End Sub
```

There is only one line of code. It is the name of the procedure followed by the two parameters. It is very important that you enter the names of the parameters in the same order as the parameters are shown in the variable declaration.

Activity Call the procedure

- Amend the code for *Button1_Click* as shown here.

- Save and run the project.

18.7 Add more buttons

Now you can add a button to every square of the grid. Using the procedure you can add code that makes each button work.

First you must copy and paste *Button1* into every square of the grid. The screenshot shows what this will look like.

Next you must add code to each button in the grid. You will use the *Choose* procedure.

The code for *Button2* will look like this:

```
        Choose(Label2, Button2)
```

The code for *Button3* will look like this:

```
        Choose(Label3, Button3)
```

And so on.

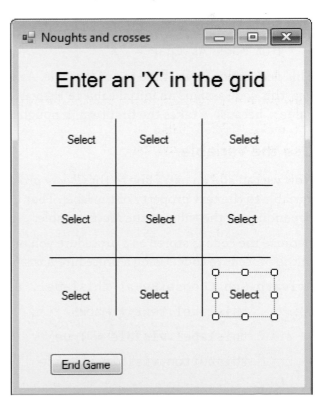

■ 18.8 Swap turns

At the moment the noughts and crosses project has a major problem. It only shows crosses and not noughts!

In this section you will add another procedure that swaps between noughts and crosses. This procedure will be called *SwapTurns*.

Declare the *Mark* variable

Some labels in the grid will show noughts and some will show crosses. This means the content of the label will be a variable. You will declare the variable, and then create a new procedure which changes the variable from X to 0 to swap turns.

We can call the variable *Mark* because it is the mark that appears in each square of the grid. We can use the data type *Char*, which stores a single character. It will store the value X or 0.

Here is the code to declare the variable *Mark*:

```
Dim Mark As Char = "X"
```

This declaration goes at the top of the code. As well as setting up the variable for use, this code assigns an initial value to the variable. The variable starts with the value *x*, because X takes the first turn in noughts and crosses.

Use the variable

Now we can add an extra line to the *Choose* procedure. This will assign the *Mark* variable to the text property of the label. That means the label will show a O or an X depending on the value of the *Mark* variable.

Because the code is stored as a procedure you only need to make this change once – in the procedure code. Using a procedure has saved you a lot of trouble.

```
Private Sub Choose(ByVal thislabel, ByVal thisbutton)
        thislabel.text = Mark
        thislabel.visible = True
        thisbutton.visible = False

End Sub
```

The new line added to the procedure assigns the value of the *Mark* variable to the text of the label.

Declare the *SwapTurns* procedure

After a mark has been added to the grid, the players swap turns. When you swap turns two things happen:

- the value of *Mark* variable changes from X to O
- the message at the top of the screen changes from 'Enter an X in the grid' to 'Enter a 0 in the grid'.

The next time you swap turns the change is from O to X. The two turns alternate until the game is over.

You will now create a procedure which carries out these actions. The procedure is called *SwapTurns*. It does not need any parameters.

Here is the procedure declaration.

```
Private Sub SwapTurns()

    If Mark = "X" Then

        Mark = "O"

        lblInstruction.Text = "Enter a '0' in the grid"

    Else

        Mark = "X"

        lblInstruction.Text = "Enter an 'X' in the grid"

    End If

End Sub
```

Looking through the lines of this procedure.

- The procedure is declared in the normal way, with the name *SwapTurns*.
- There are no parameters to this procedure, so the brackets following the procedure name are empty.
- The *If... Then... Else* structure is used. If *Mark* is X, change it to O. If *Mark* is O, change it to X.
- As well as changing *Mark*, the text of *lblInstruction* is altered.

This procedure should be declared at the top of the code. It must come after the declaration of the *Mark* variable, because this variable is used in the procedure.

- Make sure the Noughts and crosses project is open. You will declare the new variable and procedure at the top of the code, above the *Choose* procedure.

- Declare the *Mark* variable, using the code shown in this section.

- Declare the *SwapTurns* procedure, using the code described in this section.

■ 18.9 Call the procedure

Now you can adapt the *Choose* procedure. You will use the variable and the procedure that you have just declared:

- Assign the variable *Mark* to thislabel.Text.
- Call the procedure *SwapTurns* as the final line of the procedure.

The code looks like this:

```
Private Sub Choose(ByVal thislabel, ByVal thisbutton)

    thislabel.Text = Mark

    thislabel.Visible = True

    thisbutton.Visible = False

    SwapTurns()

End Sub
```

The final line of the procedure is *SwapTurns()*. This calls the *SwapTurns* procedure. There are no parameters for this procedure, so the brackets are empty.

- Amend the *Choose* procedure so that it calls the SwapTurns procedure as shown in this section.

- Save and run the project. You can now add noughts and crosses to every square of the grid.

- Try using your program to play noughts and crosses against a classmate.

■ Chapter end

Full code listing

Here is the code listing for the noughts and crosses project.

```
Public Class Form1
    'declare the mark variable
    Dim Mark As Char = "X"

    Private Sub SwapTurns()
        'swap between X and O
        If Mark = "X" Then
            Mark = "O"
            lblInstruction.Text = "Enter a 'O' in the grid"
        Else
            Mark = "X"
            lblInstruction.Text = "Enter an 'X' in the grid"
        End If
    End Sub

    Private Sub Choose(ByVal thislabel, ByVal thisbutton)
        'assign a mark to a grid square
        thislabel.Text = Mark
        thislabel.Visible = True
        thisbutton.Visible = False

        'call the SwapTurns procedure
        SwapTurns()
    End Sub

    Private Sub btnEnd_Click(ByVal -
        'close the program
        End
    End Sub
```

```
Private Sub Button1_Click(ByVal -

    'when a button is clicked the 'Choose' procedure is called

    Choose(Label1, Button1)

End Sub

'This code is repeated for buttons 2 to 9

Private Sub Button2_Click(ByVal -

    Choose(Label2, Button2)

End Sub

Private Sub Button3_Click(ByVal -

    Choose(Label3, Button3)

End Sub

Private Sub Button4_Click(ByVal -

    Choose(Label4, Button4)

End Sub

Private Sub Button5_Click(ByVal -

    Choose(Label5, Button5)

End Sub

Private Sub Button6_Click(ByVal -

    Choose(Label6, Button6)

End Sub

Private Sub Button7_Click(ByVal -

    Choose(Label7, Button7)

End Sub

Private Sub Button8_Click(ByVal -

    Choose(Label8, Button8)

End Sub
```

```
Private Sub Button9_Click(ByVal –

    Choose(Label9, Button9)

End Sub
```

```
End Class
```

Overview

In this section you learned to declare and use a procedure. You declared two procedures. One procedure had parameters, the other procedure had no parameters. Using procedures greatly simplified your coding task.

■ Questions

Answer these questions to demonstrate your learning.

The questions relate to the following procedure declaration.

```
Private Sub Makelist(ByVal Displaytimes, ByVal Listword)

    For i = 1 To Displaytimes

        Label1.Text = Label1.Text & " , " & Listword

    Next

End Sub
```

1 What is the name of this procedure?
2 How many parameters does this procedure have?
3 What are the names of the parameters?
4 A programmer wants to call this procedure to display the word 'Hello' five times in *Label1*. Write this line of code.
5 Write the full program code for an application where the user inputs a number and a word, and the output is a list showing the word repeated that number of times.
6 Give two advantages of using procedures in your code.

Further activity

Practice activities can be carried out if you finish the work in this chapter with time to spare. You can also carry out these activities in your own time to help with learning and to improve your skills.

Extension activity: If you want a challenging task, add extra code to the noughts and crosses project so that the computer detects if either player creates a winning line, and displays a message. This will involve a lot of extra coding.

19 Saving data to a text file

■ Introduction

Up until now you have not saved the output of any of the projects you created. For example, the list of drama club members from chapter 12 and the vet record from chapter 16 were not saved when the program was closed.

A text file is a file, saved in computer storage, that holds text characters. In this chapter you will learn how to write the output of a Visual Basic project to a text file. This output will be saved when the project is closed. You will also learn how to connect to a text file and read the contents back into the project to be processed or displayed.

In this way you can keep output from a project to use another time.

Learning content

3.1.7 Handling external data: use text files to read/ write data; know how to use an external text file to read and write data in a way that is appropriate for the programming language used and the problem being solved.

■ 19.1 Saving data when a program closes

When you close a Visual Basic project, all saved values are lost. In chapter 12 you entered a list of members of a drama club. In chapters 13–16 you entered a pet record for a vet. In all cases the values you entered were lost when you closed the program.

In this chapter you will learn how to save content when a project is closed. This greatly increases the power of your computer programs.

Text files

In chapter 4 you learned that text characters are stored by the computer using ASCII code. A text file is a file that contains ASCII code. If you open a text file on your computer system you will see letters and other characters including spaces.

Link

Storing different types of data – chapter 4

A text file is not the same as a Word document. A word-processed file contains other data as well as ASCII code. For example, it may include formatting and layout information, the text font and size, and images or other content. A simple text file has none of that additional data – it is just a series of letters and other characters.

Visual Basic lets you send output from any project to a text file. This is an easy way to save information from a Visual Basic project.

You will use two Visual Basic commands to work with text files:

- This command is used to put text into a text file. The text is usually from a Visual Basic textbox or variable.

      My.Computer.Filesystem.WriteAllText

- This command is used to read text from the file. The text is usually assigned to a Visual Basic object or variable.

      My.Computer.Filesystem.ReadAllText

■ 19.2 Create a text file to save high scores

If you play a computer game and you get a good score, the computer will let you save your name to the list of high scorers. In this chapter you will create a project that will let the user save their name to a list of high scorers and read the list of saved high scorers.

The project will have two forms:

- a main form that lets you add your name to the saved list
- an output form that will display the saved list of high scorers.

There is also a project module that stores the name and location of the text file as a constant.

Text file name and location

Before you begin you must decide on a name and storage location for the text file. This may be in the My Documents folder, or on a flash memory stick, or any storage location to which you have reliable access.

The first project in this chapter saves a list of high scorers for a computer game. When I created this project I used the following file name and storage location:

      "C:\Users\Alison\highscorers.txt"

You must choose a file name and storage location that suits your computer system. The program will create a file with the name that you choose in the storage location you choose. The file extension .txt tells the computer that the file is text only.

Store the file name and location as a constant

You have learned that it is useful to store any key item of information as a constant at the start of a project. You can then use the constant name throughout the project. Later, if you need to change the key information you only need to change the constant definition.

The following command will store the file name and location as a constant called *filename*:

```
Const filename As String = "C:\Users\Alison\
highscores.txt"
```

This means that wherever you want to refer to the file in your project, you don't have to give the full storage location and file name. You just enter the word 'filename' and the computer will use the name and storage location that you entered at the start of the program.

Declare the constant in a module

Most projects have more than one form. The scope of the *filename* constant must cover all of the forms in the project. You learned about scope of constants and variables in chapter 6.

To ensure the scope of the constant covers the whole project you should declare the constant as a public value in the project module. The full module code is as follows:

```
Module Module1

    Public Const filename As String = "C:\Users\Alison\
    highscorers.txt"

End Module
```

But remember you need to adapt this command to show the storage location and file name that you have chosen.

Study tip

Declare a constant *filename* in any project where you work with a stored text file. Then you can use all of the commands shown in this chapter, exactly as they are shown here. All you will need to change is the constant definition in the module.

Link

Change the scope of the variable – chapter 6

Activity Start the project

- Create a new Visual Basic project called High Scorers.

- Add a module to the project.

- In the project module declare a string constant called *filename*. Assign to this constant the storage location and file name you have chosen for your text file. Make sure the constant definition begins with the word 'Public' as shown on the previous page.

- Debug and save.

■ 19.3 The user interface

This project will have two forms:

- a start-up form called *frmMain*
- a form that displays the list of high scorers called *frmOutput*.

The following screenshots show suggested designs for these two forms.

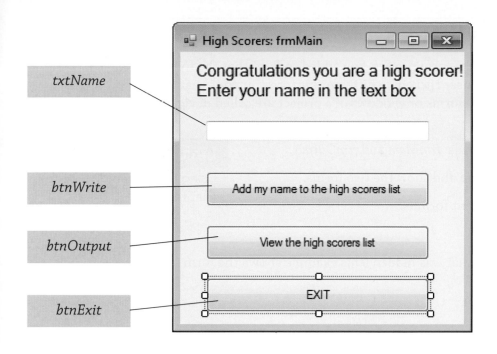

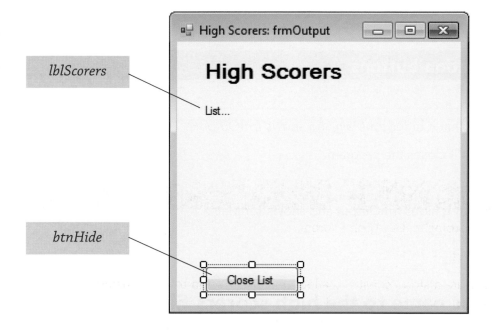

Activity Create a user interface

- Make sure you are working with the project High Scorers.

- Create two forms using the designs shown above.

- Set *frmMain* as the Startup form for the project.

- Give the buttons and text boxes suitable names as shown here.

- Debug and save.

■ 19.4 Navigation buttons

In chapter 16 you created a multi-form project. You added code so that the forms were opened and closed as the user clicked on different buttons. Buttons that control movement between the forms or windows of a project are called navigation buttons.

In this project there are two forms: *frmMain* and *frmOutput*.

The navigation buttons will hide and show the two forms.

The command to hide the current form is:

```
Me.Hide()
```

The command to show a form that was hidden (this example shows the form *frmOutput*) is:

```
frmOutput.Show()
```

Using these commands you can add code to the navigation buttons.

- Add code to *btnOutput* so that it hides *frmMain* and shows *frmOutput*.
- Add code to *btnHide* so that it hides *frmOutput* and shows *frmMain*.

Activity Enable navigation buttons

Edit *frmMain*:

- Add code to *btnOutput* so that it hides *frmMain* and shows *frmOutput*.

- Add code to *btnExit* so that it closes the program.

Edit *frmOutput*:

- Add code to *btnHide* so that it hides *frmOutput* and shows *frmMain*.

- Debug and save.

■ 19.5 Writing your name to the high scorers file

When the project starts up the user sees *frmMain*. The user can type his or her name into the text box called *txtName*. Clicking on the button that says 'Add my name to the high scorers list', means that the text in *txtName* will be copied into the text file.

Link

Using more than one form – chapter 16

In this example the text will be **appended** to the existing file. That means the new name will be added to the text file, which will grow longer. The alternative is to overwrite the text file, so that the new content wipes out the old content. In some projects that is the option you will need.

> **Key term**
>
> **Append**   To add a string or other value to an existing item, making it longer.

Syntax of the command

You will use the command *WriteAllText* to write the new content to the text file. Remember, syntax means the rules of a computer language. The syntax of the write command is:

```
My.Computer.FileSystem.WriteAllText(filename, sometext, True)
```

Here is how to adapt that command to your needs:

- Instead of the word 'sometext', enter the text you want to add to the file, in this project *txtName*.
- The final word True is a Boolean (true/false) option. If this option is set to True then the string will be appended to the text file, making it longer. If this option is set to False then the string will overwrite the text file, wiping out any previous content.

When all of these changes have been made, the finished code is:

```
My.Computer.FileSystem.WriteAllText(filename, txtName.Text, True)
```

This code will append the contents of the text that has been entered into *txtName* to the file.

Finishing touches

The code you have entered will work, but there are a couple of further touches that will improve the project:

- Make sure each name is shown on a new line by adding the command *vbNewLine* to the text.
- Once the name has been written to the text file, clear *txtName* by setting the *Text* property to "" (quotation marks with nothing between them).

If you make these changes the completed code will look like this:

```
Private Sub btnWrite_Click(ByVal –

  My.Computer.FileSystem.WriteAllText(filename, txtName.Text & vbNewLine, True)

  txtName.Text = ""

End Sub
```

Activity Write name to the High Scorers file

- Add code to *btnWrite* so that the contents of *txtName* are written to the text file when the user clicks the button.

- Debug and save.

- Check your work by adding several names to the high scorers list.

Checking your work

Using this project you can easily add new names to the file called highscorers.txt.

Close Visual Basic and look in the storage location that you chose for the text file. You will find that there is a file in that storage location called highscorers.txt. The file will open if you double click it. You will see that it contains all of the names you have entered so far.

The file may open in a basic text-editing application. You could also open the file using a word-processing program such as Word. Be careful not to make changes to the file using the word-processing program. If you save a text file as a fully formatted word-processed document this will add extra non-ASCII codes to the file, and it may not load properly in the Visual Basic project.

Activity Check your work

- Run the High Scorers project.

- Check your work by adding several names to the high scorers list.

- Open the file called 'highscorers.txt'. You will see the names you added.

A note on pseudocode

The pseudocode command to write a line to a text file is:

```
WRITELINE(file, n, value)
```

Instead of 'file' give the file name. Instead of 'value' give the string that you want to write to the file. Instead of 'n' give the line of the file you want to write to. This is not as useful a command as Visual Basic WriteAllText. You have to specify which line of the file to write to. If you pick a line that already has content then the command overwrites it.

■ 19.6 Reading from the file

The form called *frmOutput* will be used to display the list of high scorers. The contents of the text file will be displayed as the *Text* property of the label called *lblScorers*.

Load the form

The list of high scorers must be seen as soon as the form is opened (or 'loaded'). That means the event you need to code is *frmOutput_Load*.

If you double-click anywhere on *frmOutput* theCode window opens. The outline code looks like this:

```
Private Sub frmOutput_Load(ByVal -

End Sub
```

Any code added between these two lines will be carried out when *frmOutput* opens.

Read the text file

The command to read the contents of a text file is:

```
My.Computer.FileSystem.ReadAllText(filename)
```

This is a function that reads a file. Like all functions it returns a value. It returns a text string that contains the entire contents of the file.

Assign the text to a label

The returned value must be assigned to an object or variable. In this example you will assign the text string to the *Text* property of the label *lblScorers*.

So the complete command to read the high scorers file is:

```
Private Sub frmOutput_Load(ByVal -

    lblScorers.Text = My.Computer.FileSystem.ReadAllText(filename)

End Sub
```

Activity Reading from the text file

- Open *frmOutput*.
- Add code so that when the form is loaded the contents of the text file are assigned to *lblScorers*.
- Debug and save.
- Run the program a few times to add extra names to the high scorers list.

The High Scorers project is now complete. You can find the full code listing for this project at the end of the chapter.

A note on pseudocode

The pseudocode command to read a line from a text file is:

```
READLINE(file, n)
```

Instead of 'file' give the name of the file. Instead of 'n' give the line number of the file. As with Visual Basic the value read from the file can be assigned to a variable.

```
Variable ← READLINE(file, n)
```

■ 19.7 Storing an array

The High Scorers project wrote a string of text to a text file. The project also read the contents of the text file and showed it as a label. The contents of the text file was treated a single string by the program.

But sometimes saving one string of text is not enough. Sometimes you need to save an array of data. You learned how to create an array of data in chapter 12, where you declared an array and populated it with the names of members of a drama club. However, when you closed the project, all the data stored in the array was lost.

In this section you will load the Drama Club project. You will make changes to the project, so that the data in the array is stored to a file. That means that the data will not be lost when the project is closed.

You will also add code so that the saved data can be read back into the array next time you start up the project.

CSV file

A good way to store an array is to use a CSV file.

CSV stands for 'comma separated variable'. A CSV file consists of a series of strings, separated by commas. The comma stands as a marker between the different sections of the file.

In this project you will write an array to a CSV file. The elements of the array will be stored in the CSV file as separate strings, with commas in between.

Edit the Drama Club project

In section 12.4 you saved the Drama Club project, which used a simple one-dimensional array. In this section you will make changes to this project so that the array is saved as a CSV file.

As a first stage you will edit the interface so that there are two new buttons:

- A button which saves the array to a file. You could call it *btnSave*.
- A button which loads the saved array. You could call it *btnLoad*.

Element 0

In chapter 12 you did not use element 0 of the array. In this version of the project you will use element 0.

There is only one change you need to make. Everywhere in the project where you see:

```
For counter = 1 To club_size
```

change this to:

```
For counter = 0 To club_size
```

Your project now includes element 0. That means there will be one more name in the drama club array than before.

A suggested design for the amended interface is shown in the screenshot.

Link

Completed Drama Club project – section 12.4

Open the Drama Club project.

Alter the interface as shown in this section.

Name the new buttons *btnSave* and *btnLoad*.

Change both counter-controlled loops so they count from 0 to club_size.

Debug and save the project.

■ 19.8 Set up the CSV file

In this section you will add code to *btnSave* so that the contents of the *Dramaclub* array are saved to a CSV file.

Name the CSV file as a constant

In section 19.1 you declared a constant called filename. This constant stored the name and location of highscores.txt.

You must choose a suitable name and location for the Drama Club file, and save this as a constant called filename. For example:

```
Const filename As String = "C:\MyDocuments\DramaClub.txt"
```

Clear the CSV file

In the first half of this chapter you wrote high scores to a file. Every time you ran the program, the saved file got longer.

In this project you want to start each time with an empty file. Otherwise, each time you save the *Dramaclub* array the file will get longer with multiple copies of the array.

You can use the *WriteAllText* command to create an empty file. This is the command:

```
My.Computer.Filesystem.WriteAllText(filename, "", False)
```

This command writes an empty string to the file. An empty string is shown as double quote marks with nothing in between them. The Boolean value is set to False. That means the string overwrites any previous content of the file.

Of course at the moment the file is empty, but this line ensures that you always begin with an empty file at the start of the project.

Activity Set up link to CSV file

- Make sure you are working with the Drama Club project.

- Declare a constant called filename, which stores the name and location of a text file.

- Add code to *btnSave* which clears the text file as shown here.

- Debug and save.

■ 19.9 Write the contents of the array to the CSV file

In this section you will add code to *btnSave* so that the contents of the *Dramaclub* array are appended to the text file.

Counter-controlled loop

To do this you need to use a counter-controlled loop. This will count through the elements of the array one at a time. Each element will be written to the CSV file, followed by a comma.

You should be familiar with how to use a counter controlled loop. Remember the size of the array is stored as club_size. So the loop looks like this.

```
For counter = 0 To club_size
        code
Next
```

Write to the file

You will use the *WriteAllText* command to write each element of the array to the CSV file, plus a comma following each element.

The text to write to the file is:

```
Dramaclub(counter) & ","
```

Putting this into the *WriteAllText* command gives this code:

```
My.Computer.FileSystem.WriteAllText(filename,
Dramaclub(counter) & ",", True)
```

Putting it together

The complete code is:

```
For counter = 0 To club_size

My.Computer.FileSystem.WriteAllText(filename,
Dramaclub(counter) & ",", True)

Next
```

You can add a final line to the code, which tells the user that the array has been copied to the file:

```
lblClubList.Text = "Copied to storage"
```

This code comes outside the loop, as it only appears once, when the save is completed.

Activity Write members to file

- Add code to *btnSave* to write all the elements of the array to the file, as shown here.
- Add code to *btnSave* which displays a message to the user saying the save is complete.
- Run the project. Click on the first button on the interface and add names to the drama club array.
- Click on *btnSave* to save these names to the CSV file.
- Debug and save.

If you look in the storage location you have chosen, you will see a new file. It has the name you have chosen. If you open the file, you will see it contains the three stored names, separated by commas.

■ 19.10 Load the saved file into the array

You will add code to *btnLoad*. This will load the saved names into the array from the text file.

This is done in two stages:

- Load the file into a single string variable.
- Split the string to populate the array.

Load the file into a single string variable

You need to create a temporary string variable, to store the contents of the text file. This variable can be declared within the code for *btnLoad*. A good name for the variable is *temp* and it should be the string data type.

The command to declare this variable is:

```
Dim temp As String
```

You use the *ReadAllText* command to read the contents of the text file to the string variable:

```
temp = My.Computer.FileSystem.ReadAllText(filename)
```

Split the string to populate the array

Visual Basic has a useful function called *Split*. This function splits a text variable, and assigns it to an array.

The function takes two parameters:

- a string variable
- the symbol used to split the variable.

Remember you are using a CSV file. That means the elements are divided by commas, so the symbol used to split the string variable is the comma symbol.

So adding the parameters to the function you get:

```
Split(temp, ",")
```

The returned value of the function is assigned to an array. The array in this project is called *Dramaclub*. So the completed line of code is:

```
Dramaclub = Split(temp, ",")
```

Finished code

Here is the completed code to load the contents of the text file and assign it to the array:

```
Dim temp As String

temp = My.Computer.FileSystem.ReadAllText(filename)

Dramaclub = Split(temp, ",")
```

Activity Complete and run the program

- Add code to *btnLoad* which loads the content of the text file to the array, as shown in this section.

- Debug and save.

- Now you can fully test the project that you have made:

  - Add names to the array.

  - List the elements of the array.

  - Click on *btnSave* to save the array to the text file.

  - Close the project.

  - Open the project again.

  - Click on *btnLoad* to load the text file.

  - List the elements of the array.

- You should find that the elements of the array have been saved, even though you closed down the project.

The complete code for the Drama Club project is shown at the chapter end.

■ Chapter end

Full code listing: High Scorers

Here is the complete code listing for the High Scorers project.

Module1

```
Module Module1

    'declare a constant called filename which stores the

    'name and location of the text file

    Public Const filename As String = "C:\Users\Alison\
    highscorers.txt"

End Module
```

frmMain

```
Public Class frmMain

    Private Sub btnWrite_Click(ByVal -

        'write the contents of the text box to the text file

        My.Computer.FileSystem.WriteAllText(filename, txtName.Text
        & vbNewLine, True)

        txtName.Text = ""

    End Sub

    Private Sub btnOutput_Click(ByVal -

        'open the output form

        Me.Hide()

        frmOutput.Show()

    End Sub

    Private Sub btnExit_Click(ByVal -

        'close the project

        End

    End Sub

End Class
```

frmOutput

```
Public Class frmOutput

    Private Sub frmOutput_Load(ByVal -

        'read the contents of the text file to the label lblScorers

        lblScorers.Text = My.Computer.FileSystem.
        ReadAllText(filename)

    End Sub

    Private Sub btnHide_Click(ByVal -

        'Hide the output form

        Me.Hide()

        frmMain.Show()

    End Sub

End Class
```

Full code listing: Drama Club Membership

Here is the complete code listing for the Drama Club project.

```
Public Class Form1

    Const filename As String = "C:\Mydocuments\DramaClub.txt"

    Const club_size As Integer = 3

    Dim Dramaclub(club_size) As String

    Private Sub btnAddMember_Click(ByVal sender As -

        'Input values to the array

        For counter = 0 To club_size

            Dramaclub(counter) = InputBox("Enter pupil name")

        Next

    End Sub

    Private Sub btnListMembers_Click(ByVal sender As -

        'Output values from the array

        For counter = 0 To club_size

            lblClubList.Text = lblClubList.Text & vbNewLine &
            Dramaclub(counter)

        Next

    End Sub
```

```
    Private Sub btnQuit_Click(ByVal sender As -

        End

    End Sub

    Private Sub btnSave_Click(ByVal sender As -

        My.Computer.FileSystem.WriteAllText(filename, "", False)

        For counter = 0 To club_size

            My.Computer.FileSystem.WriteAllText(filename,
            Dramaclub(counter) & ",", True)

        Next

        lblClubList.Text = "Copied to storage"

    End Sub

    Private Sub btnLoad_Click(ByVal sender As -

        Dim temp As String

        temp = My.Computer.FileSystem.ReadAllText(filename)

        Dramaclub = Split(temp, ",")

    End Sub

End Class
```

Overview

In this chapter you learned how to use the Visual Basic commands to work with text files. This means writing content to the file, and reading the saved contents of the file.

- The most appropriate way to do this is to store the file details as a constant and use the constant throughout the project. To make the scope of a constant extend over an entire project it must be declared as a public constant in the project module.
- When writing to a text file there are two options: to append a string to the file, or to overwrite the contents of the file. A Boolean value is used to distinguish between these two options.
- A CSV file can be split up to populate an array.

■ Questions

Answer these questions to demonstrate your learning.

1 What is the main difference between a text file and a word-processed document file?
2 As well as letters of the alphabet, what data can a text file store?
3 What is the difference between appending a string to a text file and overwriting the file? Which option is more suitable for a list of high scorers?
4 What is the command to read the contents of a text file? What is the effect of this command?
5 What is the difference between these commands?

```
Me.Close()

Me.Hide()
```

6 How can you decide whether to declare a constant in the project module or at the top of a form?
7 What is the effect of the following command?

```
lblInformation = My.Computer.FileSystem.ReadAllText(c:\
info.txt)
```

8 What is a CSV file? Why is it more useful than an ordinary text file?
9 Explain the syntax and purpose of the *Split* command.

Further activity

Practice activities can be carried out if you finish the work in this chapter with time to spare. You can also carry out these activities in your own time to help with learning and to improve your skills.

Practice activity: Adapt the high scores project so that the list of high scorers is stored in an array.

Extension activity: Make these changes to the Drama Club project:

- Delete *btnListMembers* and all code that is linked to it.

- Declare a procedure which lists all the elements of the array in *lblClubList*.

- Call this procedure from within the code, so that if the user adds names, saves or loads the array, the elements of the array are listed.

20 Databases

■ Introduction

A program produces output. Unless this output is stored it will be lost when you close the project. A database is a structured collection of stored data. Using a database is the most practical way to save the output from a programming project.

In this chapter you will learn how to use databases to store information that is useful for your computer projects.

■ 20.1 What is a database?

You have learned that a computer is a machine that turns data into information. Data is a general term for facts and figures. Computers process data to make useful information.

One of the ways that computers do this is by organising data into a **database**. A database is a collection of data that relates to a particular task or project and is organised in a structured way. There are specialist software applications that let you make databases and work with the data. This type of software is called a database management system (DBMS), or more commonly just a database system. You may be familiar with Microsoft Access which is a DBMS and is part of the Microsoft Office suite.

In this chapter you will work with an Access database.

A database is a collection of data. The data is organised into one or more tables. A **table** is all of the information about a type of entity. An **entity** can be anything – a person, an object or an event for example. So, a database in a library might contain a table of information about the books. A database in a hospital might contain a table recording details of patients. A database in a travel agent might contain a table recording holiday bookings, and so on.

Learning content

3.1.15 Database concepts: understand the basic concepts of a relational database as a data store; explain the terms 'record', 'field', 'table', 'primary key', 'relationship'.

3.1.15.2 Connecting to databases from applications and web-based apps: be able to use databases from within their own applications.

Key terms

Database   A collection of information stored in a structured and organised way.

Table   Part of a database, storing all of the information about a particular type of entity. It is usually shown in the form of a grid.

Entity   Anything about which you can store data, such as objects, people or events.

Tables, records and fields

A database table holds data about a group of entities (such as objects, people or events). Each entity has its own **record** in the database. A record is all of the information about a single entity.

For example, a social networking site stores information about everyone who signs up to belong to that site. Users have a user name. In this example the user name is one word beginning with @. The database also stores the user's real name, their gender (M or F) and their relationship status (single or attached).

Here is the table that stores this data. It is called the user table.

UserName	Surname	FirstName	Gender	Current status
@SeanyBoy	O'Brien	Sean	M	Single
@TopGirl	Durrant	Tarryn	F	Single
@Batman99	Singh	Manjinder	M	Single
@GagaFan	Billington	Lucy	F	Attached
@MrFixIt	Khan	Ali	M	Attached
@Electrify	Phillips	Shuna	F	Single

Each row of this table represents one record. This table contains six records. Of course in real life, social network sites have literally millions of records, and they store a lot more information than this. This is a simplified made-up example.

Each record contains several items of information. Each item of information is called a **field**. This table has five fields. Every record in the table consists of the same fields in the same order. The fields are shown as columns in the table.

So:

- the rows of the table are records
- the columns of the table are fields.

When you create a data table you have to decide what fields to include. For each field you need to choose a field name and a data type. The field names are shown in the table as the column headings. You learned about the different data types in chapter 7 and you have used them throughout this book.

> **Key term**
>
> **Record**   All of the information about a single entity. Usually shown as one row of a table.

> **Key term**
>
> **Field**   One item of data. Every record in a table has the same fields. Fields are usually shown as the columns of the table. The column heading is the field name.

> **Link**
>
> Data types – chapter 7

One field in each table is the **primary key**. This stores a unique value that identifies each record. There are no duplicates. In this example the user name is the primary key. The user name is different for each user. There may be more than one user with the same real-life name, but each user will have a different user name. When you join the social network you have to pick a unique name. It won't accept a name that is already taken.

In other cases the primary key is a code number that is generated automatically by the database software.

Relational databases

So far you have looked at a simple database with one table. A relational database contains more than one table, and there are links between the tables. The links are called relations.

For example, in the social network database there is a table that stores the messages which users post. Each user can post several messages a day. People can read each other's messages. Here is the table that stores the messages. It is called the Message table. Four messages are shown.

Message code	Date	Time	UserName	Message
1000405	20/01/2014	13:00	@MrFixIt	This snow is never going to stop!
1000406	20/01/2014	13:03	@TopGirl	I've got exams next week. I hope I can get into college.
1000407	20/01/2014	13:03	@MrFixIt	@TopGirl Don't stress about it. I'll give you a lift.
1000408	20/01/2014	13:10	@Batman99	@MrFixIt Yeah, right. If you can get your car to start.

This table has five fields:

- **Message code:** This is the primary key. It is a unique code generated automatically by the software.
- **Date:** This is taken automatically from the system clock.
- **Time:** This is taken automatically from the system clock.
- **UserName:** This is taken from the table of users.
- **Message:** This is the only field the user has to type in by hand.

UserName makes a link between the message table and the user table. A link like this is formed when the key field of one table is used as a field within another table.

UserName	Surname	FirstName	Gender	Current status
@SeanyBoy	O'Brien	Sean	M	Single
@TopGirl	Durrant	Tarryn	F	Single
@Batman99	Singh	Manjinder	M	Single
@GagaFan	Billington	Lucy	F	Attached
@MrFixIt	Khan	Ali	M	Attached
@Electrify	Phillips	Shuna	F	Single

Message code	Date	Time	UserName	Message
1000405	20/01/2014	13:00	@MrFixIt	This snow is never going to stop!
1000406	20/01/2014	13:03	@TopGirl	I've got exams next week. I hope I can get into college.
1000407	20/01/2014	13:03	@MrFixIt	@TopGirl Don't stress about it. I'll give you a lift.
1000408	20/01/2014	13:10	@Batman99	@MrFixIt Yeah, right. If you can get your car to start.

When the key field of one table is used in another table it is called a foreign key.

When a user writes a new message they don't have to give all of their user details. Instead they just enter their unique user name. That is enough to identify them. All of the other information about that user can be found by looking in the user table. This relationship between tables is shown above.

Advantages of relational databases

Imagine if all of the information in the social network database was stored in one big table. All of the information about a user would have to be repeated every time that user created a new message. Instead, the information about users is stored separately in the user table. Whenever that user creates a message, they only need to enter their unique user name and that will identify them and link to their full details.

In a relational database each item of data is stored in only one table – apart from the key fields which are used to make links. Having no repetition in the database has many advantages:

- It saves on storage space.
- It speeds up data entry.
- It reduces the chance of an error.
- If a change is needed, it is made in one place only.

Database programming

You can work directly with databases using DBMS applications such as Access.

You can also work with databases using a programming language such as Visual Basic. Visual Basic can work with single data tables or with relational databases that have many different tables. In this chapter you will work with a single data table. But more advanced database work is common for professional programmers.

Visual Basic allows you to perform many different actions with the database. For example you can:

- look at the data records
- make changes to the data – for example add records or change field contents
- search the database for particular records.

In this chapter you will learn to do all of these things.

■ 20.2 Connect to a data source

In this section you will start a new Visual Basic project and begin the actions that will link it to the database that can be downloaded from the website. This database file is called Social Network Data.

Add new data source

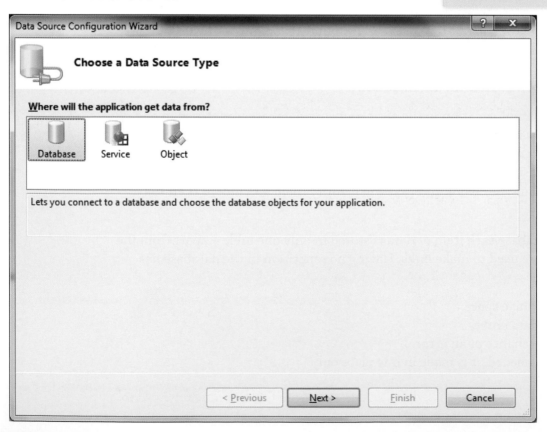

To connect to a database you open the Data menu and select the option Add new data source. This starts a feature called the Data Source Configuration Wizard. This takes you through a series of choices step by step. By making the right choices you can:

- establish a connection to the database
- create a dataset within the program that will hold the database tables and fields.

The wizard is a series of five windows. The first window is shown in the screenshot. This window is called Choose a Data Source Type. When you see this window you need to select the Database option, and then click on the button that says Next.

The next table lists the five windows of the wizard in order. For most of these windows your actions are very straightforward.

Window title	Your actions
Choose a Data Source Type	Select Database and click Next
Choose a Database Model	Select Dataset and click Next
Choose Your Data connection	You need to establish a connection to the Access database. Instructions about how to do this are given below
Save the Connection String	Click Next
Choose Database Objects	Select Tables and click Finish

This chapter will now guide you through the five windows of the Data Source Configuration Wizard. Carry out the activities in order.

Activity Start the wizard

Carry out the following actions to start the Data Source Configuration Wizard:

- Start a new Visual Basic project and call it Social Network.

- Open the Data menu and select Add new data source (see Study tip).

- When you see the first window of the Data Source Configuration Wizard, select Database and click Next.

- The second window is called Choose a Database Model. Select Dataset and click Next.

- The third window is called Choose Your Data Connection. Go to the next section to learn how to do this.

Study tip

If you are using Visual Basic 2012, you will find the command 'Add new data source' on the Project menu, not the Data menu.

Choose your data connection

The third window of the wizard is called Choose Your Data Connection. You need to set up a new connection to the database.

Find a button on the window that says New Connection. If you click on this button you will see a window that lets you choose the database file. You can see this window in the screenshot.

Find the Browse... button. If you click on this button the Browse window opens. The Browse window lets you look through your storage areas to find any file. Using this window you can find the database file called Social Network Data. When you have selected and opened the file, click on OK to create the connection.

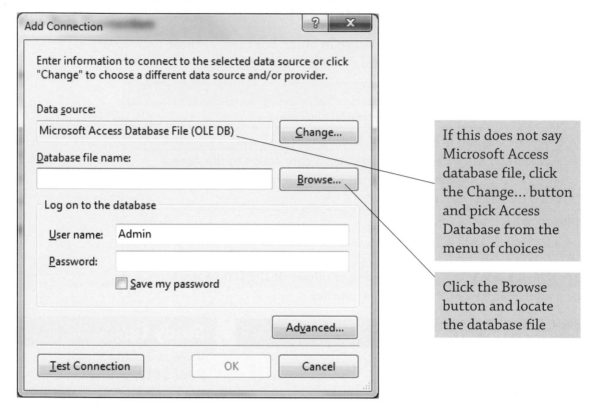

If this does not say Microsoft Access database file, click the Change... button and pick Access Database from the menu of choices

Click the Browse button and locate the database file

A small window may appear, asking whether you want to make a copy of the database. If you have connected to a shared file, then click Yes so that you have your own copy. Otherwise click No.

Activity Add a data connection

The third window is called Choose Your Data Connection. Carry out the following actions to create a data connection to the database:

- Click on New Connection.
- On the Add Connection window click the Browse... button.
- Find the database file, open it and click on OK.
- When the small window appears asking whether you want to make a copy of the database, pick No (unless you have connected to a shared file).
- You have now created a link to the database. Go on to the next section to complete the wizard.

Complete the wizard

You now complete the final two windows of the wizard.

The next window is called Save the Connection String. The connection string is the information that Visual Basic needs to connect to the database. You don't have to do anything with this. Just click Next.

The final screen of the wizard is called Choose Your Database Objects. This window is shown in the screenshot. From this window you pick Tables and you have finished the Data Source Configuration Wizard.

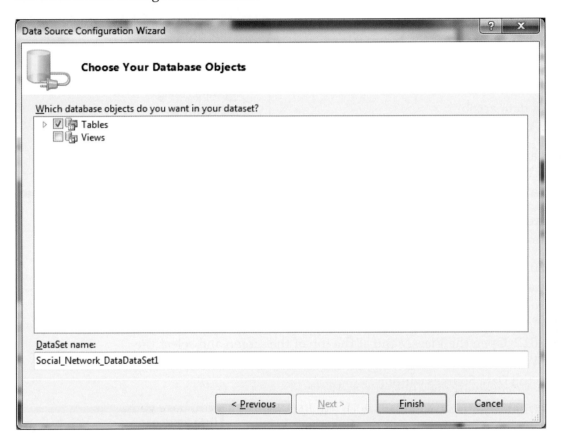

Activity Complete the wizard

Carry out the following actions to complete the Data Source Configuration Wizard:

- On the window called Save the Connection String, click Next.
- On the window called Choose Your Database Objects, select Tables and click Finish.

■ 20.3 Create a form

The database is a very simple one. It contains only one table. In this section you will create a form that lets you view and edit the table and add new records.

Changes to the screen display

The database is now connected to your Visual Basic project. Take a moment to see where it appears on the screen.

The Solution Explorer, at the top right of the screen, shows all the components of the project. You can see this in the next screenshot. Two new components have been added: these are the elements that connect the project to the database.

- Social network data.accdb
- Social_network_dataDataSet.xsd

You don't need to amend these elements in any way.

Open list of data sources

To look at the contents of the database you need to open a new window called Data Sources. The method varies slightly between Visual Basic 2010 and Visual Basic 2012:

- Visual Basic 2010: Look on the left of the screen, where the toolbox is. There are three tabs at the bottom of this part of the screen. These tabs let you select between the toolbox and two other screens called Database Explorer and Data Sources. Select the tab for Data Sources.
- Visual Basic 2012: Open the View Menu at the top of the screen and select the option Other Windows. A list of options opens. Find Data Sources on this list and select it to see the Data Sources window.

The Data Sources window shows the tables which you have loaded. The current database has only one table. It is called User Table. It contains five fields. These correspond to the columns of the table. This is shown in the next screenshot.

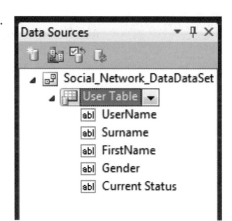

Create a form

It is very easy to create a form that is linked to the database table. You simply drag the table from the Data Sources window to the form. Visual Basic does the rest.

The finished form is shown in the screenshot.

The large object on the form that shows the data table is called the DataGridView. You can drag the sides of the DataGridView and the form. Make them wide enough so that you can see the whole table, as shown in the screenshot on page 237.

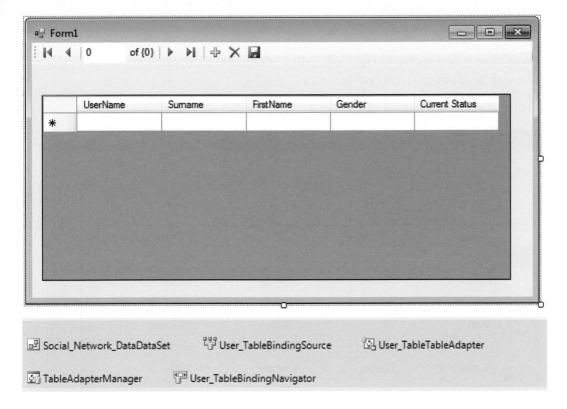

There are two other changes:

- Below the form you can see a range of objects with names like TableAdapterManager. These are components that help the program to connect to the database. They have been added automatically by Visual Basic. You don't have to do anything with these.
- If you look at the code for *Form1*, you will find that a lot of new code has been added. Again, this is added automatically by Visual Basic, and you don't need to do anything with it. Just be careful not to delete or change the code.

Activity Create a data form

Carry out the following actions to create a data input form:

- Drag the User Table onto *Form1*.
- Make the DataGridView and the form wider so you can see the whole table.
- Save the project.
- Go on to the next section to use the form to view and edit the data table.

■ 20.4 Use the form

You have created a form that is connected to the User Table. When you run your project you can view and edit the data in this table.

When you run the project the form will look like this:

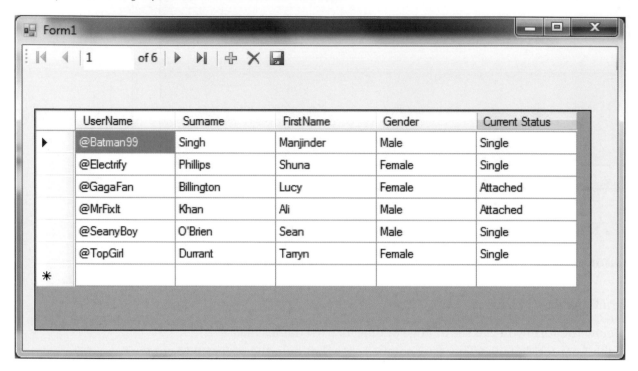

The form displays the complete User Table, with all the records.

The tools at the top of the table let you view and edit the data:

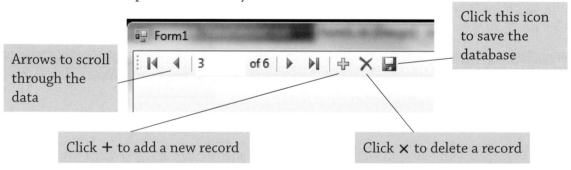

Arrows to scroll through the data

Click this icon to save the database

Click **+** to add a new record

Click **×** to delete a record

Activity Use the data form

- Run the project using Debug.

- Use the data form to make any changes you like to the records in the User Table.

- You may like to add records, perhaps adding yourself and your classmates to the table. Remember to give each user a unique user name.

- Click the icon to save the data to the database.

■ Chapter end

Overview

In this chapter you learned how to link a Visual Basic project to an Access database, and how to use a Visual Basic form to view and edit the records in a database.

You learned the meaning of key database terms such as 'table', 'record' and 'field'. You learned about the structure of a database, and about the use of a primary key to identify records. You learned that a relational database is made when the primary key from one table is used in another to link them together.

■ Questions

Answer these questions to demonstrate your learning.

1 What is a primary key and why is it needed in a database table?
2 A Hotel has 40 rooms where guests can stay. What information would the hotel store about each room? Design a database table to store this data. Remember to include a key field which uniquely identifies each room.
3 The hotel also stores information about all the guests who have stayed at the hotel or made bookings. Design a database table to store information about guests. Remember to include a key field.
4 The hotel manager needs to store information about room bookings. For this reason he adds another table to the database. The new table stores the date of the booking, the room number and the guest. Design this table.
5 Explain how foreign keys are used to link the booking table to the room table and the guest table.
6 A principle of good database design is to store each item of information once only. Explain the advantages of this approach.

Further activity

Practice activities can be carried out if you finish the work in this chapter with time to spare. You can also carry out these activities in your own time to help with learning and to improve your skills.

Extension activity: In section 16.7 you learned how to print out a form. Add a button to *Form1* that will print out the form.

Extension activity: Carry out the following activity if you know how to create an Access database.

In chapter 13 you created a data structure to store information about pets for a veterinary practice. Look back at this chapter to remind yourself about the items of data that were included in the data structure.

- Create an Access database with a single table that stores pet records.

- Link this to a Visual Basic project and create an input form that lets you view and edit pet records.

21 Database queries

Introduction

In the last chapter you created a project that was linked to a database. Using the form you could view and edit the database records. In this chapter you will learn how to use search criteria to extract records and fields from the database. The SQL language is used to create database queries and you will learn to create SQL queries to find information in a database.

Learning content

3.1.1 Constants variables and data types: be able to use NOT, AND and OR when creating Boolean expressions.

3.1.15 Database concepts: explain the terms 'query', 'index' and 'search criteria'; be able to create simple SQL statements to extract, add and edit data stored in databases; have experience of using SQL statements.

21.1 Database queries

A **database query** is a command that extracts data from a database. A large database may have thousands or even millions of records. You rarely want to see all of the records in a database. A query lets you pick out just some of this data:

- You can pick out records from a table according to a search criterion.
- You can choose to see only some of the fields in the table.
- You can sort the records into order, such as alphabetical order.
- Some queries also display summary data such as totals and averages.

Key term

Database query   A command which extracts data from a database. It finds records that match a search condition.

The SQL language

In this chapter you will learn how to create queries using SQL. SQL stands for Structured Query Language. It is pronounced 'sequel'. SQL is a different programming language to Visual Basic. It is used to work with databases.

When you are typing SQL commands it doesn't matter whether you use upper- or lower-case letters. But by convention, SQL commands are given in UPPER CASE. Names of tables and fields and other items are given in lower case.

If a field name or table name has more than one word in it, like [User Table], you have to put it in square brackets.

SQL queries

With SQL you can write short commands called 'queries'. A SQL query tells the computer what data you want to see. The computer will find that data in the database and display it.

You can select which fields in the database you want to see. For example, you might only want to see the field showing Firstname. The SQL command for that is:

```
SELECT Firstname from [User Table]
```

You can find particular records or groups of records in the table. For example, you might only want to see the names of first names of male users. The command for that is:

```
SELECT FirstName FROM [User Table]

WHERE Gender = "M"
```

You will learn how to create SQL queries in this chapter.

■ 21.2 Common SQL commands

This section describes some commonly used commands in SQL. Using these you can create a wide range of database queries. You can specify which fields and records you want to select from the database.

Selecting fields

The SELECT statement is used to extract records from a database. The results are stored in a new table called the result-set. The following SQL statement will select all of the records in the User Table:

```
SELECT * FROM [User Table]
```

The asterisk (*) stands for 'everything'. So this statement tells the computer: 'Select everything from User Table'.

Sometimes you don't want to select everything, you just want to select particular fields from the table. The following SQL statement will select just UserName from the table:

```
SELECT UserName FROM [User Table]
```

If you want to select more than one field, give the field names in order, separated by commas. For example:

```
SELECT UserName, Gender FROM [User Table]
```

This will list the username and gender from the user table.

Search for records

You have learned that a data query finds records that match a search criterion. In SQL the word WHERE is used to search for records.

WHERE and SELECT are used together. For example, to select the UserName of male users:

```
SELECT UserName FROM [User Table]

WHERE Gender = "M"
```

As you can see from this example, it is all right to split a SQL statement over more than one line. The name of the search string is given inside double quotation marks.

Relational operators

Link

Relational operators – chapter 9

The search criterion in the previous example was:

    Gender = "M"

This example of a search criterion uses the equals sign. The equals sign is a relational operator that finds exact matches. Relational operators are used to compare two values. In the example given, the equals sign is used to compare the Gender field of each record with the string M. The records where there is an exact match are selected.

There are several relational operators. The most common are:

Relational operator	Meaning
=	Equal to
<>	Not equal to
>	More than
<	Less than

The operators = (equal) and <> (not equal) can be used to search for either string values or numerical values.

The operators > (more than) and < (less than) can only be used with numerical values. They will search for records where numerical values are greater or smaller than the search condition.

Where a string is used in a search criterion it is enclosed in quotation marks. Where a value is used it is not put in quotation marks.

■ 21.3 Create a query

In this section you will create a simple query to extract data from the Social Network database. In this example you will create a query that extracts the records of users who are single.

Create a query

The Social Network database is displayed on *Form1* as a table. A table like this is called a DataGridView. Before you begin to create a query you must click on the DataGridView on *Form1*. The query will be attached to this data grid. The results of the query will be displayed in the data grid.

On the Data menu there is an option called Add Query. If you select Add Query a new window will open called Search Criteria Builder. You can use this window to define SQL search criteria. This window is shown in the screenshot on page 243.

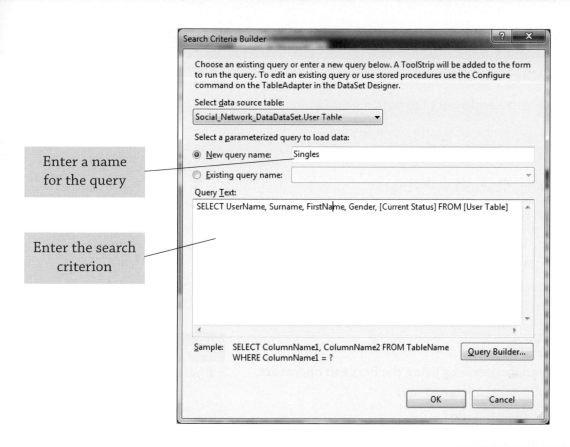

Enter a name for the query

Enter the search criterion

You must enter a name for the query. This example is called Singles. The next step is to add a search criterion that finds all of the records where the current status is Single.

The computer has started to create a SQL query. The content has been generated automatically. It looks like this:

```
SELECT UserName, Surname, FirstName, Gender,
[Current Status] FROM [User Table]
```

This query selects all the fields in the User Table. Now you can amend the query so that it will only show the records of people who are single. You need to add the following additional line to the query:

```
WHERE [Current Status] = "Single"
```

When you click on OK, a new tool is added to *Form1*. It has the title Singles. When you run the project, you can click on this tool and it will restrict the data table to only those records that match the criteria.

Study tip

Some versions of Visual Basic do not include a Data menu. If you do not see a Data menu, here is another way to make a query. Below the form are several database objects. See the screenshot on page 237 to remind yourself what they look like. One of the objects is a 'table adapter'. In this example it is called User_TableTableAdapter. Move the mouse pointer to this object. Right click on the object. A small menu appears. Pick `Add query' from the menu.

Activity Create a query

- Select the DataGridView on *Form1*.

- Open the Data Menu and select the option Add Query.

- Next to New query name enter the name Singles.

- Add a line to the query text that says:

  WHERE [Current Status] = "Single"

- Click on the OK button to save the new query.

- Run the project. The word 'Singles' appears at the top of *Form1*. Click on this word to carry out the saved query. The computer will display all the records with the status Single.

- Save the project.

Boolean operators

You can combine search criteria by using the **Boolean operators**. The most common Boolean operators are:

          AND   OR   NOT

These terms are used to combine criteria. The meaning of the terms is similar to their normal use in everyday language.

The Boolean operator AND combines two criteria, and only finds records where both criteria are true. Here is an example:

          SELECT * FROM [User Table]

          WHERE Gender = "M" AND [Current Status] = "Single"

This example will find all records where the gender is M and current status is single.

The Boolean operator OR finds records where one or both of the criteria are true. Here is an example:

          SELECT * FROM [User Table]

          WHERE FirstName = "Sam" OR FirstName = "Samantha"

This example will print out the full details of all users with the first name Sam or Samantha.

The Boolean operator NOT finds records that do not match a particular criterion. Here is an example:

          SELECT FirstName, Surname FROM [User Table]

          WHERE NOT Surname = "O'Brien"

This search criterion will list the names of all users except those with the surname O'Brien.

Key terms

Boolean operators
  Operators that produce a single Boolean value by transforming one or more Boolean values.

Study tip

Boolean operators are also called logical operators.

Study tip

The search criteria on either side of the Boolean operator can use the same field or different fields. In either case, state the search criteria in full.

Sorting

You can also use SQL statements to sort the output into order. Any field in the table can be used to sort the table. The ORDER BY keyword is used to sort the output. It can be added to the SELECT command.

```
SELECT FirstName, Surname FROM [User Table]

ORDER BY Surname
```

This will show the names of all users sorted in alphabetical order. If you use a string field the records will be sorted in alphabetical order. If you use a number field the records will be sorted in numerical order.

The records will be sorted in ascending order. If you want to sort the records in reverse or descending order, add the word DESC at the end of the command.

```
SELECT Title FROM tblBook

ORDER BY Title DESC
```

Indexes

An index can be added to a SQL table. Computer users cannot see the index, but it speeds up searches and queries. An index uses one field in the table. An index makes it quicker for the computer to find matches using that field.

There are advantages and disadvantages to using indexes with your tables:

- Searches for data work much faster if the table has an index.
- The index takes up some computer resources.
- Updating the table with new data will be slightly slower if there is an index.

These are important considerations for professional database developers who might be working with database tables containing thousands or even millions of records. For your starter projects, indexes will not make a big difference to speed or efficiency.

The SQL statement to create an index is:

```
CREATE INDEX indexname ON table (column)
```

Instead of the lower-case words in this example, add the names of a table and a column from your database. Give the index a suitable name.

Here is an example:

```
CREATE INDEX ndxSurname ON [User Table] (Surname)
```

This command creates an index in Surname order.

Combining SQL statements

You can create long commands by adding several SQL statements together. For example, you could select particular fields, use a search criterion and sort the results into order.

Here is an example:

```
SELECT FirstName, Surname FROM [User Table]

WHERE FirstName = "Sam" OR FirstName = "Samantha"

ORDER BY Surname
```

Can you tell what this query does?

Activity SQL statements

Here is an example of a database table. It is called tblSavings.

SavingsCode	Surname	FirstName	AmountSaved
S0056	Brown	Judith	245.50
S0057	Harris	Tom	620.00
S0058	Bains	Sandeep	350.10
S0059	Wittington	Lionel	100.00

The following questions relate to this example table.

1 What data would be output by the following SQL statements?

   a SELECT Surname, AmountSaved FROM tblSavings

   b SELECT Surname FROM tblSavings WHERE AmountSaved > 300

   c SELECT * FROM tblSavings WHERE Firstname = "Judith"

2 The following SQL statements have errors in them. Write the corrected version of each command.

   a SELECT AmountSaved WHERE AmountSaved > 100

   b SELECT * FROM tblSavings WHERE Surname = "Bains" OR "Harris"

   c SELECT SavingsCode FROM tblSavings ORDER "AmountSaved"

3 Create SQL statements that will produce the results described:

   a An index for the table that uses the field SavingsCode (you can decide for yourself what the name of the index should be).

   b A list of surnames and first names, sorted in order of the amount saved.

   c All details of savers with the surname Brown and savings of more than 500 (this command will produce no matches).

■ Chapter end

Overview

In this chapter you learned how to use the SQL language to create database queries.

- You learned how to select fields, search for records that matched a criteria, and sort the output into alphabetical or numerical order.
- You learned about the relational operators that are used to create search criteria.
- You learned about the Boolean operators that are used to combine search criteria.

■ Questions

Answer these questions to demonstrate your learning.

1 What is the purpose of a database query?
2 How are square brackets [ ] used in SQL?
3 How are double quotation marks used in SQL?
4 Give the symbol and meaning of three common relational operators.
5 Explain how relational operators are used to define search criteria.
6 Give the SQL statement to sort a table called tblCars using a field called CarType.
7 What are the three main Boolean operators?
8 What does this SQL statement do?

```
SELECT JobTitle FROM tblJobs WHERE Salary > 10000
```

9 What are the advantages and disadvantages of using an index when searching through a database?
10 In what circumstances would a database developer be most likely to use an index?

Further activity

Practice activities can be carried out if you finish the work in this chapter with time to spare. You can also carry out these activities in your own time to help with learning and to improve your skills.

Practice activity: Continue to work with the Social Networks project. Create a range of queries for *Form1*. Here are some suggestions:

- Create a query called Show all, which shows all the records in the table.
- Create a query called Show names, which shows the first and second name of all records.
- Create a query called Male, which shows the user name of all the male users.
- Create a query called Single girls, which shows the first name and surname of all users who are female and single.

You may have to resize *Form1* and move the DataGridView to make room for the new queries at the top of the form. Run the project to test the queries.

22 Debugging your code

■ Introduction

In this book you have carried out a series of programming projects. As you complete projects you debug them to detect and remove errors. In this chapter you will learn about more advanced methods for finding and correcting errors at every stage of the programming process.

■ 22.1 The programming process

To understand how errors occur in programming, you need to understand how programs are created and made ready to use. The part of a computer system that carries out processing is called the CPU. The CPU only understands instructions that are in the form of an electronic number code called machine code.

Nowadays programmers hardly ever prepare instructions for the CPU by writing machine code. Instead programmers write the instructions in a programming language. There are many different programming languages. Before the CPU can carry out the instructions they must be converted from the programming language into machine code. This is called compiling the code.

When you **compile** a program the computer converts the program into machine code and stores it. There are several ways to do this in Visual Basic:

- When you run Debug the compiled code is executed (carried out) straight away so that you can see the effect and spot any errors.
- The *Build* and *Publish* commands are used to compile finished projects and to create software application files that can be shared with users.

A Visual Basic programmer will use Debug to check the way a program works and to make improvements. This is essential for the testing process. Only when testing is complete will the programmer release the file to the user.

■ 22.2 Detecting errors

It is common and normal for computer programs to have errors while they are being developed. All programmers, including

Learning content

3.1.6 Error handling: know how to test your code for errors; know how to detect errors from within code; be able to use trace tables to check code for errors; know how to recover from errors within code; understand that computer programs can be developed with tools to help the programmer detect and deal with errors, for example watch, breakpoint, step).

3.1.5 Scope of variables: identify what value a variable will hold at a given point in the code.

Key term

Compile   Convert a complete program to machine code.

Link

Build and release an application – chapter 27

professionals, make errors at some stage in their work. These errors must be detected and removed so that the program can work properly.

The Visual Basic interface provides several helpful ways to spot any errors in your programs. It also offers advice about how to correct the error. In this chapter you will learn more about how to find and correct errors.

You have learned that there are three types of error:

- **Syntax errors** are errors that break the rules of the programming language. This includes mistyping key words and putting words in the wrong order. These errors prevent the computer from turning the program into machine code.
- **Run-time errors** are errors that occur when the computer tries to run the machine code. Sometimes this is because the input data causes an error. For example, a variable may be integer data type, and the user tries to enter a string.
- **Logic errors** occur when the machine code runs without problems, but it doesn't do what you want it to do. These errors are harder to spot. For example, a payroll program might add tax to pay instead of taking it away. Programs must be tested to spot and correct logic errors.

In this chapter you will look at two important ways to find and correct errors:

- error warnings and messages that appear as you write the code
- structured error handling during debugging.

The third important way to detect errors is to thoroughly test your program. Testing is covered in chapter 26.

> **Link**
>
> Testing – chapter 26

■ 22.3 Warnings and error messages

As you are writing code, if the Visual Basic IDE spots a problem it will underline the code with a wavy line. The colour of the underlining tells you the type of problem. There are two main types of underlining in Visual Basic: green and blue. Green underlining is for a warning. Blue underlining is for a mistake.

Warnings

Green underlining gives you a warning. The underlining is accompanied by a warning message. For example, if you declare a variable but you have not used it in the program, then the variable declaration will be underlined with a green wavy line.

The screenshot shows an example of this. The user has declared a variable called *Counter* but has not yet used that variable in the program code.

The computer also displays a warning message at the bottom of the screen.

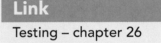

```
Public Class Form1

    Private Sub Button1_Click(ByVal sender As Syste
        Dim Counter As Integer

    End Sub
End Class
```

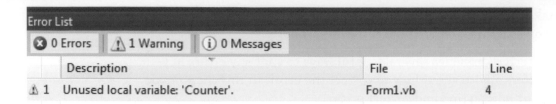

Note that even if this warning is ignored, the program will still compile into machine code. A variable has been declared and not used, but that will not stop the program from working.

Error messages

Blue underlining marks a more serious error that will prevent the program code from compiling into machine code. Blue underlining is accompanied by an error message at the bottom of the screen.

In this example the programmer has mistyped the word 'integer'. The mistyped word is underlined:

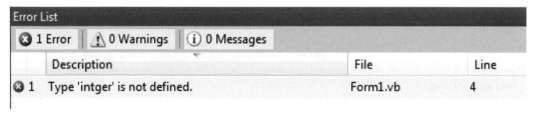

and an error message is seen at the bottom of the screen:

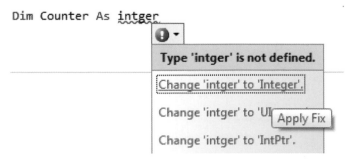

Notice that the error message has explained the problem and said what line of the code has the problem.

There is another helpful feature: if you move the mouse to the underlined word, you will see a red exclamation mark. If you click on that, you will see a drop-down list of suggested fixes for the error.

The first of these fixes is to change the word *intger* to *Integer*. This is the right solution, and if you select it the computer will apply the fix and correct the code.

You must correct all errors that are underlined in blue or the program will not compile into machine code.

Activity Error messages

- Pay careful attention to error messages in all programming projects. Although green warning messages will not prevent your program from running, they should not be ignored.

- To practice finding and removing errors from code, look at the examples of 'deliberate mistakes' on the website which accompanies this book. Find and correct the errors.

■ 22.4 Run-time errors

Debugging is the stage in project development when the lines of program code are converted into machine code and executed (carried out) by the CPU. Debugging is used to detect errors in the program before final compilation.

Further coding errors may be revealed during debugging. They are called run-time errors.

Some run-time errors in a program are caused when input values do not match the data type of the variable used to store the input. For example, a program asked users to input how many children they had. The value was assigned to a variable called *HowManyChildren*.

A user meant to enter the number zero (0) but typed the letter 'o' by mistake. This produced a run-time error. The debug process paused and an error message appeared on the screen. This is what the error message looked like:

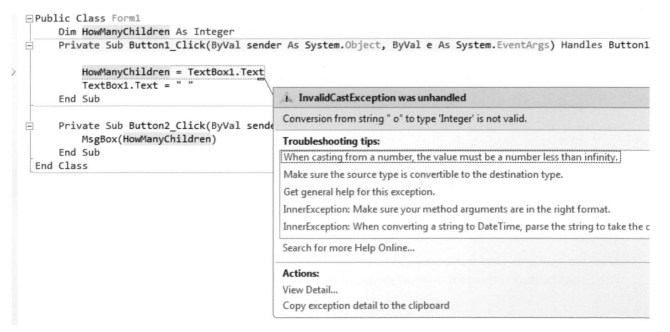

The main error message says 'InvalidCastException was unhandled'. This is not very helpful. However, under that message you can see an explanation: 'Conversion from string " o" to type 'Integer' is not valid.'

This is a helpful message. It clearly explains what the problem is. The letter 'o' cannot be stored as an *Integer* data type.

Below the error message are some troubleshooting tips. The second of the troubleshooting tips gives a good solution to this problem: 'Make sure the source type is convertible to the destination type.'

To avoid this problem you can use a Visual Basic function called *IsNumeric()*. This function tests a value and returns a True/False answer. If the value is numeric, the answer is True, if the value is not numeric, the answer is False.

You can use this function within an *If...Then* statement like this:

```
If IsNumeric(TextBox1.Text) Then

    HowManyChildren = TextBox1.Text

    TextBox1.Text = ""

End If
```

The contents of *TextBox1* is only copied to the variable **if** the value is numeric.

To improve the code even further, use an *If...Then...Else* statement to give an error message if a non-numeric value is entered. Here is the complete code

```
Private Sub btnOK_Click(ByVal sender As System.Object, ByVal e As System.EventArgs) Handles btnOK.Click

    If IsNumeric(TextBox1.Text) Then

        HowManyChildren = TextBox1.Text

        TextBox1.Text = ""

    Else

        MsgBox("Please enter a numerical value")

    End If

End Sub
```

Activity Run-time errors

- Create a project with one form. Users are asked to enter into a text box the number of children that they have.

- Add two buttons. One button assigns the contents of the text box to an integer variable. The other button displays the value stored in the variable using a message box.

- Debug and save the program. Enter a non-numeric string in the text box and notice the run-time error message.

- Use the *IsNumeric()* function to prevent this run-time error.

- Debug and save the improved program.

- Test the program by entering various values and strings into the text box.

■ 22.5 Debugging tools: step through

Sometimes it is harder to spot the error that has occurred or to see how to fix it. Visual Basic offers two very useful debugging tools to help programmers find and correct the errors in their code. These are:

- **step through**
- breakpoint.

Programming problem – calculate factorials

In this section we will look at a simple programming problem. This is a program to calculate the factorial of any number.

> **Key term**
>
> **Step through**   To execute a program one line at a time, observing the results at each step.

The factorial of a number is the result of multiplying together all of the numbers from 1 to that number. The symbol for factorial is an exclamation mark.

Here are some examples

$$3! = 1 \times 2 \times 3 = 6$$

$$4! = 1 \times 2 \times 3 \times 4 = 24$$

$$5! = 1 \times 2 \times 3 \times 4 \times 5 = 120$$

So the value of 5 factorial is 120. This is written as:

$$5! = 120$$

A student tried to write a program that calculated the factorial of any number. The screenshot shows the user interface.

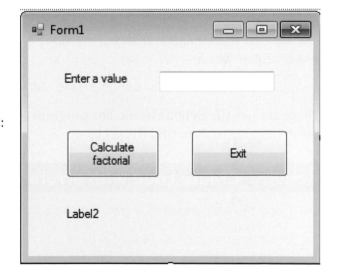

Here is the code which goes with that user interface. It has several errors in it.

```
Public Class Form1

    Dim n As Integer

    Dim result As Integer = 1
```

```
Private Sub btnShow_Click(ByVal sender As -

    Dim counter As Integer

    n = TextBox1.Text

    For counter = 1 To n

        result = result * n

    Next

    Label2.Text = Str(n) & "! = " & Str(result)

End Sub

Private Sub btnOK_Click(ByVal sender As -

    End

End Sub
```

End Class

> WARNING: This program has deliberate errors in it. Do not use it as an example of correct programming.

This code compiled without problems and there were no run-time errors. However, when the number 5 was entered in the text box, instead of the correct result:

        5! = 120

the result was:

        5! = 3125

The student tried it again, entering the value 3 in the text box. This time the answer was given as:

        3! = 84375

These are not the right answers. The program was not working, so the student used the debugging tools to find the problem.

Activity Create code with errors

- Copy the user interface shown in this section.

- Enter the program code shown here.

- Run the program, and enter different values to see the incorrect results that it produces.

- Save the code.

Step through

Step through is a way of controlling the execution of the code during debugging. The first line of code is carried out, then the program pauses and waits for the user signal, then the next line is carried out and the program pauses again. There is a pause after every line. This gives you a chance to check that every line works properly.

Step through is even more useful when it is combined with the Watch tool. 'Watch' lists the value of every variable so that you can see how the values change as the program code is run.

To start step through, open the Debug menu on the menu bar at the top of the program. This menu is shown in the screenshot.

Step Into is an option on this menu. Selecting this option will start the step through. The Step Into symbol is also found as an icon on the toolbar. You can click this icon instead of using the Debug menu.

The first line of the program is carried out and the program halts like this. The yellow arrow shows where you have got to in the program.

If you click on Step Into again, the program will go to the next line and so on. When you get to the line that requires user input, the interface will appear so you can enter a value.

You can step through the whole program line by line.

The Watch window

There are three variables in this program:

- *n*
- *result*
- *counter*.

Now you will use the Watch window to see the value of each variable as you step through the program:

- Open the Debug menu and begin step through.
- Open the Debug menu again and select the first option on the menu, Windows.
- On the small menu that opens, select the option Watch.

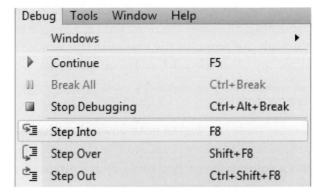

Study tip

Pressing the F8 key (F11 key in Visual Basic 2012) on your keyboard is another way to step through the program.

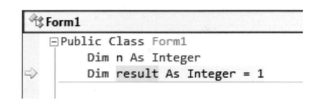

Study tip

If you open the Debug menu when you are not doing step through you will not see the Windows option.

A small Watch window appears at the bottom of the screen, below the program code. Type the names of the three variables into this window. It will look like this:

Watch			
Name	Value		Type
n	0		Integer
result	0		Integer
counter	'counter' is not declared. It may be inaccessible due to its protection level.		

As *counter* is a local variable declared within the *btnOK_Click* procedure, the program does not recognise it yet. As you step through the program the values in this window will change to show the value of each variable at each step.

Study tip

Use pseudocode or a flowchart to plan and set out the algorithm for this program code.

Trace table

A trace table is a way to note down the value of each variable at each step of a program. It is a way to record the results of the step-through process. A trace table has a column for each variable in the program, and a row for every step as you step through the program.

Here is a trace table for this program with the first few lines filled in. In this example the user entered the number 4.

Step	n	result	counter
1	0	0	n/a
2	0	1	n/a
3	4	1	0
4	4	1	1
5	4	4	1
6			

Activity Step through

- Use step through and Watch to trace the values of the variables used in this program.

- Enter an input value and trace the values of all variables.

- Create a trace table showing the values at each stage of the program.

- If you can see how to improve the program code to give a more accurate result, make that change now (if you can't see how to make improvements go on to the next section).

- Save the project.

■ 22.6 Debugging tools: breakpoint

As a result of tracing the values of the variables the student was able to improve the program. The new program code looked like this:

```
Public Class Form1

    Dim n As Integer

    Dim result As Integer = 1

    Private Sub btnOK_Click(ByVal sender As –

        Dim counter As Integer
```

```
    n = TextBox1.Text
    For counter = 1 To n
        result = result * counter
    Next
    Label2.Text = Str(n) & "! = " & Str(result)
End Sub
Private Sub btnShow_Click(ByVal sender As –
    End
End Sub
End Class
```

When the student ran the program it calculated the first factorial correctly. However, if the student entered further values the results were always wrong.

For this reason the student wanted to continue debugging, this time using the **breakpoint** method.

Key term

Breakpoint   A point in a program where the execution will pause so the programmer can observe results.

Breakpoint

The step through process is useful, but it takes a long time. You have to step through every line of the program one line at a time. The example program shown here has a loop in it, so there are a lot of repetitions. It takes a long time to go through the whole program.

The breakpoint method allows you to set one or more breakpoints. The debug process runs automatically without stopping until it reaches the breakpoint. Then it pauses. You can note the values of variables in the Watch window. You can write them down in a trace table. Then press Debug again and the program continues until it reaches another breakpoint.

To enter a breakpoint you go to the line in the code where you want to place a breakpoint. Then you open the Debug menu and select Toggle Breakpoint. The screenshot shows the program code with a single breakpoint entered.

```
Public Class Form1
    Dim n As Integer
    Dim result As Integer = 1

    Private Sub Button1_Click(ByVal sender As Sys
        Dim counter As integer
        n = TextBox1.Text
        For counter = 1 To n
            result = result * n
        Next
        Label2.Text = Str(n) & "! = " & Str(resul
    End Sub

    Private Sub Button2_Click(ByVal sender As Sys
        End
    End Sub

End Class
```

Debug with breakpoint

Once the breakpoint is entered you can start Debug.

- Click the Debug tool on the toolbar.

The program code will run as usual until it reaches the breakpoint. Then it will stop.

- Note the values of the variables as shown in the Watch window.
- Press the Debug tool to continue.

The student carried out the debug using the breakpoint shown above, entering the values 5, 3 and 2 in turn.

This was what the trace table looked like after these three calculations.

Breakpoint	n	result	counter
1	5	1	0
2	3	3125	0
3	2	84375	0

As you can see, the result field gets larger and larger each time. Looking at this the student realised what the mistake in the program was. The *result* variable was not reset to 1 between calculations, so it kept getting bigger.

The student changed the code so that the variable *result* was reset to 1 at the start of each calculation. The corrected program code is shown at the end of this chapter.

Remove breakpoints

When you have successfully debugged your program you will need to remove the breakpoints that you added. If you open the Debug menu you will see that Delete Breakpoints is a menu option.

Activity Breakpoint

- Enter a breakpoint as shown in this chapter and debug the program.

- Create a trace table as shown here.

- If you know how to correct the program so that it works properly, make the changes.

- Run Debug again to see if your changes have fixed the problem.

- Save the code.

■ Chapter end

Code listing

Here is the corrected code for the factorial program described in this chapter.

```
Public Class Form1
    'declare variables
    Dim n As Integer
    Dim result As Integer

    Private Sub btnShow_Click(ByVal sender As -
        Dim counter As Integer
        'reset 'result' to 1
        result = 1

        'input number to use for factorial
        n = TextBox1.Text

        'multiply 'result' by all numbers from 1 to n
        For counter = 1 To n
            result = result * counter
        Next

        'output result
        Label2.Text = Str(n) & "! = " & Str(result)
    End Sub

    Private Sub btnOK_Click(ByVal sender As -
        End
    End Sub

End Class
```

Pseudocode

Here is a pseudocode version of the factorial program.

```
n ← USERINPUT
    result ← 1
```

```
    FOR counter ← 1 TO n
        result ← result * counter
    ENDFOR
OUTPUT result
```

Overview

In this chapter you learned about the tools that are provided with Visual Basic to find and correct errors in programs.

- You learned that the code editor adds underlining to alert you to syntax errors. It also provides an error message and suggests corrections.
- You learned that the Debug tool halts execution when there is a run-time error. When the program stops, an error message appears with suggestions about what the problem is and how to correct it.
- You learned how to use step through and breakpoint to go slowly through a program as it executes. You created trace tables to show the values of variables at each stage of program execution.

■ Questions

Answer these questions to demonstrate your learning.

1 As well as syntax errors, what are the main types of coding error?
2 Why does a program need to be compiled before it can be executed?
3 A variable called *age* was declared as integer data type. The user entered the value *twenty* into this variable. Why did this cause a run-time error?
4 Explain what function you could use to avoid this error.
5 What happens when you run the step through feature?
6 What is the advantage of using breakpoint rather than step through when debugging a program?
7 What is shown in the Watch window?
8 Explain what a trace table is and how it can help you to debug a program.

Further activity

Practice activities can be carried out if you finish the work in this chapter with time to spare. You can also carry out these activities in your own time to help with learning and to improve your skills.

Practice activity:

1 Create a program that allows the user to enter a series of ten values and outputs the largest value in the list.

2 Run the program using Debug and enter ten values. Use step through to create a trace table showing the value of all variables at each step of this program.

3 Now add a single breakpoint at a suitable point in the program. Run Debug and create a trace table showing the value of the variables each time the program reaches the breakpoint.

23 External code sources

Introduction

You do not need to develop every piece of code in your projects from scratch. Examples of ready-made code and working software are available for public use. Professional programmers use external code sources to speed up their work and to make the most of programming techniques developed by others. In this short chapter you will learn how to use code developed by other people to enhance your projects.

Learning content

3.1.14 Use of external code sources: know of the existence of external code sources; know how to integrate code from these sources; be able to explain the advantages and disadvantages of using such sources.

23.1 Helpful advice and examples

You can find helpful advice and examples of Visual Basic code in books and on the Internet. There are many websites where Visual Basic programmers discuss program code and share examples of code. In general, professional programmers remember when they were learners, and they want to encourage young people who are keen to develop their skills.

Online you may find:

- discussions between experts about tricky programming problems
- questions posted by beginners with answers from more experienced programmers
- samples of working code
- educational sites to support learners.

If you are stuck when developing code you may find that Internet research will help you. It can be difficult to find a site with advice at the right level. Some sites are suitable for learners while others are aimed at experts.

Samples provided online or in books will need to be adapted for your own programming projects. You may have to change the names of variables and objects in the sample code to match the names you have used within your project.

Remember that you should always understand why and how a code sample works, rather than simply cutting and pasting it into your project. If you cut and paste without understanding, you are quite likely to find that the code sample does not work properly.

Unfortunately there are also sites that offer code which is not safe or suitable. If you are copying and pasting code in plain text form then the risk is minimised. Before using it, read the code for yourself and check that it is all right.

To be on the safe side:

- only use code from recognised sources with a good reputation
- only insert code into your program if you understand what it does and how it works.

Activity Sources of advice

- Look in your school or college library to find out what books are available to support Visual Basic code development.

- Search online for sites that provide advice which is helpful for beginners learning to program.

- As a class, compile a short list of recommended books and websites.

■ 23.2 Insert code snippet

Visual Basic has a code library called IntelliSense Code Snippets. This is a collection of ready-made code samples. A **snippet** is a little piece of code that performs a single task. You can insert a snippet into your project.

Each snippet performs a programming task. Examples include:

- sending an e-mail message
- including graphics in the screen display
- error handling.

Code snippets are available via the text editor that you use to write code.

Snippets can help you to develop good programming code. But there are two challenges when using code snippets in your own work:

- finding the right snippet to meet your current programming needs
- adapting the snippet to fit in with your program code.

In general it is best to learn the basics of coding before you start to use snippets.

How to insert a snippet

To insert a code snippet into your code:

- In the code editor, make sure the cursor is in the spot where you want to insert the code snippet.
- Right-click the mouse and then select the Insert Snippet command on the shortcut menu.
- Find a code snippet from those available.
- Press Enter to insert it into your code.

The collection of snippets is shown in the screenshot.

Key term

Snippet A code fragment that the user can insert into a program and adapt to their needs.

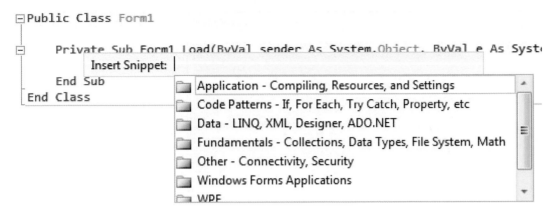

You can see that snippets are arranged into categories. There are seven categories including Application, Data and Fundamentals. Within each of those main categories there are further subcategories. Click on any category to see the snippets that are available.

How to adapt the snippet to your code

The code in each snippet is just a basic outline. Usually you will need to make changes to the code. For example, you may need to change the names of variables in the snippet to match the variables in your program, or set a string to show the location of a text file on your own computer.

The places where you may want to make changes are called replacement points. If you rest the mouse pointer over a replacement point you will see a short note explaining what information is needed.

Snippets from the Internet

Code snippets are also available on the Internet. Some are provided by experienced programmers to help other programmers. Some may be from unreliable sources. It is possible that these code snippets could cause security problems for your computer. Sometimes they have hidden computer viruses. Be very careful before using a code snippet imported from a website. It may be best to stick to snippets provided within the Visual Basic programming environment.

Example: random number

A student decided to create a maths quiz game based on random numbers.

The game would work like this:

- The computer generates two random numbers between 1 and 12.
- The computer shows the two random numbers as a multiplication question.
- The user enters an answer to the question.
- The computer says whether the answer is right or wrong.

The screenshot shows the interface the student designed. When the user clicks on *btnQuestion*, a new question is generated and displayed as the text of *lblQuestion*.

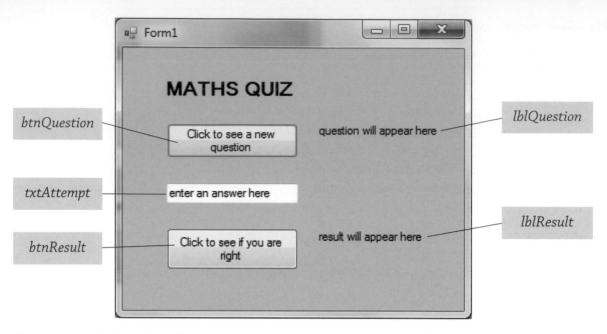

The student double-clicked on *btnQuestion* to begin coding. The first thing that needed to be done was to generate two random numbers.

Here is how the student found the code to generate a random number:

- Right-click the mouse button.
- Select Insert Snippet from the menu.
- Select Fundamentals and then Math.

A list of maths snippets appears. The screenshot shows that 'Get a random number' is on the list of snippets.

```
Private Sub Button1 Click(ByVal sender As System.Object, ByVal e As System.EventArgs) Handl
        Fundamentals - Collections, Data Types, File System, Math  >  Math  >
End Sub
Class
```

| Calculate a Monthly Payment on a Loan |
| Calculate the Cosine of a specified Angle |
| Calculate the Sine of a specified Angle |
| Calculate the Sum-of-Years Depreciation |
| Calculate the Tangent of a specified Angle |
| Get a Random Number using the Random class |

- Double-click on the chosen snippet to insert it into the code.

The random number snippet looks like this when it is inserted into the code:

```
    Private Sub btnOK_Click(ByVal sender As –

      Dim generator As New Random

      Dim randomValue As Integer

      randomValue = generator.Next(10, 100)

    End Sub
```

Two replacement points are highlighted in yellow. They are the numbers 10 and 100. These numbers must be replaced by suitable values. The student hovered the mouse pointer over the highlighted replacement points. An explanatory message appeared next to each number.

- The message for the first number was 'Replace with the smallest integer you want in the results set'.
- The message for the second number was 'Replace with one more than the largest integer you want in the results set'.

The student wanted the random number to be between 1 and 12. That meant the smallest integer in the results set was 1 and 'one more than the largest integer' was 13. These figures were inserted into the code at the replacement points.

The code looked like this:

```
Private Sub btnOK_Click(ByVal sender As -

    Dim generator As New Random

    Dim randomValue As Integer

    randomValue = generator.Next(1, 13)

End Sub
```

This code creates a random number and places it in a variable called *randomValue*. The student wanted two random numbers, so changed the code again to look like this:

```
Public Class Form1

    Private Sub btnOK_Click(ByVal sender As -

        Dim generator As New Random

        Dim random1, random2 As Integer

        random1 = generator.Next(1, 13)

        random2 = generator.Next(1, 13)

    End Sub

End Class
```

The two random numbers are stored as two variables called *random1* and *random2*.

Next the student added code that would use those two numbers to create a multiplication question and display it on the screen.

Activity   Random maths quiz

- Create a new application called Maths Quiz with the interface shown here.

- Add code to *btnQuestion* so that when it is clicked the program generates two random numbers between 1 and 12 and displays them as a multiplication question in *lblQuestion*. Make sure your code shows the question, not the answer.

- Add code so that the program works out the right answer to this multiplication sum.

- Add code to *btnResult* so that when it is clicked the program takes the answer in *txtAttempt* and compares it to the right answer to the multiplication sum.

- The result – a message saying whether the answer is right or wrong – should appear in *lblResult*.

Run the Maths Quiz a few times to check results. The completed code for this problem is shown at the end of the chapter.

23.3 Advantages and disadvantages

There are two ways to find and use code samples:

- Ordinary code samples are provided on websites and elsewhere as plain text that you can cut and paste into your program.
- Code snippets are not plain text; a code snippet includes replacement points and advice messages to help you to adapt the code to your own program.

There are advantages and disadvantages to using samples of code created by other programmers.

Advantages:

- Visual Basic includes many useful functions. Code snippets show you those functions and help you to add them to your code.
- There is no need to invent new solutions from scratch when other programmers have already developed ways to solve problems.
- Snippets created by the software development team will show best practice as recommended by the experts.
- It is quicker to insert a code snippet than to type out a piece of code by hand.

Disadvantages:

- You may insert a code snippet that you don't properly understand, and your program will not work the way you want it to.
- You may not be able to find a code snippet that suits your needs.
- You have to adapt the code snippets to your program. Unless you do this properly they will not fit in to the rest of your code.
- There are security issues if you use code snippets obtained from unknown sources.

As well as using snippets from other programmers, experienced programmers create their own code libraries. They can reuse code that they have developed on previous projects. This makes their work faster, and they learn from experience. In this way programmers can produce more effective program code with less effort.

■ Chapter end

Full code listing

Here is the completed code for the random maths quiz project in this chapter.

Note that most variables are declared within the procedures in which they are used. However, the variable *answer* is used in both procedures so it is declared at the top of the code.

```
Public Class Form1
    'declare variable 'answer' for use in all procedures
    Dim answer As Integer

    Private Sub btnQuestion_Click(ByVal sender As -
        'declare variables for use in this procedure only
        Dim generator As New Random
        Dim random1, random2 As Integer

        'assign random numbers to variables
        lblResult.Text = ""
        random1 = generator.Next(1, 13)
        random2 = generator.Next(1, 13)

        'display the question
        lblQuestion.Text = random1 & " x " & random2 & " = ?"

        'store the right answer in variable 'answer'
        answer = random1 * random2
    End Sub

    Private Sub btnResult_Click(ByVal sender As -
        'declare variables for use in this procedure only
        Dim Attempt As Integer

        'Assign user input to variable 'attempt'
        Attempt = txtAttempt.Text

        'compare user input with the right answer
        If Attempt = answer Then
            lblResult.Text = "YES: This is the right answer"
```

```
        Else
            lblResult.Text = "NO: The answer is " & answer
        End If
    End Sub

End Class
```

Overview

In this chapter you have learned how programmers can make use of samples of code created by other programmers.

- Advice and samples of code that you can cut and paste into your program are available on many websites. Code snippets are provided as part of the Visual Basic development environment.
- Both types of code can be very helpful. They save you time and they show you the recommended way to solve programming problems. The code must be adapted to suit your particular needs.
- There is a security risk in using code from a source that you are not familiar with.

■ Questions

Answer these questions to demonstrate your learning.

1 A friend has found a site that provides samples of code. What advice would you give your friend about making use of the code?
2 You want to use a code snippet in your project. Explain two challenges you face if you want to do this.
3 What are replacement points in a snippet? How would you use replacement points when adapting the code to your own use?
4 Which loop structures are available on the Code Snippets selection that you can access in Visual Basic code editor? (You will have to open Visual Basic and use the code editor to answer this question.)
5 Discuss the advantages and disadvantages of using code snippets in your projects.

Further activity

Practice activities can be carried out if you finish the work in this chapter with time to spare. You can also carry out these activities in your own time to help with learning and to improve your skills.

Further activity: Adapt the maths quiz given here so that the program keeps track of how many questions the user has answered and how many they have got right. The score is to be shown at the top of the main form.

Extended activity: Create a large maths tournament project that generates a range of different types of maths questions at different levels of difficulty. Extend your maths tournament by adding an option that allows two users to play against each other.

24 Networking

◼ Introduction

Modern computers are able to communicate with each other and share data. Networks are formed when computers are linked. The Internet is a system of links between millions of computers all over the world. Software applications can be run over remote links. In this chapter you will learn more about networking and web applications.

◼ 24.1 Networks

A network is a system that connects computers together. The connections transmit electronic signals. These signals are used to communicate between computers. Most schools and colleges have networks. A typical network has a central computer called a server, which controls the network and stores software and data files. The other computers in the network are connected to the server. The way that the computers are connected to the server varies. The different network shapes are called 'network topologies'. In this chapter you will learn about the different network topologies

The alternative to a networked computer is a stand-alone computer. The computer you use at home may be stand-alone.

Advantages

For a medium to large organisation there are many advantages to linking computers with a network:

- **Shared resources:** A network allows a group of computers to make use of shared resources such as printers. Printers are quite expensive and each user only needs access to a printer occasionally, so it makes sense to share.
- **Shared access to the Internet:** The network server is generally connected to the Internet. Everyone who logs on to the network has access to the Internet.
- **Sharing software:** Software can be held on the central server of a network or on the individual networked computers. There are different ways that software can be shared over a network. Learn more about this in section 24.3.
- **Storage:** In chapter 4 you learned about data storage. Data files can also be stored on the network server. A big advantage of using central networked storage is that your files can be accessed from any computer on the network.

- **Communicating:** It is easy to send messages of all kinds to other computers that are on the same network. For example, a teacher could send a message to all the pupils in a class telling them about homework. Or a head teacher could send a message to all the pupils in the school telling them about a school event.
- **Roaming profile:** Users can log on to the network from any computer. They immediately have access to their email account, their stored work and any other personal settings.

Disadvantages

The main disadvantages of installing a network are the additional costs and new risks that arise due to the use of the network.

Costs:

- Initial expenses include buying the central server and the cabling or wireless system used to connect the computers.
- There are also maintenance costs. If an organisation runs a network then it will need one or more technicians or system administrators to look after the network, fix errors and make sure everything is operating correctly.

Risks:

- Because files are shared and transmitted through the network, security and privacy of data is a concern. Passwords are used to ensure data is kept private.
- Data may be lost due to hardware faults or user error. Regular backups are taken so that if data is lost from the server it can be restored from a recent copy.
- If the server or the data connections fail, the network will cease to operate. If most of the software and data files are stored centrally this may mean that nobody in the organisation can get any work done until the network is fixed.

■ 24.2 Types of network

Networks vary according to the type of connection and the structure or **topology** of the network. Learn more about topology in section 24.3.

> **Key term**
>
> **Topology**   The study of shapes. Network topology is a way of classifying networks by their different shapes: line, star or ring.

- **Wireless and wired:** Some networks are connected by cabling, which transmits the electronic signals that represent data. Fibre-optic cabling is a modern alternative that transmits signals by light pulses. Wireless networks use radio waves, microwaves or infrared signals to transmit data.
- **LAN:** A network that covers a single building, or perhaps a nearby group of buildings, is called a Local Area Network or LAN. It is a private network, operated by an organisation, to link people who are connected to that organisation (such as employees of a company, or students of a college). Typically the organisation that runs the LAN has bought and installed all the cables or the Wi-Fi that connects the computers.

- **WAN:** A private network that covers a region or country is a Wide Area Network or WAN. An example would be a company which has offices in London and Cardiff, which may be connected by a private network. Typically a WAN is linked together using a national telecom service, and the company pays a fee for this service.
- **Internet:** The Internet does not have one central server. It is like a huge network with millions of different servers connected over great distances. The Internet includes the 'world wide web' of websites, which use an agreed communication protocol to share information. There is more information about protocols in the final section of this chapter.

■ 24.3 Network topologies

There are various different ways that computers can be connected together by wires. These are called different network topologies. These topologies only apply to local networks, connected by wires. There are three main network topologies:

- ring
- bus
- star.

Ring

In a ring network each computer is connected to two other computers in the network. Signals are passed round the network from computer to computer (always in the same direction).

Some advantages of this design of network are:

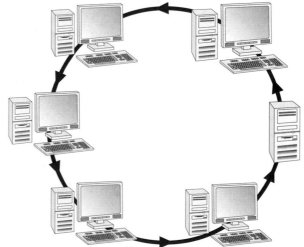

- compared to a star topology it uses less cabling, so is less expensive
- it can operate over larger distances and handle more data than a bus topology
- because the signals only go one way round the ring, they do not interfere with each other.

The main disadvantages are:

- if one computer in the network stops working then the whole network goes down because it can no longer pass on the signal
- it can be difficult to expand a ring network because adding a new computer means interrupting the whole communication ring.

Ring networks were once quite common, but nowadays this topology is rarely used.

Bus or linear network

In a bus network all of the computers and other items are connected to a single cable called the bus. The cable sends signals and allows the computers to communicate with the server, with each other and with devices such as a shared printer. Signals are passed up and down the data bus.

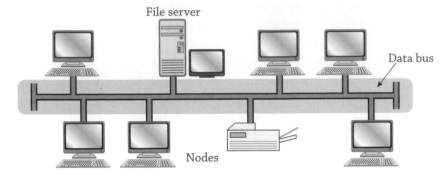

Some advantages of this design of network are:

- it is easy to add more computers to extend the network
- it uses less cabling than the other network designs
- if a single computer breaks it does not disable the whole network.

Some disadvantages are:

- a break or fault anywhere on the cable will disable the whole network
- the size of the network is limited by the capacity and length of the bus
- a single bus is not suitable for networks with a lot of computers and lot of data being transmitted.

Star network

All computers and other devices in a star network are connected by separate wires to the central server or hub.

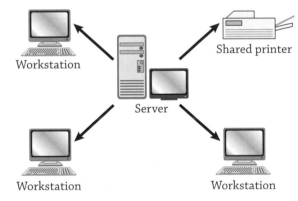

A wireless network has a star topology. But in this case the connections are typically made via radio signals. Some advantages of this type of network are:

- if one connection breaks, the rest of the network is unaffected
- as each computer has its own cabling, the load on each section of cabling is less
- if there is a fault it is easier to find and correct, for example by replacing one section of cable.

The main disadvantages are:

- it uses more cabling than other topologies, which can be expensive
- if the central server or hub breaks down, the whole network fails.

In many networks each group of computers is connected to a local hub or router. Each local hub sends signals to the main network server. This is still called a star topology.

The star topology is probably the one used in your college or school. It is the most common type of modern network. It has become more popular as cabling and wireless connections have become less expensive.

■ 24.4 The client–server model

A computer connected to a network, which holds data or software to share with other computers, is called a server. Data and software can be passed down the communication links of the network from the server to other computers. The networked computer where the user sits and works is called the client computer. The way the network is used depends on the relationship between the client and server computers. There are two main models: thick client and thin client.

Thick client

In some systems every computer in the network has its own software. Processing is carried out by each computer working on its own. The network connection is only used to send data to central storage and to send output to the printer. This is called a thick client system.

This system has several advantages:

- If the network connection fails, each computer in the network can still function. Work can be saved locally until the network connection is restored. Working without connection to the server is called working offline.
- Different computers on the network can have different software systems in place, so this system is more flexible.
- The central server does not need to be so powerful or fast, as it does little processing.
- Because all processing is done locally, the response time can be quicker and is not affected by increased workload.

The main disadvantages are:

- each computer needs to have its own software installed
- each computer in the system must be modern and powerful enough for all processing tasks.

Because each computer must be of a high specification, this approach can be expensive, particularly in large networks with hundreds of computers.

Thin client

In other cases the software is held on the central server of a network. The processing is carried out centrally. A system like this is called a thin client system.

The main advantage of a thin client system is that the client computer only needs to do a small amount of processing. This means that cheaper, older and smaller computers can be used. As they do little processing they don't need to be powerful.

The main disadvantage is that the client computers are not much use if the network breaks down. This system is only suitable for online working.

Variations on the client–server model

The way the work is divided between the client and the server can vary:

- In a dumb terminal system no processing is carried out locally. The local client works only as a keyboard and monitor screen. All of the processing is done remotely at the server end.
- In a thin client system, very little processing is carried out by the local computer. Most of the software is held centrally, and data is processed on the main server.
- In a typical web application some of the processing is carried out by the web browser software on the local computer, and some is carried out by a computer at a distance via an Internet connection.

■ 24.5 Web applications

Any computer that connects to the World Wide Web uses a web browser (for example, Microsoft Internet Explorer, Google Chrome or Mozilla Firefox). Your web browser requests data from other computers and uses it to display information on your own computer. This is how you can see webpages when you connect to the Internet.

People who create webpages make the content of the pages available in a digital form that can be understood by web browsers. The browser turns the digital content into a display on the computer screen and other output such as sound.

A typical web application uses the web browser of a client computer to run an application stored on the server. This means some processing is carried out at the client end. Most of the processing is carried out at the server end.

For example, when you buy goods over the Internet you use your browser to prepare and send the details of your order. But your order and payment details are processed on the main computer of the online store. Amazon and iTunes work like this.

Most web applications make use of the web browser. Some make use of other types of client software such as e-mail software or online chat software.

In a few cases you have to download special software that lets your computer work with the remote server. For example, some computer games operate over the Internet. You have to download some special software on to your own computer to start playing the game. But most of the processing that makes the game work happens on the computer owned by the games company.

Protocols

If two computers are to communicate with each other, they must send signals in the same general format. They must agree to use the same formats, codes and conventions. A communication agreement of this kind is called a 'protocol'. That means an agreed communication method that both computers understand.

The Internet uses two common protocols:

- **IP:** This stands for Internet Protocol. IP is the communication system that gives every computer on the Internet an 'address'. IP ensures that information is sent to the right 'address'.
- **TCP:** This stands for Transmission Control Protocol. This protocol ensures that computers send each other blocks of data in a secure and orderly way. TCP is the protocol used by webpages and email.

The two protocols work together to create a smooth world-wide communications network. The combined procol is called TCP/IP.

Handshake

There are a number of risks and problems when running web applications:

- The client and the server must use the same communications protocol.
- The client and server must correctly identify each other, and the signals must be kept separate from other applications that might be running at the same time.
- Security is a risk with all web applications. For example, when you buy goods from an online store you need to send information about your bank account to the server. If a computer hacker could get hold of that information they could steal your money.

To prevent these problems, a process takes place that allows the two computers to recognise each other and confirm the protocol and connection before they begin to share information. This is known as a handshake.

The diagram shows the 'handshake' process for the TCP protocol. It has three stages:

The 3-step TCP 'handshake'

1. The client computer sends a 'Synchronise' signal (labelled 'SYN' in the diagram) to the server. This asks the server to establish a connection.
2. The server sends back a 'Synchronise acknowledgment' signal (SYN-ACK). This agrees to establish a connection with the client.
3. The client completes the handshake with a final acknowledgement of the process (ACK). Communication can now go ahead.

After the communication is completed the connection is closed (this final signal is sometimes called FIN). If a connection is kept open for too long without being used, then it closes automatically: the connection 'times out'.

This is a slightly simplified description of the process. A more complete picture is given in the next section, on client–server 'states'.

Client–server 'states'

A computer which is communicating is in a different 'state' to a computer which is just resting. Both the client computer and the server pass through different states during the handshake process. The client side initiates the connection. It performs an **active** connection. The server agrees to respond. It performs a **passive** connection.

Let us look at this in a bit more detail.

1 At first there is no link between the two computers. The server is in a state called 'listening'. That means it is ready to receive messages from other computers. But no messages have come yet.

2 Then the client sends the SYN command to the server. The client computer is now in a state called 'SYN-SENT' and the server is in a state called 'SYN-RECEIVED'.

3 If the server agrees to establish a connection it moves to a state called 'ESTABLISHED'. This means the connection is established and ready to go. The server sends the SYN-ACK signal to let the client know it has agreed.

4 When the client receives the SYN-ACK the client computer also moves into the 'ESTABLISHED' state. It sends the final ACK signal back to the server. Now both computers are in the right state to communicate.

5 Either side can finish communicating by sending the FIN signal. When this happens both computers move out of the ESTABLISHED state and back to listening.

You may find a diagram easier to understand than a description. The next diagram shows the changing states of the two computers.

Creating client–server applications

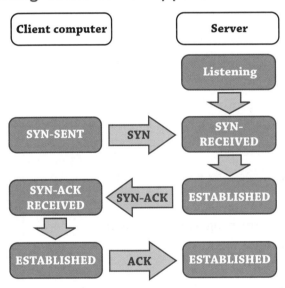

At the completion of the handshake both computers are in the established state and communication can go ahead.

Coding a **client–server application** means that the code must be designed to make use of software on the client computer. All web browsers work in much the same way and recognise the same codes. A client–server application works by interacting with this software to produce the required result.

Many web-based applications make use of databases. The database will be created, updated and stored on the central server. The client computer will send information that is used to update the central database, and queries to extract data. Think of what happens

Key term

Client–server application An application for which most of the processing is carried out on a distant server rather than on the local computer.

when you buy goods from Amazon or other online retailers. They have records of all their customers, all their products and all the orders. When you make an order this information is used to record your transaction and prepare the parcel for shipping to the right address.

There are several advantages of putting most of the data and software at the server end:

- The business retains control over all the data related to its work and finances.
- Customers only have access to their own data, through queries and updates, and cannot see or change anyone else's data.
- The system can be used by many different customers on different types of computer.
- The software is standardised and designed by the business, and it operates in a predictable way.
- The central system represents a major investment for the business, and time and money is spent to ensure it is robust and reliable.

For these reasons it is most common in the client–server model for all processing and information storage to be centralised. The only work that is done at the client end is preparing transactions to be sent to the central database.

Programming web applications

If you want to create web applications there are a number of programming routes that build on the Visual Basic skills that you have already learned.

Visual Basic Express, the programming system used in this book, is part of Visual Studio Express, which includes a web application module called Visual Express for Web. New versions of Visual Express will be released from time to time by Microsoft.

Learning more about this software will enable you to extend your experience and understanding in order to develop web applications.

Creating web applications has additional challenges for the programmer compared to creating simple applications to run on a single computer.

- Browsers: Users connect to web applications through web browser software. There are a number of different browsers available, so any web application must be designed to work well with all web browsers.
- Accessibility: Well-designed web applications should be usable by people of all abilities and disabilities and give all users equal access to the information and functionality. This can include spoken text options for visually impaired users, for example.
- Continuity: A user can connect to a web application more than once (these are called 'sessions'). A well-designed web application 'recognises' the user, and 'remembers' the information that the user has entered in a previous session. An application can ensure continuity between sessions by copying a small packet of data, called a 'cookie', onto the client computer. Next time the user connects to the application, the cookie provides information about the users' previous sessions.

■ Security: Most web applications store information about their users, so data security is a very important consideration. Firstly, it is important that data is not lost or accidentally deleted. For this reason a 'backup' copy of all data must be made and stored somewhere safe. Secondly, it is important that data is not accessed by an unauthorised person. For this reason data may be password-protected or encrypted (stored using a code).

■ Chapter end

Overview

In this chapter you learned about the advantages and disadvantages of linking computers to form networks. You learned about the main types of networks and the most common network topologies. You also learned about the client–server model and how this is used in modern web applications.

■ Questions

Answer these questions to demonstrate your learning.

1 State four major advantages to a business or other organisation installing a network.
2 What are the major costs and risks associated with installing and using a network?
3 What strategies can a business use to reduce these risks?
4 Draw diagrams representing the main network topologies and explain their advantages and disadvantages.
5 How does the client–server model make use of network connections to control processing?
6 Describe a modern web application that makes use of the client–server model. What advantages are there to this way of handling transactions?
7 What are the two main Internet protocols, and what is the purpose of each?
8 What three signals are sent during the TCP 'handshake' process? Which signals are sent by the client and which by the server?

Further activity

Practice activities can be carried out if you finish the work in this chapter with time to spare. You can also carry out these activities in your own time to help with learning and to improve your skills.

Further activity:

1 Investigate the network in use at your school or college. What network topology is used?
2 If possible speak to a network technician and find out how applications are handled on your school/college network – is the software stored centrally or locally? Are client–server applications used, for example by teachers completing class registers?
3 Write a report on the network and how it helps the staff and students of your school or college.

25 The software development life cycle

■ Introduction

In this book you have learned a lot about writing computer code to carry out identified tasks. In this chapter you will see how writing computer code is part of a larger process of software development that includes several stages.

■ 25.1 Software development

A software application is developed by programmers to meet a need. Some software is generic. That means it is developed for general use to help with many different tasks. An example is a word-processing application. Other software is developed to meet a particular need or solve a specific problem.

In all cases software development must be driven by the identified need. The whole process of development must be directed at delivering a finished application that solves the initial problem or fulfils the initial requirements.

Getting to a finished solution that does what it is supposed to do is a complex process. Writing computer code is only part of that process. A programmer has to understand the process and work within it, as part of a team, to reach the goal of the process.

Software development is expensive. For this reason the software development process continues while the software is in use. Ideally software will be maintained and developed further in order to keep it useful and relevant for as long as possible.

Eventually the software will no longer be useful, and the process must begin again with new software taking the place of the old applications. Because software develops, grows and is eventually replaced, the process of development is called a life cycle.

■ 25.2 Life-cycle models

In order to keep control over the software life cycle, developers use models. Models are a bit like maps of the development process. A model will give you an idea of where you are in the **systems development life cycle**. It will tell you what needs to happen at any stage of the process. It will tell you what you need to do next after the current stage is completed.

Learning content

3.1.11 Software development life cycle: understand the software development life cycle; be able to explain what commonly occurs at each stage of the software development life cycle; be able to identify at which stage of the software development life cycle a given step will occur; understand that there are several life-cycle models that can be used (for example, cyclical, waterfall, spiral); be able to discuss the advantages and disadvantages of these life-cycle models.

3.1.11.1 Prototyping: understand what prototyping is; be able to discuss the advantages and disadvantages of using prototyping when developing solutions; have experience of using prototyping to create solutions to simple problems.

Key term

Systems development life cycle   The entire process of software development from analysis of requirements to implementation and maintenance of the software.

In this section you will look at three well-established life-cycle models: waterfall, cyclical and spiral.

Waterfall

The waterfall model divides the process of software development into stages. The outcomes of each stage feed into the next stage.

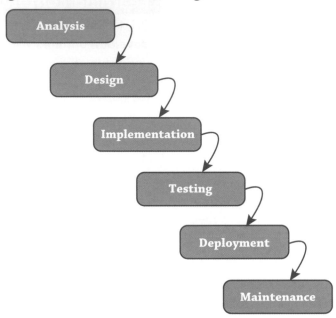

1 **Requirements analysis:** The development team determines exactly what is needed and set this out in a requirements specification.
2 **Software design:** The development team takes the requirements and produces a design for the software that will meet the requirements. They may use algorithms such as flow charts and pseudocode. They may analyse the input and output values. They may break the program down into smaller chunks that can be developed separately. The output of this stage is a design brief.
3 **Implementation:** The programmers take the design brief and write computer code to match the design. The output of this stage is computer code that may still contain errors.
4 **Testing:** The programmers test the code to remove all errors. The output of this stage is tested and reliable software.
5 **Deployment:** The software is installed on computer systems and used by the client to perform tasks. Deployment may include training and support for users.
6 **Maintenance:** Finally, the software can be maintained, including upgrades and improvements, to keep it useful for as long as possible.

This model has advantages and disadvantages:

■ **Advantages:** The waterfall is a simple and straightforward model. It is easy for members of the development team to use the model to understand where they are in the process. The output of each stage is clear. Work is linked to the outputs.

- **Disadvantages:** Many people think the waterfall model is too rigid and does not match the real process of software development. They argue that there is no need to wait for one stage to be finished before the next begins. The stages can overlap. Also they argue that sometimes it is necessary to go back up the waterfall. For example, the testing stage may reveal problems with the code, so the implementation stage must begin again.

Cyclical

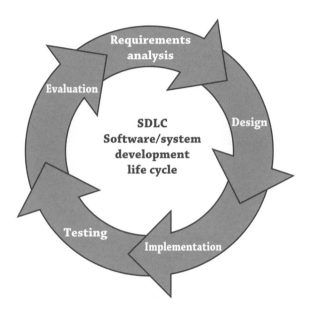

The cyclical model of software development has similar stages to the waterfall model. But the cyclical model emphasises the continuous process of keeping software up to date.

The process begins with the stages of requirements analysis, program design, implementation and testing, as seen in the waterfall model. However, the next stage of the process is not final deployment and maintenance. Instead there is an evaluation of how well the sofware meets client requirements. This may lead to a new requirements analysis. And so the whole process begins again.

This model has advantages and disadvantages:

- **Advantages:** Like the waterfall model it is quite clear and well defined. Programmers can understand the model and see how their work fits into the process. It is an improvement on the waterfall model because it shows a constant productive cycle of work, rather than a decline and ending.
- **Disadvantages:** This model has also been criticised for being too rigid. It is argued that modern software is more likely to be developed as a series of small modules. Different modules are at different stages of development at any time. Like the waterfall model, the cyclical model describes a process that goes in one direction, from design to program implementation to evaluation. But in real life the process can work in the other direction, with implementation leading to changes in the design.

Spiral

The spiral model of software development is a cycle, but the cycle does not return to the same place each time. Instead each turn of the cycle (called an iteration) has greater cost, risk and complexity.

Each iteration includes several tasks. These are shown by the four quarters of the spiral.

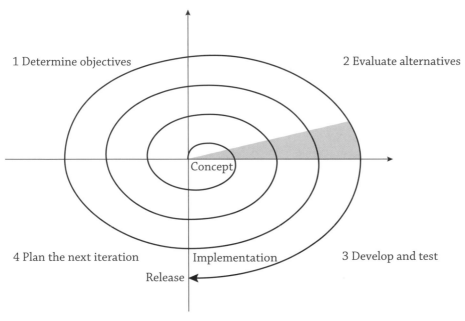

1 Determine objectives or requirements.
2 Evaluate alternative approaches, including risks, and choose a solution.
3 Develop and test the chosen solution.
4 Plan the next iteration.

At each turn of the spiral the software is more developed:

- At first the team comes up with the idea or concept of the software.
- Next the team progresses the concept into a **prototype** or early version.
- Finally the team develops the software fully into a finished product that can be released for sale.

The exact number of iterations required will depend on the difficulty of the project.

There are advantages and disadvantages to this model:

- **Advantages:** There is careful testing and planning at each stage. Alternatives and risks are considered. It is a less rigid model than the waterfall or spiral. This model includes the opportunity for more design and coding at the next iteration.
- **Disadvantages:** This model is slow and expensive to follow. It is not suitable for a quick fix. It is complicated to understand where you are in the process. It is not always clear how much more work there is to do.

> ### Key term
>
> **Prototype** A prototype is an early version of a new product that can be tested by real-life users. A prototype may be used during the development process.

Conclusion

The choice of development model depends on the time available and the complexity of the final project. Most programming teams pick and choose from the different models depending on their needs.

■ 25.3 Prototyping

Prototyping means developing an early working version of software that can be shared with the final user. Often a prototype will include the full user interface, but some of the functions will not work yet. For example, the user may be able to see all of the buttons and menus, but not all of the menu options will work.

Rapid application development

Rapid application development (RAD) is a software development model that uses prototyping. It emphasises:

- breaking a software project down into small chunks that are developed rapidly and then combined
- involving the final user at every stage of the design, development and testing process
- producing a good enough working prototype to get the system up and running, even if it is not perfect
- putting the user interface into place as quickly as possible, even if all of the functions have not yet been added
- a process of constant small improvements to the software while it is in use.

If you want to get the opinions of real users, a prototype should be used. This is because a typical user will not understand program algorithms or designs. A real-life example of the software application is much easier for the user to understand. Users can give helpful and realistic feedback on the prototype. They might say they can't understand the interface, or that there are buttons missing that they expected to see, etc.

Advantages and disadvantages

The advantages of RAD are that it gets software in place as quickly as possible. Close involvement by the end user means there is a strong focus on understanding and meeting user needs. Because the prototype is put in place very rapidly, programmers get the benefit of real-life user feedback.

The disadvantages of RAD are that it can lead to more work overall if the prototype needs a lot of revision. Some programmers feel that end users do not have the expertise to be so involved in the development process. There is also concern that a prototype with errors in it might give the user a bad impression.

Using prototyping in your programming

In this book there is an emphasis on producing a user interface quite early in the coding process. Visual Basic is designed to make this easier: code is added to objects on the user interface. You can design the interface at the start of the project. As soon as you have a working interface with some code you can test it like a prototype. The debugging that you do at every stage of your coding gives you the chance to review your program as if you were the user.

When you are developing your skills there are two ways that you can use prototyping:

1 You can try to act as your own user. That is, you can test and use your own software. Try to be unbiased about the strengths and weaknesses of the prototype. Try to approach the interface as if you were new to it.
2 Get friends to act as the user. Ask them to try to use the program. Ask them for feedback. Observe if they get anything wrong or use the interface in a way you were not expecting. This is a better way of testing your system than doing it yourself.

And of course, when you come to develop programs for real users, you can involve them in design and development. Use prototypes to demonstrate your program and to get feedback on whether it suits the eventual user.

Prototyping is an example of testing. The testing process is described in more detail in the next chapter.

Link

Testing – chapter 26

■ Chapter end

Overview

In this chapter you learned about software development.

- Creating software is part of a larger development process that includes analysis, design and testing.
- The traditional software development models are the waterfall, the cycle and the spiral. Each model has advantages and disadvantages, and many program teams will pick and choose from these models according to circumstances.
- Prototypes can be used to engage the user at all stages of the development process. Visual Basic makes it easy for coders to create a user interface early in the process, and to work with users during development.

■ Questions

Answer these questions to demonstrate your learning.

1 The following stages of the software development process are in alphabetical order. Put them into the order in which they are carried out by the development team according to the waterfall model:
> Deployment
> Implementation
> Maintenance
> Requirements analysis
> Software design
> Testing
2 Put the stages of the software development process into a waterfall diagram.
3 What is the output from each stage of the waterfall model?
4 What is the main difference between the waterfall model and the cyclical model?
5 Some programmers have said that the waterfall and cycle models do not match the real programming process. Give two examples of this.
6 What are the advantages and disadvantages of the spiral model?
7 Explain how prototypes are used to increase the involvement of ordinary users in the development of software.
8 What are the advantages and disadvantages of involving the user in software development?

Further activity

Practice activities can be carried out if you finish the work in this chapter with time to spare. You can also carry out these activities in your own time to help with learning and to improve your skills.

Practice activity: Pick any of the projects that you have undertaken during your study – for example the Vet Record program or the Social Network project. Analyse and write up the requirements of this project. What is the purpose of the program and what functions should it have? You can use these requirements as a guide when thinking about how to test the program.

26 Testing

■ Introduction

All of your software needs to be tested before it is completed and installed. You have learned about ways of testing software and finding errors. This chapter pulls the topic together and explains how to ensure your testing is complete and effective.

■ 26.1 The need for testing

Testing pulls together a lot of the subjects that you have learned about in this book:

- You have learned that it is important for software to be robust and reliable (see chapter 10).
- You have learned that there are many kinds of errors that can prevent code from working properly (see chapter 22).
- You have learned that coding is part of a development cycle that includes testing (see chapter 25).
- In almost every chapter you have created programs and debugged them during development.

Testing is essential because all programmers, even the most experienced, can make mistakes. Programming a successful application can be challenging. Testing is a way of making sure your programs are the best they can be. All software in use in the modern world has been thoroughly tested to make sure it works the way it should.

■ 26.2 Types of testing

In this section you will learn about the different types of test that you can carry out. When a program is finished, the programmer will carry out a full range of tests to ensure that the application meets the requirements.

Learning content

3.1.6 Error handling: test for errors; detect errors.

3.1.12 Application testing: understand the need for rigorous testing of coded solutions; understand the different types of tests that can be used, including unit/modular testing; be able to create suitable test plans and carry out tests to demonstrate that solutions work as intended; be able to hand-test simple code designs/algorithms using trace tables.

3.1.16 Use of computer technology in society: evaluate the effectiveness of computer solutions.

Link

The need for robust and reliable systems – chapter 10

Detecting errors – chapter 22

The software development life cycle – chapter 25

Syntax errors

The first stage of debugging is spotting and removing syntax errors from the code. The Visual Basic development environment will identify and highlight syntax errors and help you to correct them. There is more about this in chapter 22.

Link

Locating syntax errors – chapter 9

Creating a trace table – chapter 22

Trace tables

In chapter 22 you learned how to create a trace table to track the value that a variable has at each stage of the process. You can create trace tables using debugging tools like step through and breakpoint, together with the Watch window. You can also trace the value of variables as you read through a pseudocode algorithm.

Trace tables can be used alongside test data to see what happens to variables within a program when different user input is entered.

Test data

Test data is used to find runtime and logical errors. You can run the program using the debug feature. Then test the program by entering test data wherever user input is required. The method for testing software is:

1 input test data
2 see what the output is
3 compare the output you see with the output you want
4 if the program is not doing what you want, make corrections and then test again.

Key term

Test data   Inputs used during testing to check that a program functions correctly in a range of circumstances.

To ensure that you test the program thoroughly you must use three types of test data:

- **Normal** data. This is data that a typical user would input when using your program in normal use. For example if the user has to enter 'age' then test the program by entering a typical age of a user, for example 18 or 25. Your program must work properly when normal data is input.
- **Extreme** data, such as very long strings or very large or small numbers. Extreme data is also known as 'boundary' data. This data is at the limit, or boundary, of what is acceptable for the program. Boundary data lets you test the limits of the software. For example if you allow users to enter any age from 0 to 99, then 0 and 99 will be the 'boundary' values. The program should accept boundary values without causing an error.
- **Invalid** data, such as entering a negative number for age. Invalid data is data that is outside the limits of what is allowed by the software. The program should reject invalid input, preferably with a sensible error message which explains the program. In chapter 22 you learned how to add code to trap invalid input before it causes a run-time error. Entering invalid data allows you to test this functionality.

You cannot be sure what users will input when they are using your program. So you must test all the possibilities.

Test parts and the whole

In general a computer project consists of different parts that work together. In Visual Basic your project will typically have several forms, such as a main menu, an input form and an output form. The exact design will depend on the project.

It is a good idea to test every part of the project separately. Then you can test the entire project with all of the forms in place.

User testing

Ideally your program will be tested by the person who will use the finished program. This is the ideal type of test because it is the most realistic. The user may not have your expertise or understanding of the interface, so the testing will be more challenging.

Users can be involved at any stage of testing. A good way to engage users in testing is to create a prototype. You learned about prototypes in chapter 25. A prototype is a version of an application. It has a working user interface, but it may be incomplete or unfinished. The user can try out the program and see what the interface is like. Ask the user to note any problems encountered and to give you critical feedback that will help you to improve your work.

If you can't get the user involved then it is good to test the program on someone who does not know in advance how the program is supposed to work and who has the same general level of skill as a typical user.

If you can't arrange for either of these types of test, then you must try to test the program like a real user would. Try to put yourself in the place of a new user, and try out all of the parts of the program as if you were using them for the first time. This is harder than getting a real user involved.

> **Link**
>
> Prototyping – section 25.3

■ 26.3 Test planning

Your test plan will set out the tests that you are going to do. Your plan should include:

- a test for every input control on the user interface, including all buttons and text boxes
- all three types of test data (normal, extreme and invalid), in every place where data is input
- a check against all of the user requirements that you were given
- testing each part separately and testing how the parts fit together.

A good way to make a test plan is to challenge yourself to describe the tests so clearly that you could give the plan to another person and he or she would understand how to do the test.

You can set out your test plan in a table that looks something like this. The table is half empty, ready to enter the test results:

Reason for test	Test data	Expected output	Actual output	Next steps
1 Test Main Menu button works	Click Main Menu button	Main Menu form is displayed		
2 Test age input box works	a Normal data: 25	Age appears on the form		
	b Extreme data: 120	Age appears on the form		
	c Invalid data: ZZ	Error message: 'Please enter a number'		

This example shows four tests. You will have more tests than this.

When testing a simple button with one function you cannot use test data. Just click the button and see if it works. But in other cases, where the user has to input some data, you should cover all three types of test data.

■ 26.4 Carrying out tests and recording results

Once you have made your test plan you can carry out each test in turn. Record the results of your tests in the test table. Here is an example of the test table with all columns filled in.

Reason for test	Test data	Expected output	Actual output	Next steps
1 Test Main Menu button works	Click Main Menu button	Main Menu form is displayed	Main Menu did not open	Make corrections to Main Menu button
2 Test age input box works	a Normal data: 25	Age appears on the form	Age appears on the form	None – passed the test
	b Boundary data: 120	Age appears on the form	Age appears on the form	None – passed the test
	c Invalid data: ZZ	Error message: 'Please enter a number'	Program crashes. See screenshot 2c	Make corrections to data validation

In this example two tests produced the expected results and two tests produced unexpected results. The programmer has noted the results. Where the program has failed the test the programmer notes that corrections are needed.

You can use screenshots to keep evidence of the results of the tests. You can include screenshots in the document following the test table. In this example the programmer has given the screenshot a number (2c) and refers to the screenshot by number in the table.

Remember: finding a mistake in a program is not a sign that you are a bad programmer. It is a sign that you are a good programmer who has carried out a sensible set of tests and found the places that need to be corrected.

■ 26.5 Evaluating effectiveness

The outcomes of the testing process are:

- finding and removing all errors so that the program functions correctly
- evaluating the **effectiveness** of the solution.

Effectiveness is more than just working correctly without errors. A program can be free of errors, but not effective.

You learned in chapter 25 that software development begins with a requirements analysis. To evaluate whether a program is effective you must compare the output of the program to the requirements that you started with. If the software meets all of the requirements then it is effective.

So, for example, if the requirement was to output a list of all members of a drama club, you would look at the output of the program and see whether it correctly shows that list. Or, if the requirement was to keep on online diary, you would look at the functions of the program and see how useful it was as an online diary.

> **Key term**
>
> **Effectiveness** The degree to which a solution meets initial requirements. Software is developed to meet a need; if it meets that need it is effective.

> **Link**
>
> Requirement analysis – chapter 25

In general, effectiveness is not a simple yes/no judgement. There may be several requirements and you will need to evaluate the effectiveness in terms of each requirement.

Some requirements will be simple to evaluate. For example, if the requirement is to input date of birth and output age, then you can see from your test results whether this has been achieved.

Other requirements will be harder to evaluate. For example, if the requirement is that output should be clear and well formatted, you may have to use your judgement to decide how well the output meets that requirement.

Sometimes when the software is finished, the user will realise that there are additional requirements, or further work is needed. This is because software development is a cycle rather than a process with a clear end point.

■ Chapter end

Overview

In this chapter you learned about testing your program and evaluating its effectiveness.

- Testing is needed to make sure that software is robust and reliable.
- Testing is done throughout the software development cycle.
- You must find and remove syntax errors during coding.
- You must enter test data during debugging to make sure the program can deal with all types of input: normal, extreme and impossible.
- Before passing on software to the user, a complete set of tests must be carried out. The tests should be planned and the results carefully recorded. When errors are found they can be corrected.
- The effectiveness of software is evaluated by comparing the completed software with the original requirements. The result may be further work or a revision to the requirements to reflect the user's needs.

■ Questions

Answer these questions to demonstrate your learning.

1 In chapter 25 you learned about the software development cycle. Pick one of the system life-cycle models that you have learned about. Explain where testing occurs in this model.
2 In chapter 10 you learned about how computer systems are important in many different contexts. Pick one important modern use of computing and explain why it is important for the computer software to be fully tested so that it is robust and reliable in use. What could happen if the software has errors in it?
3 A programmer created a prototype for the user to test. What are the advantages of asking a real-life user to test an application?
4 Explain how a prototype might differ from the final version of an application.
5 Why do tests include impossible data?
6 A programmer created an application with no coding errors, but it was not effective. Explain how that can happen.

Further activity

Practice activities can be carried out if you finish the work in this chapter with time to spare. You can also carry out these activities in your own time to help with learning and to improve your skills.

Practice activity:

1 Pick any programming project that you have completed as you worked through this book. Carry out a complete test of the project and record the results against a test plan.
2 Ask a helpful assistant who is not a computer programmer (perhaps a family member or friend) to try out the project. Ask for feedback, either in writing or as a verbal briefing.
3 Evaluate the effectiveness of the program you created.
4 Set out your next steps for improving and correcting the project.

27 Building and publishing a software application

Introduction

In this book you have learned a lot about programming and how to use programming methods to solve problems. You have also learned how to use different methods to document the program design (the algorithm) and to set out the program code. You have learned how to test a program and remove errors. You have also learned how programming fits into an overall software development cycle, which begins with a set of requirements. You have learned that the effectiveness of software is determined by how well it meets the requirements of the user.

In this section you will see how these different techniques and skills come together to enable you to design, build and successfully publish a software application.

27.1 Design and plan

Analysis of requirements

The software development cycle begins with an analysis of requirements. Before you begin software development you must be clear about the final outcome that you want to achieve. Typically this requirement will come from a user or client and not from the person developing the software.

Software developers must be certain that they understand the user's needs and the problem which the software will solve for that person. This may involve working carefully with the user to help them to state their needs clearly. Developers often use interviews and questionnaires to collect information, and they may observe the user at work to see what tasks can be supported by software.

The requirements should be set out in full in a document called the 'Statement of Requirements'. At the end of the software development process the software will be evaluated by comparing it with the initial requirements. A solution is effective only if it meets those requirements.

Overview plan

An overview plan will set out the general overall structure of the program. This could include:

- a general description of the approach you will take
- a diagram showing the different forms that make up the solution and what they are used for (for example, main menu, input form and output form)

Learning content

4 Assessment objectives: in the context of the knowledge and skills that make up the subject content:

- recall, select and communicate knowledge and understanding of computer technology
- apply knowledge understanding and skills to solve computing or programming problems
- analyse, evaluate, make reasoned judgements and present conclusions.

- a design sketch of the user interface
- a table showing the variables that will be required and how they relate to each other (a data dictionary)
- details about how data will be stored, for example in a text file or database
- an overview of the calculations and data processing that will take place.

In chapter 25 you learned that developers do not always stick firmly to initial plans, and you may need to come back later and make amendments to this documentation. However, doing this work before you begin will help you to make quicker progress as you develop the software. It is like having a map before you set off on a journey; it guides you and lets you know how you are progressing towards your goal.

> **Link**
>
> The software development life cycle – chapter 25
>
> Data dictionary – chapter 8

Describe the algorithm

You have learned how to use flowcharts and pseudocode to describe an algorithm. These are ways to set out the logical structure of your code, showing conditional statements, iterations and the assignment of values to variables.

In general you should create a separate algorithm for every processing task in your project. For example, if there are three forms in your project you might create three separate algorithms. In other cases you may find that a form has two buttons, and each button is associated with completely separate activities. In this case you might create a separate algorithm for each button.

The goal is to create an algorithm that is clear enough to be understood by another programmer or by you if you return to the work at a later date. That means that for each algorithm there should be a clear explanation of its purpose and what it shows.

■ 27.2 Develop and document

Once your preparation and planning is done you can begin creating the software. You have learned a lot of programming techniques that you can apply to the task.

Remember that the IntelliSense facility will provide on-screen advice about how to complete a line of code, and usually there will be a menu of choices to pick from. Also remember that you can use snippets to add ready-made blocks of code to your programs. You will find more advice and examples online.

If your code does not work correctly the first time, revise it and try again – this is part of the normal development process.

Develop in modules

It is safest and easiest to develop the different parts of your program separately and to make sure that one section works properly before going on to the next. For example, if you have a main menu form, add code so that the buttons on the main menu work properly. Make sure that these buttons allow you to open the other forms in your project. When the main form is functioning correctly, go on to develop another form. And so on until all the parts of your application work properly.

Print out your code

You can print out code so that you have a record of your programming. A well-designed program will be easy for the reader to understand. The programmer will:

■ use sensible and explanatory names for procedures, functions, variables and constants
■ name objects such as buttons, labels and text boxes with explanatory names instead of always using the default names such as *Button1*.
■ add comments at the start of blocks of code.

Comments

At all stages of programming you should add comments to explain the code. Comments are messages to readers, which are ignored by the compiler.

Comments will help you if you come back to look at your work after a break, for example if you decide to add extra functions to your project weeks or months after it is finished. The comments you added will remind you of the function of each part of the code. This will save you time.

Comments will also help other programmers to understand your code. They can look at the code listing and immediately see the purpose of each section of your code. Even if they disagree with your approach they can understand what you were trying to achieve.

Adding comments also forces you to think carefully about the purpose of each section of code. If you can't describe the purpose of a block of code then you should think carefully about your project plan and implementation. Perhaps the application is badly structured, or the code has errors. You may need to go back and study the coding methods you have used.

You have learnt how to add comments to code. If you start a line with a single apostrophe (') then the line will be treated as a comment. That means Visual Basic will ignore the line. Visual Basic displays the line in green, to show that it is a comment.

■ 27.3 Test and evaluate

In chapter 26 you learned how to plan a range of tests, carry them out and document the results. According to the waterfall model, testing follows software development. However, you will probably find that there is a two-way flow between testing and coding. Your tests will show you problems and faults in your code, and you can go back and make changes.

Link

Testing – chapter 26

For example, you will need to add code to your solutions so that the program does not crash if the user enters data of the wrong type. The process of checking data to make sure it is of the right type is called validation. If you forget input validation during your initial development, your testing will produce problems when you enter invalid data. Simply go back and revise your code to prevent the problem.

Evaluating the program means comparing it to the initial statement of user requirements. A program that meets all of the requirements is fully effective. Your evaluation may produce a list of requirements that have been met and others that have not. This could give you a plan for the next stage of your coding.

Modern methods of prototyping and user involvement mean that it is common for program developers to share an early version of the software with users, who give feedback. The coders then develop the software further on the basis of this feedback.

■ 27.4 Create an application to share with others

Up until now you have run your Visual Basic code within the Visual Basic software environment. When your software is fully tested and developed you can create a stand-alone machine code file. The file has the extension .exe which means it is an **executable file**. The file can be installed onto any Windows-compatible computer. Once it has been installed on a computer the user can run the file at any time. They do not have to have Visual Basic installed.

> ### Key term
>
> **Executable file**   This consists of machine code. The computer can execute the file. That means the computer will carry out the instructions in the file. This is also called running the file.

For example, you could create a maths quiz program that generates random maths questions. You could compile it and then e-mail the file to friends to challenge them to the quiz. Or you could copy the file onto a CD and send it to a friend in another town. You could also publish it on a website so that other students could use it. And of course professional programmers offer their software applications for sale to people.

Build and publish

The Visual Basic development environment includes three commands that allow you to prepare an exe file:

- **Debug:** this command runs the file immediately so you can check how it works
- **Build:** the command creates an exe file but does not run it
- **Publish:** the application is compiled and a setup file is created that allows a user to install the application on any computer.

The publish command uses a system called ClickOnce, which is designed to simplify the process of downloading and installing applications. For example, when you publish your application you can add commands so that the application automatically checks for updates.

Build the application

To create an executable file:

- open the Visual Basic project
- make sure the project is fully tested and debugged
- look on the menu bar at the top of the Visual Basic screen, and find the menu called Build
- select Build from this menu.

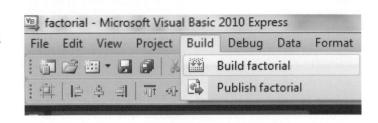

This is shown in the screenshot, which uses the factorial project from chapter 22 as an example.

When the build is completed you will see a small message at the bottom left of the screen saying Build succeeded. If there are any errors in the code the message won't appear, and you need to continue debugging.

Assuming that the build succeeds, you will now see that there is an exe file within the storage area where you have saved the Visual Basic project. The screenshot shows this for the factorial project.

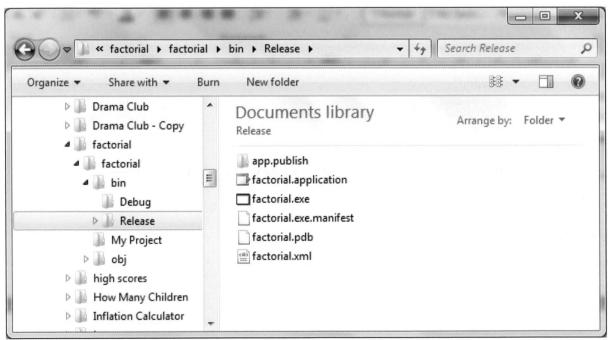

Within the factorial project folder there is a subfolder called bin. This stands for binary (machine code) files. The exe files are stored here. The exe file created during debugging will be found in the Debug folder. The finished exe file that was created by the Build command will be found in the Release folder. It is called factorial.exe.

- Double-click on the exe file to run the application.

You can send this exe file to anyone so that they can run the application from their own computer.

Publish the application

Publishing the application gives you some additional options to make your application more useful to users.

- To begin publishing open the Build menu and select Publish.
- The Publish wizard opens. This takes you through a series of screens:
  - First select a location where you want the exe file to be published. Pick a suitable storage area on your system and click Next.
  - The screen that follows asks where users will install the application from. Pick CD-ROM and click Next.
  - The screen then asks whether you want your application to check for updates. Select 'The application will not check for updates', and click Next.
  - Finally, you will see a screen that says 'Ready to publish!' and on this screen you can click Finish.

As well as the exe file that runs the app, the wizard will create a file called setup.exe. This file will help users to install the app on their computer. You will find setup.exe in the chosen storage area. To install the application you double-click on this file. The file will then install on your computer like any other software application.

You can vary the responses that you enter in the Publish wizard. For example, you might enter different responses if you want to publish your application to a website.

■ 27.5 Exploring the alternatives

There are a number of different development environments that you can use to develop Visual Basic applications. The example used in this book is Visual Basic 2010 Express. There are other versions of Visual Basic Express, and these may vary slightly in the presentation of the interface.

Visual Studio Express is a free integrated development environment that includes:

- Visual Basic Express
- Visual Web Developer Express
- Express for Windows Phone.

In addition Microsoft have produced Visual Studio, which is a larger development environment designed for professional programmers. Under arrangements between schools or colleges and Microsoft, students may have access to the full Visual Studio IDE.

Explore these alternatives if you want to specialise in developing web or phone applications. You can make use of Visual Basic code as you develop these applications, and the development environment will help you to create specialist applications for users to access by web or phone.

Microsoft has also developed a simple programming environment which can be accessed through a mobile phone. It is called TouchDevelop. You write scripts by tapping on the screen. You do not need a separate PC or keyboard. You may find this an interesting alternative approach.

■ Chapter end

Overview

In this chapter you learned how to pull together all of the skills you have learned to create a complete software application.

- You reviewed all the stages of the development process: requirements analysis; planning and design; development of code; testing; publishing.
- You learned how to create an exe file from your code and how to share it with users so they can install and run the software.

■ Questions

Answer these questions to demonstrate your learning.

1 What should be set out in the statement of requirements at the start of a programming project?
2 List the items that should appear in the overview plan for a programming project.
3 Describe three ways that you can make your program code easy for other programmers to understand.
4 What is the difference between building and publishing an application?
5 What is the function of the file called setup.exe and why would you provide it alongside your application file?

Further activity

Practice activities can be carried out if you finish the work in this chapter with time to spare. You can also carry out these activities in your own time to help with learning and to improve your skills.

Practice activity: Pick a programming project that you have completed this year and compile it as a software application. Share it with friends and invite them to install it on their own computer systems.

Index